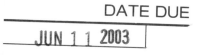

Presidents from
Reagan through Clinton,
1981–2001

Recent Titles in
The President's Position: Debating the Issues

Presidents from Washington through Monroe, 1789–1825
Amy H. Sturgis

Presidents from Theodore Roosevelt through Coolidge, 1901–1929
Francine Sanders Romero

Presidents from Hoover through Truman, 1929–1953
John E. Moser

PRESIDENTS FROM REAGAN THROUGH CLINTON, 1981–2001

Debating the Issues in Pro and Con Primary Documents

LANE CROTHERS
and
NANCY S. LIND

The President's Position: Debating the Issues
Mark Byrnes, Series Editor

GREENWOOD PRESS
Westport, Connecticut • London

3 1218 00352 0708

Library of Congress Cataloging-in-Publication Data

Presidents from Reagan through Clinton, 1981–2001 : debating the issues in pro and con primary documents / [compiled by] Lane Crothers and Nancy S. Lind.
    p. cm. — (The president's position : debating the issues)
    Includes bibliographical references (p.) and index.
    ISBN 0–313–31411–X (alk. paper)
    1. Presidents—United States—History—20th century—Sources. 2. United States—Politics and government—1981–1989—Sources. 3. United States—Politics and government—1989—Sources. 4. Reagan, Ronald—Political and social views.
5. Bush, George, 1924—Political and social views. 6. Clinton, Bill, 1946—Political and social views. I. Crothers, Lane. II. Lind, Nancy S., 1958– III. Series.
    E176.1.P922   2002
    320'.6'097309048—dc21   2001023308

British Library Cataloguing in Publication Data is available.

Library of Congress Catalog Card Number: 2001023308
ISBN: 0–313–31411–X

First published in 2002

Greenwood Press, 88 Post Road West, Westport, CT 06881
An imprint of Greenwood Publishing Group, Inc.
www.greenwood.com

Printed in the United States of America

The paper used in this book complies with the
Permanent Paper Standard issued by the National
Information Standards Organization (Z39.48–1984).

10 9 8 7 6 5 4 3 2 1

Cover photos: Reagan: Courtesy Ronald Reagan Library; Bush: George Bush Presidential Library; Clinton: Library of Congress.

CONTENTS

Series Foreword   xi

Acknowledgments   xv

Timeline   xvii

Introduction   1

1 RONALD REAGAN (1981–1989)

Introduction   15

DOMESTIC AND ECONOMIC POLICY

The First Reagan Economic Program (July 1981)   20
Air Traffic Controllers Strike (August 1981)   24
Enterprise Zones (March 1982)   28
The 1986 Tax Reform Act (May 1985)   33
Balancing the Budget (October 1985)   40
Immigration Reform (November 1986)   45
Welfare Reform (February 1987)   50
The Nomination of Robert Bork to the U.S. Supreme
Court (September 1987)   55
Housing and Community Development (February 1988)   62

MILITARY AND FOREIGN POLICY

Arms Control and the MX Missile (July 1983)   68
Peacekeeping in Lebanon (October 1983)   72
Invasion of Grenada (October 1983)   79
Strategic Defense Initiative (July 1985)   84

Economic Sanctions on South Africa (September 1985)   88
Bombing of Libya (April 1986)   92
Iran-Contra Scandal (March 1987)   98
Intermediate-Range Nuclear Forces Treaty (December 1987)   103
Recommended Readings   109

2   GEORGE H. W. BUSH (1989–1993)

Introduction   113

DOMESTIC AND ECONOMIC POLICY

The Bush Economic Plan (February 1989)   118
Drug Control (September 1989)   123
Americans with Disabilities Act (July 1990)   127
Family and Medical Leave Act (June 1990)   131
Education Reform (May 1991)   135
Nomination of Clarence Thomas to the U.S. Supreme
Court (July 1991)   141
Welfare Reform (April 1992)   147
Balanced Budget Amendment (June 1992)   152
North American Free Trade Agreement (December 1992)   157

MILITARY AND FOREIGN POLICY

Invasion of Panama (December 1989)   162
The Persian Gulf War (January 1991)   166
Strategic Arms Reduction Treaty (July 1991)   171
Economic Support for the Former Soviet Union (April 1992) 175
Recommended Readings   182

3   WILLIAM (BILL) CLINTON (1993–2001)

Introduction   187

DOMESTIC AND ECONOMIC POLICY

National Service (May 1993)   193
Most-Favored-Nation Trade Status for China (May 1993)   197
Homosexuals in the Military (July 1993)   202
The First Clinton Economic Plan (July 1993)   208
Health Care Reform (September 1993)   212
North American Free Trade Agreement (November 1993)   217
Gun Control (The Brady Bill) (November 1993)   222
Drug Control (April 1996)   226
Megan's Law (May 1996)   230
Investigation and Impeachment (January 1999)   234
Tax Cuts and Budget Surplus (September 1999)   240

MILITARY AND FOREIGN POLICY

Peacekeeping in Somalia (October 1993)   245
Peacekeeping in Yugoslavia and Bosnia (February 1994)   249
Intervention in Haiti (September 1994)   254
Peacekeeping in Rwanda (March 1998)   258
Air Strikes on Sudan and Afghanistan (August 1998)   263
Peacekeeping Through Bombing in Kosovo (March 1999)   268
Nuclear Test Ban Treaty (October 1999)   273
Recommended Readings   278

Bibliography   281

Index   285

SERIES FOREWORD

When he was running for president in 1932, Franklin D. Roosevelt declared that America needed "bold, persistent experimentation" in its public policy. "It is common sense to take a method and try it," FDR said. "If it fails, admit it frankly and try another. But above all, try something." At President Roosevelt's instigation, the nation did indeed take a number of steps to combat the Great Depression. In the process, the president emerged as the clear leader of American public policy. Most scholars see FDR's administration as the birth of the "modern presidency," in which the president dominates both domestic and foreign policy.

Even before FDR, however, presidents played a vital role in the making of public policy. Policy changes advocated by the presidents—often great changes—have always influenced the course of events, and have always sparked debate from the presidents' opponents. The outcomes of this process have had tremendous effects on the lives of Americans. The President's Position: Debating the Issues examines the stands the presidents have taken on the major political, social, and economic issues of their times as well as the stands taken by their opponents. The series combines description and analysis of those issues with excerpts from primary documents that illustrate the position of the presidents and their opponents. The result is an informative, accessible, and comprehensive look at the crucial connection between presidents and policy. These volumes will assist students doing historical research, preparing for debates, or fulfilling critical thinking assignments. The general reader interested in American history and politics will also find the series interesting and helpful.

Several important themes about the president's role in policy making emerge from the series. First, and perhaps most important, is how greatly the president's involvement in policy has expanded over the years. This has happened because the range of areas in which the national government acts has grown dramatically and because modern presidents—unlike most of their predecessors—see taking the lead in policy making as part of their job. Second, certain issues have confronted most presidents over history; tax and tariff policy, for example, was important for both George Washington and Bill Clinton, and for most of the presidents in between. Third, the emergence of the United States as a world power around the beginning of the twentieth century made foreign policy issues more numerous and more pressing. Finally, in the American system, presidents cannot form policy through decrees; they must persuade members of Congress, other politicians, and the general public to follow their lead. This key fact makes the policy debates between presidents and their opponents vitally important.

This series comprises nine volumes, organized chronologically, each of which covers the presidents who governed during that particular time period. Volume one looks at the presidents from George Washington through James Monroe; volume two, John Quincy Adams through James K. Polk; volume three, Zachary Taylor through Ulysses Grant; volume four, Rutherford B. Hayes through William McKinley; volume five, Theodore Roosevelt through Calvin Coolidge; volume six, Herbert Hoover through Harry Truman; volume seven, Dwight Eisenhower through Lyndon Johnson; volume eight, Richard Nixon through Jimmy Carter; and volume nine, Ronald Reagan through Bill Clinton. Each president from Washington through Clinton is covered, although the number of issues discussed under each president varies according to how long they served in office and how actively they pursued policy goals. Volumes six through nine—which cover the modern presidency—examine three presidencies each, while the earlier volumes include between five and seven presidencies each.

Every volume begins with a general introduction to the period it covers, providing an overview of the presidents who served and the issues they confronted. The section on each president opens with a detailed overview of the president's position on the relevant issues he confronted and the initiatives he took, and closes with a list of suggested readings. Up to fifteen issues are covered per presidency. The discussion of each issue features an introduction, the positions taken by the president and his opponents, how the issue was resolved, and the long-term effects of the issue. This is followed by excerpts from two primary documents, one representing the president's position and the other representing his opponents' position. Also included in each volume is a timeline of significant events of the era and a general bibliography of sources for students and others interested in further research.

As the most prominent individual in American politics, the president receives enormous attention from the media and the public. The statements, actions, travels, and even the personal lives of presidents are constantly scrutinized. Yet it is the presidents' work on public policy that most directly affects American citizens—a fact that is sometimes overlooked. This series is presented, in part, as a reminder of the importance of the president's position.

Mark Byrnes

ACKNOWLEDGMENTS

No book is ever the product of individual effort but is the product of cooperation, effort, and growth. This is our opportunity to thank those who helped us make this book possible.

First, Dr. Mark Byrnes of Middle Tennessee State University deserves our thanks for the opportunity to do this book. His invitation set in motion the work that became this volume. Second, Dr. Manfred Steger of Illinois State University provided invaluable advice that shaped this project and its outcome. Dr. Jamal Nassar, Chair of the Department of Political Science at Illinois State University, also supported this project, as did Dr. Tom Eimermann of Illinois State University. Their help made this a better book.

We also owe incalculable thanks to Steven Rich, whose patient and careful work on the book's many drafts literally made this work possible. We would also like to thank those who granted their permission to use their work as well as the staffs of the various presidential libraries who provided us with some ideas on key issues. In addition we would like to thank Karen Hult, Robert Maranto, and Charles Walcott for the initial encouragement they provided for undertaking this work.

Finally, we both would like to thank our families, without whose support we would not have had the opportunity to accomplish this project.

As is always the case, this book benefited from the help of all of these individuals; its flaws are entirely our own.

TIMELINE

RONALD REAGAN (1981–1989)

1980

November 4	Election

1981

January 20	Inauguration
March 30	Assassination attempt
April	Passage of the first economic package: substantial tax cuts without substantial savings
April	Aid cut off to Sandinista government of Nicaragua; policy supports contra rebels
July	First economic plan advanced; major tax cuts made to stimulate economic growth and major increases in defense spending without major cuts in social spending
August 5	Striking air traffic controllers fired
September 25	Sandra Day O'Connor named as first woman to serve on the U.S. Supreme Court; confirmed by the U.S. Senate in the same month

1982

November	Long-time leader of the Soviet Union, Leonid Brezhnev, dies; is replaced by Yuri Andropov
November 2	Argentina invades Falklands; war with Britain follows
November 2	Midterm elections; Republicans lose substantial numbers of seats in the House and retain the Senate with a narrow majority

1983

March 8   "Evil Empire" speech calls for efforts to undermine the Soviet Union; foundation of the "Reagan Doctrine" attempting to undermine Communist countries around the world

September 1   Destruction of Korean Air flight 007 by Soviet Union over Kamchatka Peninsula

October 23   Killing of U.S. Marines in Lebanon

October 25   Invasion of Grenada

1984

February   Soviet leader Yuri Andropov dies; is replaced by Konstantin Chernenko

November 6   Reelection

1985

January   Congress eliminates funding for the contras in Nicaragua

January 20   Second inauguration

March   Soviet leader Konstantin Chernenko dies; is replaced by Mikhail Gorbachev

1986

January 28   Space shuttle *Challenger* explodes, killing all aboard

April 14   Air strike against Libya

April 28   Chernobyl nuclear reactor explodes in Soviet Union

October 22   Tax Reform Act

November 4   Midterm elections: Democrats regain control of the Senate

November 13   Reagan acknowledges trading arms for hostages held by Iranian-supported groups in Libya; foundation of Iran-contra scandal

1987

May   Congressional hearings on Iran-contra open

May 17   Iraqi aircraft attack and destroy USS *Stark* in Persian Gulf

August 7   Central American Peace Accords signed; end of contra war in Nicaragua

December 5   Intermediate-Range Nuclear Forces Treaty signed with Soviet Union

1988

February   Panamanian leader Manuel Noriega indicted for drug trafficking

April 14   Agreement with Soviet Union signed for withdrawal of Soviet forces from Afghanistan

May–June   Reagan visits Soviet Union for the first time

July 3   U.S. naval vessel destroys Iranian airliner over Persian Gulf

| December 16 | Relations with Palestine Liberation Organization opened after it recognizes Israel's right to exist; foundation of peace agreement signed under Clinton in 1993 |

1989

| January 20 | Leaves office |

GEORGE H.W. BUSH (1989–1993)

1988

| November 8 | Election |

1989

January 20	Inauguration
February	Soviets leave Afghanistan
June 3	Tiananmen Square incident: China represses internal dissenters; international tensions follow
August 18	Solidarity labor movement wins election in Poland; beginning of the end of Communist East Europe
October 18	East German leader Erich Honecker removed from power
November 12	Collapse of the Berlin Wall
December 20	Invasion of Panama

1990

January 3	Manuel Noriega, leader of Panama, surrenders to U.S. forces
February 11	Nelson Mandela, leader of opposition movement in South Africa, freed after twenty-nine years in prison
June 1	Nuclear and other weapons control treaty signed with Soviet Union
July 26	Americans with Disabilities Act signed: sweeping civil rights reforms benefiting people with disabilities in areas of education, employment, and access to public goods and services
August 2	Iraq invades and occupies Kuwait
September	Bush economic package advanced: tax increases and spending cuts
October 3	Germany reunified
October 22	Bush Vetoes Civil Rights Act
November 6	Midterm elections: Democrats retain control of both Houses of Congress; Republicans lose several seats in the House of Representatives
November 15	Clean Air Act signed

1991

| January 12 | Congress authorizes the use of force against Iraq |

January 16	Air war against Iraq begins
February	Ground war against Iraqi troops occupying Kuwait begins, ends February 28
April 6	Iraq agrees to surrender terms: creation of "no fly" zones in northern and southern Iraq; limitations of sale of oil; requirement to allow United Nations inspectors to search for weapons throughout Iraq; limitations on the size of Iraq's military and its weapons programs
June 12	Boris Yeltsin elected president of Russia
June 25	Croatia and Slovenia announce their independence from Yugoslavia; disintegration of Balkans begins
August 19–21	Communist hard-liners attempt coup in Russia but are defeated; Communist party outlawed in Russia
October 11–14	Clarence Thomas–Anita Hill hearings held to determine whether Supreme Court nominee Clarence Thomas sexually harassed Anita Hill when he was her supervisor in a previous government job
December 15	Last U.S. hostage in Lebanon freed; original reason for the arms-for-hostage trades of the Reagan administration
December 25	Soviet Union dissolved
1992	
April	Civil war breaks out in the former Yugoslavia
April 7	Europe recognizes independence of Bosnia-Herzegovina, former provinces of Yugoslavia
April 29	Riots occur in Los Angeles in aftermath of verdict on police officers alleged to have beaten Rodney King during a traffic stop
November 3	Bush loses election to Bill Clinton
December	Troops sent to Somalia to intervene in civil war and allow for the provision of emergency aid to starving citizens
December 17	Bush signs NAFTA, the North American Free Trade Agreement, linking the economies of the United States, Canada, and Mexico in a common market
1993	
January 3	START II Treaty with Russia signed, commits United States to substantial reductions in its nuclear arsenal
January 13	Air strikes ordered against Iraq for noncompliance with terms of surrender
January 20	Bush leaves office

WILLIAM (BILL) CLINTON (1993–2001)

1992

November 3	Election

1993

January 20	Inauguration
February 4	Hillary Clinton appointed to direct national health care plan development
February 17	First economic plan submitted to Congress: some new taxes and increased domestic spending
February 22	Airlift of supplies to Bosnia-Herzegovina in response to civil war
February 26	World Trade Center bombed in New York City
July 19	Clinton announces "don't ask, don't tell, don't pursue" policy regarding homosexuals in the U.S. military
July 20	Clinton aide Vince Foster commits suicide; Whitewater investment deal revealed; independent prosecutor begins investigation soon thereafter
August	Revised economic plan submitted to Congress
September	Reinventing government/National Performance Review introduced; systematic review of government operations with the idea of eliminating waste, reducing redundancy, reducing bureaucracy
September 13	Israel-Palestinian peace pact signed
October 3	U.S. Army troops killed in Somalia; political controversy ensues
October 27	National health care proposal introduced; pronounced dead on arrival in Congress
November 20	NAFTA passed by U.S. Congress
November 30	Clinton signs Brady Bill, major gun control legislation named for Reagan aide shot during assassination attempt made on Reagan

1994

February	Limitations placed on use of U.S. forces in Somalia
April	Civil war in Rwanda leads to deaths of hundreds of thousands in ethnic killings
April 19	Branch Davidian compound in Waco, Texas, destroyed in standoff with Federal Bureau of Investigation and Bureau of Alcohol, Tobacco and Firearms
July	Congressional investigation of Whitewater begins; culminates in impeachment and trial in 1998–1999

August 26	Haiti occupied to restore political stability and democracy
November 8	Midterm elections: Republicans take over both Houses of Congress

1995

April 19	Destruction of Alfred P. Murrah Federal Building in Oklahoma City, Oklahoma
July	Diplomatic relations reopened with Vietnam
December	Budget showdown with Congress; Clinton refuses to sign several spending bills; federal government shuts down twice

1996

January	Second economic plan announced
August 22	Welfare Reform Act passed
November 5	Reelection

1997

January 20	Second inauguration
May	Balanced budget agreement worked out with Congress: tax increases and spending cuts agreed to
May 20	*Clinton v. Jones* decision announced; Supreme Court rejects presidential claim of executive privilege against being sued on a civil matter while serving as president

1998

January 21	Independent Counsel Kenneth Starr receives authorization to expand investigation of Whitewater affair to include alleged sexual relations between the president and Monica Lewinsky
August 7	U.S. embassies in Kenya and Tanzania bombed
August 17	Clinton admits to relationship with Monica Lewinsky
August 20	U.S. military forces bomb Sudan and Afghanistan in retaliation for the bombing of U.S. embassies in Nigeria and Tanzania
September 9	Independent Prosecutor Kenneth Starr's report released
November	Clinton settles Paula Jones sexual harassment suit out of court for $850,000
November 3	Midterm elections: Democrats almost regain control of House of Representatives; Republicans retain firm control of the Senate
December 11–12	House Judiciary Committee votes in favor of four articles of impeachment against Clinton
December 19	House of Representatives votes two articles of impeachment against Clinton

1999

February 12	Clinton acquitted on both articles of impeachment

March	U.S. forces begin bombing in Kosovo and Yugoslavia to stop human rights violations
2000	
October	Conflict reemerges between Israel and the Palestinians
November 7	Election Day
November 17	Clinton visits Vietnam
2001	
January 20	Clinton leaves office

INTRODUCTION

In some ways, historians have it easy.

Historians will, no doubt, object to this statement. They struggle to find records and evidence of long-past events; they debate the proper ways to interpret what evidence they find; and they act in an arena in which the next discovery could undermine a life's careful work. There is nothing, they would say, easy about history.

While historians will be right to raise these objections, they have one advantage over students of contemporary life: time. Time filters political, social, economic, gender, racial, and ethnic biases and assumptions. Time makes it possible to take more dispassionate positions on an array of events that seem vitally important at the moment but lose their significance over the years. Most important, time assists in assessing what is and is not important. Those issues and items that capture our attention today are those that have come down through history and that, accordingly, history has judged important. It is, of course, the inevitable case that history misses much, and much of what it misses it overlooks because of various biases and inattentions. However incomplete history is, it is nonetheless a basis for choosing some issues to include in a work like this while avoiding others.

When engaging the recent past, or even the unfolding present, there are no filters of time working to highlight certain events or reduce the significance of others. President William (Bill) Clinton has just finished his term as this book is being published. Which of his initiatives, crises, or points of personal character will be considered important in fifty years? Will the Persian Gulf War, fought under President George Bush, be considered important, or will his deemphasis of international human rights after the protests at Tiananmen Square in China draw history's attention? Will President Ronald Reagan's policy of pressuring Communist countries to undermine their governments—the so-called Reagan Doctrine—be considered a significant part of the end of the Cold War, or will the massive budget deficits run up during his time in office be regarded as the most important aspect of his administration?

This book represents our best judgments, unaided by the filter of time, about which issues, initiatives, and events were the most important in the presidencies of Ronald Reagan (1981–1989), George H.W. Bush (1989–1993), and William (Bill) Clinton (1993–2001). At the very least, we are confident that most of these issues will retain their relevance for understanding the nature, context, and actions of these presidents. Time, of course, will be the ultimate judge.

THE CONTEXT: POLITICAL, SOCIAL, AND ECONOMIC CHANGE IN THE 1980s AND 1990s

There is a tendency in popular discussions of politics to equate politics and political events with the individuals who hold office during the period. Thus, popular discussions of politics tend to emphasize the roles played by individuals in shaping events. One implication of this, obviously, is that whenever things go badly (or, for that matter, when they go well), it is entirely the result of the actions and choices of those in office at the time. Good outcomes equal good leaders, and vice versa.

This linkage of politics and personality is particularly evident at the level of the U.S. presidency. Presidents are the most easily distinguishable political figures in the United States, and perhaps the world. Accordingly, much analysis of what happens in politics is reduced to the simple-minded notion that individual presidents, by strength of their will, character, and skill, are responsible for making sure that things "go well" for Americans. When times are rough, it is seen as the obvious result of the failure of presidential leadership; when times are good, the president is generally viewed as good, or even great.

This simple-minded understanding of presidents and their actions is unfortunate for a number of reasons. First, *presidents are individuals acting in a complex political system.* They operate in a set of institutions—Congress, the courts, the bureaucracy, state and local governments, and so on—that seriously limit their independence of action. These institutions may or may not support individual presidents for reasons that are entirely outside of the president's control: Congress may be controlled by members of a different political party, for example. Assuming presidents are entirely responsible for events during their time in office misses much of the complexity of what actually occurs.

Second, *presidents inherit the policies of prior administrations.* No president comes to office with unlimited opportunity to make the world anew; billions of budget dollars and intricate patterns of political support are already allocated toward some programs, policies, and goals. It is not possible wholly to reject standing commitments nor is it even desirable to do so. What is actually important is what presidents do with the programs in place—how they adapt them, support them, oppose them, and so on—as well as how they develop their new ideas. Assessments of presidential successes and failures must account for this inheritance if they are to be realistic.

Third, *presidents inherit social and political contexts*. In addition to policies and programs, presidents encounter social and political contexts when they come to office. War, for example, may limit a president's ability to make choices. Similarly, tight economic times can seriously hinder the nation's ability to develop new programs or even pay for existing ones. And dramatic social changes, such as mass immigration or significant social movements, can influence what is possible at a given political moment. Acknowledging these forces must be part of any interpretation of a particular presidency.

This introduction focuses on five contexts that can be seen to have shaped the choices and actions of the three presidents covered in this volume: (1) the era of divided government, (2) the increase in budget deficits and the growth of the national debt, (3) the end of the Cold War, (4) globalization, and (5) changing social and political demographics that have reshaped the character of the American electorate. Each of these factors have influenced what all three of the presidents presented here were able to achieve. Accordingly, each deserves some discussion before moving to the main text of the work.

The Era of Divided Government

One of the central conditions affecting each of the presidents covered in this volume was *divided government*. This term means that while the president was from one political party, control of one or both Houses of Congress was generally in the hands of a different political party. For example, Ronald Reagan (Republican) faced a Democratic-controlled House through his entire administration, and a Democratic-controlled Senate during his final two years in office. George Bush (Republican) faced a Democratic Congress during his entire administration. Bill Clinton (Democrat) enjoyed a Congress controlled by his own party from 1993 to 1995; after 1995, both the House and Senate were taken over by the Republicans—the House for the first time in forty years.

Divided government makes it more difficult for presidents to achieve their political agendas. To the degree that presidents and members of Congress share similar ideas and attitudes about what government ought to do, they can cooperate to make new government policies and reform existing programs. However, when presidents and Congress disagree, it can be almost impossible for presidents to achieve their goals. While it is not necessarily the case that members of Congress will agree with a president who is a member of the same political party, it is more likely that this will be the case. Accordingly, divided government implies that control of each branch of government is in the hands of people with very different political ideas and agendas. It is, therefore, more difficult for presidents to achieve their goals in such an environment, and any consideration of what specific presidents did and why they did it must acknowledge the effect of divided government on their administrations.

The Budget Context

Budget politics in this era were tough, to say the least. Owing to a combination of such factors as a rise in entitlement programs (welfare, social security, unemployment insurance, and the like), a rise in oil prices, changes in the world economy, and the Vietnam War, the United States began to face budget shortfalls in the 1960s. These intensified in the 1970s. When Ronald Reagan promoted, and Congress supported, massive tax cuts as part of his first economic package, without cutting spending to an equal degree, the United States entered an era of massive budget deficits. From 1981, when Ronald Reagan took office, to the beginning of 2001, the end of the era being covered in this volume, the accumulated debt of the United States rose from $1.5 trillion to $5.8 trillion dollars—almost 400 percent in just twenty years.

Enormous budget deficits—over $350 billion per year in the latter years of the Bush administration—put extraordinary pressures on the political system. Current programs, many of which have well-entrenched supporters who do not want the programs altered in any way, require funding. But so do any new policies that may be developed. Money for these programs can be generated in only three ways: borrowing, which builds up the debt and has long-term consequences for the nation; redistribution, taking money out of some programs and either reducing the size of the overall budget or transferring funds from one program to another; and tax increases, transferring money from citizens to government. All of these options are difficult and unpopular, although borrowing in this period was more popular than redistribution or tax increases.

It is difficult to be a president in an era of tight budgets. It is virtually impossible to sponsor new, potentially popular programs. Furthermore, it is often necessary to argue for program redistribution or tax increases to make budget numbers at least approach a balance. If national emergencies, such as wars, occur, the budget makes it increasingly difficult to respond—even the Persian Gulf War was affected since it was through substantial contributions from Kuwait, Saudi Arabia, and other interested nations that the United States was able to afford to send its military to the region without incurring even greater levels of debt.

Beginning in 1998, the United States began to enjoy budget surpluses. The result of a combination of strong economic growth, tax increases, and changes in the world economy, the U.S. budget surplus through the years 2000–2010 is projected to be as high as $1.7 trillion. While this surplus is a source of political debate—some wish to return the surplus to voters in the form of tax cuts, others wish to pay off the accumulated debt, and still others want to fund new programs—it is fair to say that all of the presidents covered in this volume would have preferred to deal with the complications and opportunities provided by an era of budget surpluses instead of massive budget deficits.

The End of the Cold War

The central factor of U.S. foreign policy making in the post–World War II era was the Cold War—the competition between the United States and the Soviet Union for allies, resources, and political and military dominance. This conflict, which turned World War II allies into competitors armed with over 20,000 nuclear weapons each, was global: small disputes between seemingly minor nations often escalated into proxy wars in which both the United States and the Soviet Union supported opposing sides and poured in supplies, money, aid, and training for their cause. These proxy wars substituted for direct military conflicts, which both sides carefully avoided since, for the first time in human history, the world's two leading powers had the ability to destroy the planet, not just large portions of the other nation's population.

Working from the premise that the Soviet Union was engaged in a slow process of world domination through the subversion of democratic regimes and the installation of Communist governments in their place, the United States undertook a policy of containment in the initial postwar years. This meant that the United States gave substantial political, economic, and military support to non-Communist governments and organizations around the world. The United States became directly involved in military conflicts in Korea and Vietnam. Finally, the United States selectively engaged the Soviet Union and the world's other great Communist power, China, in economic and diplomatic relations called *détente*. The aim of détente was to reduce the scope of U.S.–Communist conflicts in favor of wary cooperation.

Later, under Ronald Reagan, the United States changed its policy regarding the Soviet Union from containment and détente to an active strategy to undermine Communist regimes. The United States gave substantial support to anti-Communist groups and forces, and also undertook a massive weapons and military technology program intended to push the Soviets into a competition they could not afford. Cumulatively, the intent of these policies was to undermine the Soviet Union and make it financially and politically impossible for the Soviets to continue the Cold War.

Regardless of specific policies pursued by individual presidents during this era, the Cold War provided a fundamental focus to U.S. policy. Concerns for human rights, ethnic tensions, and global economics were generally suppressed in favor of promoting stable anti-Communist governments. Indeed, both the United States and the Soviet Union helped local governments control dissident groups and individuals in the name of Cold War stability. The Cold War, then, justified and shaped U.S. policy: anything that was understood to limit or reduce perceived Soviet expansion was justified as being necessary to prevent either Communist world domination or nuclear war. Other concerns were secondary at best.

Then, suddenly, the Soviet Union collapsed. Republicans generally claim that it was Ronald Reagan's policies that caused this collapse; a more developed view acknowledges that there were many problems in the Soviet Union well before Ronald Reagan became president, and while his policies may have influenced the timing of events, they were not the sole cause. In any case, starting with the fall of the Berlin Wall separating East from West Germany in 1989, the Iron Curtain separating Eastern, Communist Europe from Western, democratic Europe came down. In 1991 the Soviet government collapsed and was replaced by a new, Russian, somewhat democratic regime. The Cold War was over.

The end of the Cold War ended the clarity that had shaped U.S. foreign policy. Questions of human rights, ethnic diversity, and global economic changes became more significant. No longer could the United States justify supporting the repression of political dissent in anti-Communist countries; thus, years of accumulated tensions exploded in violence in nations around the world. Similarly, the Russians could not, and did not desire to, continue to support repressive regimes around the world; long-repressed ethnic, economic, and other tensions began to emerge in formerly Communist countries. What, then, was the United States to do?

As of the time of the publication of this volume, there is no clear answer to this question. Some believe that the United States has an obligation to support human rights struggles around the world regardless of cost or effort. Others believe that the United States should engage other countries only when its direct military or economic interests are at issue. Most occupy a middle ground arguing for intervention in some places but not in others for reasons that are usually inconsistent. To be president in the new era of foreign policy is to lack clarity of purpose and to face inevitable criticism from many points.

Globalization

Another significant international force began to shape the context in which these three presidents acted: globalization. Globalization describes a process by which the economies of the world's nations move beyond the control of individual governments in favor of new, multinational, transnational conglomerates. More, the world's cultures become interlinked through mass media like television: people in the Middle East can watch the Cable News Network (CNN) cover school shootings in Oregon as easily as Americans can view ethnic conflict in Bali. Thus, economics and politics in the global era become "supranational": they transcend the national boundaries that traditionally have been the organizing limits of political control.

In practice, globalization makes it more difficult for nations to control their own destinies. For example, where once a nation was able to ensure its citizens a decent income by requiring companies based in their country to provide a minimum hourly wage, today companies move around the globe in search of ever-cheaper sources of labor, goods, and materials. Well-developed transportation systems and the internet make the notion of a "national" economy somewhat out of date. In return, goods and services are provided to consumers at higher levels of quality and at lower costs. But, since governments have to tax in order to fund their operations, globalization makes it hard for governments to function: a company facing a high tax load simply moves its operations to a low tax zone. In the era of globalization, accordingly, decisions made in Washington, D.C., may no longer influence companies very much: they move, find new sources of products, and establish new markets. Making government policy, then, is difficult at best.

Another important economic consequence of globalization is vast inequity in the distribution of wealth. Stockholders and managers of transnational corporations generate vast profits and can gather great fortunes on the backs of Third World laborers making as little as $1 a day. Indeed, whether in the developed or developing world, those people engaged in economic enterprises that can compete on the world market thrive; those who are tied to less competitive industries suffer. Unfortunately, some of the jobs that thrive entail low pay and benefits; jobs with high pay and benefits are lost to cheaper labor markets. The people who lose their jobs in this transition often move from a condition in which a person with a high school education or less can raise a family to a condition in which two college-educated parents struggle to make ends meet. Circumstances can be worse for less educated people. Competition is always difficult; placed on a world stage, in the context of vast disparities in wealth and opportunities, it becomes more intense and potentially costly.

In addition, there is a cultural dimension to globalization. As transnational entertainment and service corporations like Disney, Microsoft, Wal-Mart, and McDonald's spread across the globe, a homogenization of local culture begins. McDonald's makes hamburgers one way because that is the cheapest, most efficient way. Their product is desirable and inexpensive. People flock to the restaurants. But, as a consequence, local businesses lose customers, and customers lose local choices.

The "globalist" answer to this consequence is simple: people prefer McDonald's, so why worry about the lost restaurants, local entertainment venues, software alternatives, or department stores? Opponents of this homogenization give two answers to the question, "Why worry?" First, those people who once worked at local restaurants, stores, and other businesses lose their jobs; while some find jobs in the new enterprises, most do not. They then put pressure on government for services like unemployment insurance and welfare—services government struggles to pay for since they cannot tax the transnational corporations effectively. People frustrated by the inability of government to provide for their needs often become angry at the transnational companies. This anger can, at its worst, promote ethnic nationalist or separationist groups. Since the international conglomerate hurt me in favor of its stockholders, the logic goes, we should hold an ethnic or separationist revolt to drive the transnational corporations and their supporters out of the country. Many contemporary conflicts in world affairs are the result of this kind of angry global-local confrontation.

Second, local flavor is lost, often forever. The traditions and patterns of life that are also part of the fabric of society can be sacrificed for the sake of economic efficiency and competitiveness.

Cumulatively, globalization makes the job of being president more difficult. Presidents have to shape their policies in light of the demands both of voters and of economic forces they cannot fully control. These tensions and demands have the potential to cause internal disruption at home or ethnic and other conflicts in those nations with which the United States interacts. Tilting too far either way has enormous consequences for the nation. So does not tilting too far. The choices presidents make in this globalized environment must be accounted for in interpreting the successes and failures of any individual president.

The Changing of America

The final context to be addressed here is the changing of America—the increasing demographic, cultural, and ideological diversity occurring within the United States. Simply put, the United States once was made up of roughly three groups: whites, the overwhelming majority, most of whom emigrated from Europe; African Americans, largely the children and grandchildren of people brought to the United States as slaves; and

Native Americans pushed aside as the European population spread across the American continent. This led to a type of stability in American politics as policies reflected the ideas, opinions, and experiences of the majority population. This representation often hurt minority populations, but it was a type of stability nonetheless.

The nation's demographic and cultural diversity has increased in the last thirty years, however. The Latino population is increasing rapidly and is expected to surpass that of African Americans by 2020. Asian Americans are becoming increasingly numerous and constitute large percentages of the population in some states. Each of these groups is itself a compilation of peoples who may not have similar experiences—Latinos include expatriate Cubans whose families fled Cuba after the revolution there in 1959, Puerto Ricans who have been in the United States since the United States took possession of the island in 1898, and more recent immigrants from the Caribbean and Central and South America. Each of these groups has its own interests and desires that it presses within the political system. Other groups are seeing similar gains and experiencing similar levels of diversity. Even the "established" groups—the whites—are experiencing greater sensitivity to the ethnic and religious differences among themselves. The United States, in other words, is becoming a much more diverse nation, and to the degree that peoples' different life experiences shape different political desires and demands, the pressures on the political system can be expected to become more complex over time.

Additionally, the United States is aging. The fastest growing age group in the United States comprises people over eighty. Increased awareness of health maintenance earlier in life, combined with powerful (and often expensive) medical treatments for aging people, has led to a remarkable increase in the number of people living for decades after retirement. Given that the Social Security and Medicare systems were established to help older citizens with their retirement and health concerns, this increase in the older population puts substantial stress on the political system to fund these programs. Moreover, the interests of older citizens may differ from those of younger people: older citizens may be concerned with property tax control, for example, because they cannot easily pay higher property taxes on fixed incomes; younger people may want taxes increased to fund new school construction, the development of computer labs, and other programs aimed at children. As more and more people live well into their postretirement years, these pressures intensify.

Such demographic changes are complemented by cultural and ideological changes in the nation as well. Women have entered the workforce in increased numbers. Demands for the protection of workforce rights, especially in the areas of access to jobs and sexual harassment law, have intensified over the last few decades. Others, such as gays, lesbians, and the disabled, have made similar gains and have placed similar pressures on the political system in the last twenty years. Additionally, the nation has developed a substantial environmental movement since the early 1970s. Questions of abortion rights, prayer in school, and other lifestyle issues have proliferated. Finally, beginning in the 1980s, Christian conservatives began to demand that the political system act to advance their interests and preferences.

In many ways, these changes are to be embraced and encouraged. Diversity has meant that peoples' rights are more carefully treated and less easily ignored. Questions of environmental and lifestyle quality are central issues of life; however, cumulatively, these changes profoundly influence the presidency. It is telling, for example, that both major party candidates in the 2000 presidential election—Texas Governor George Bush (R) and Vice President Al Gore (D)—speak Spanish. The concerns women express have become centerpieces of political campaigns—more women than men voted in 1996, and Bill Clinton's reelection was contingent on the broad support he drew from women. Political leaders throughout this period were forced to engage in a delicate game of coalition politics among groups and attitudes that were increasingly sensitive to their differences. Ronald Reagan's two elections were based on a working coalition of conservative Republicans and working-class Democrats upset, to some degree, with the policies their party had advanced in favor of minorities; George Bush's loss was related to his inability to maintain the Reagan coalition; and Bill Clinton's victories, as suggested, were the result of a new coalition of voters. Since Congress reflected the same patterns of diversity that influenced campaigns, presidential interactions with Congress became more difficult: a president and a member of Congress might be from the same party, but they may not reflect the same demographic and ideological values. Making policy in this environment is difficult at best.

SCOPE, ORGANIZATION, SELECTION CRITERIA, AND METHODOLOGY

The readings and issues on each president covered in this volume are divided into two main sections: Domestic and Economic Policy, covering those issues that affect Americans in such areas as crime control, roads, education, and other public goods and services, as well as control over the economy, the promotion of economic growth, and taxes; and Military and Foreign Policy, involving the use of military force, the development of doctrines guiding the use and purchase of weapons, the nature of the United States' relationship with foreign nations, and why the United States does or does not intervene in events around the world. Each of these areas saw substantial presidential involvement during the period of this study. They also cover the central issues that any president must inevitably face.

In order to understand why these areas have emerged as the organizing themes of this work, it is necessary to understand that this volume is grounded in an approach to politics and political life that is historical and institutional in nature. What this means, in practice, is that our understanding of what goes on in politics, why things happen, and why they matter is based on an analysis of the way in which history shapes political events and the ways in which political institutions—the presidency, the Congress, the Supreme Court—filter and respond to political happenings in real-world situations. To understand the reasons for the selection of issues in this volume, it is necessary to understand four factors that shaped our thinking: the purposes of government, the unique characteristics of the United States, which events and issues were significant in the context of the moment, and the ways in which political leaders act to shape political events.

The Purposes of Government

In general, government—all governments, of every type, everywhere—has at least three purposes: to defend national and community frontiers, to protect the domestic security of citizens, and to provide goods and services to citizens.

The first purpose, to defend national and community borders, is crucial to every government. Unless a government can control its borders, it cannot function or survive. As a practical matter, this makes the areas of foreign policy—diplomatic relationships with foreign governments—and national security policy—military and secret relations—an important area of government action. This is particularly the case in the United States during the period under study here: the United States has become the world's premier military and foreign policy superpower. Accordingly, this volume contains selections related to the military and foreign policies of the United States: each of the three presidents covered here undertook substantial initiatives in these crucial areas.

The second purpose, to protect the domestic security of its citizens, refers to practices in the areas of criminal and civil law—how people relate to each other, and how the government acts to prevent citizens from harming each other. In the context of this volume, such policies fall in the area of domestic policy. Each of these presidents undertook a number of domestic policies intended to deal with the issue of crime. The important ones are addressed in this volume.

The final purpose, to provide goods and services to its citizens, largely informs the domestic and economic policy sections of this work. Citizens want things from government. They want, for example, roads, schools, and a national banking system. Which demands to address is a crucial question faced by all presidents. Accordingly, this volume includes a section on domestic policy (which encompasses crime-control issues) and economic policy.

Unique Characteristics of the United States

It has been said that the United States is an experiment intended to discover whether people of widely varying backgrounds, attitudes, and opinions can govern themselves effectively through democracy. While this idea can lead to a kind of thoughtless patriotism (i.e., America's policies are always good because it is a democratic, free nation), it is a useful way of considering an important dimension of the nation: its *exceptionalism*.

Exceptionalism is a concept that highlights certain characteristics of the United States that are of relevance for the policies it makes, the way in which it interacts with the outside world, and the ideas and values its citizens bring to bear when they express opinions and evaluate what government does. For the purposes of this volume, the dimension of exceptionalism that is most important to consider is *Americans' understanding of the purpose of their nation*. Simply put, many Americans, including those who have shaped the way in which the nation makes and justifies its laws over time, believe that the United States has a unique mission to promote freedom and democracy through the practices of limited government and selective engagement with other nations. This means that the leaders and citizens of the United States tend to insist that the nation undertake policies and actions that promote global freedom and democracy—as the people at the time see it—and that do not restrain individual choice within the United States.

The exceptionalist impulse to establish freedom and democracy both globally and in the United States is the foundation of the foreign and military policy sections of this volume: the role of the United States in world affairs and the role of the federal government in U.S. politics. Policies involving international relations are rarely made without invoking some justification that touches on the sense of mission that shapes American political culture. Similarly, few policies that affect the United States directly are made without a consideration of how they fit in the United States' unique mission. Accordingly, to understand what the presidents wanted, why they wanted it, and what their opponents had in mind during the debate, it is important to address the underlying philosophical issues that were at play during specific policy debates.

The Events and Issues That Were Significant in the Context of the Moment

Every president emphasizes some issues and downgrades the significance of others. Such issues must be considered in a volume such as this. Additionally, the push of events sometimes causes issues to rise in significance outside of an individual president's desires and hopes. Both types of issues and circumstances shape what is important in any administration.

This work is made up of readings related to both types of issues—those of presidential choice and those of circumstance. The directors of Reagan's and Bush's respective presidential libraries—institutions developed after presidents leave office to house important papers, honor the work of, and provide a central research location for issues and events of a president's career—were asked what were the most important issues advanced by the president during his time in office. We also used our personal judgments as experts in the field to select our issues. In the case of President Clinton, we used our judgments about which issues he had advanced most aggressively during his time in office. These issues are examined in this text.

In addition, external events occur that can demand presidential attention, and political circumstances can change in ways that may or may not favor the president's position. Accordingly, we surveyed the record of each president's time in office, focusing on those circumstances (e.g., the fall of the Berlin Wall, impeachment, or the Republican takeover of Congress in 1994) that placed new pressures on the president's agenda. Such issues and events are also considered within this volume.

Together, this approach allowed us to develop a list of core issues, ideas, and circumstances that were central to each president's administration. As might be expected, given the close linkage in time among these leaders, many of the issues and events are common to all three administrations; others are not. What really matters was the significance of the issue in the context of the moment.

The Ways in Which Political Leaders Act to Shape Political Events

Politics is complicated. Political outcomes are inevitably the result of cross-cutting factors including the interests of the people making decisions, the opportunities and problems that exist at a given moment, the constraints of time and patterns of support for and against different ideas, and the choices individuals make in the context of the moment.

Leaders are central to the process of political decision making. They help define which issues rate concentration, and the choices they make significantly influence the successes and failures of particular political programs. Rhetoric—the words and arguments leaders use to advance a political debate—is a vital part of all leaders' arsenals in the political process. Leaders use words to advance specific programs, denigrate others, and shape the debate in terms favorable to their agendas.

This volume focuses on the words and arguments used by different political leaders—presidents and their opponents—to advance their own positions while challenging opponents' rhetoric. While the interaction of the president's words with those of his opponents does not fully explain why particular policies won or lost, it is an important part of the story. Fuller understanding of why things happen in politics, then, requires an attention to the words through which politics is practiced. Accordingly, this volume presents representative examples of the rhetoric used by presidents and their challengers and places them in their political context to help understand why some policies and programs were successful, while others failed, in American political life.

CONCLUSION

In sum, this volume represents our understanding of what the crucial issues and policies of the 1980s and 1990s were, how presidents acted to shape these issues in the ways they preferred, and how their opponents fought the presidents' agenda to mold it in their image. To anyone interested in the politics of the era, the rhetorical summaries and political analysis that constitute each section of the text should allow a better grasp of why things happened the way they did. At the very least, we hope to have provided a foundation for further analysis and study. In any case, the readings and discussions throughout this work demonstrate the infinite intrigue and excitement of politics.

1

RONALD REAGAN

(1981–1989)

INTRODUCTION

In many ways, Ronald Reagan's presidency set the tone, general direction, and political character of all three presidencies covered in this volume. Decisions made in the early days of his administration established the context within which subsequent presidents operated. In addition, his optimism and ideology inspired a new generation of conservative politicians who have become an enduring power in the Republican Party. Together, these factors have shaped contemporary political life.

Reagan was elected in a time of economic, social, and international turmoil. Unemployment and inflation were high. The legacy of the Vietnam War and the Watergate scandal and the government's ineffective responses to the social disruptions caused by these events led many Americans to grow more cynical about government. In addition, the 1979 Soviet invasion of Afghanistan, the 1979 Communist Sandinista takeover of Nicaragua after a long civil war, and the 1980 Islamic fundamentalist revolution in Iran caused many people to believe that the power of the United States was declining and its national security was at risk. Thus, the political context in which Reagan became president was generally unfavorable.

In the 1980 presidential election, Reagan offered simple, optimistic answers to these problems. Key among his proposals was a substantial tax cut, particularly for high wage earners and investors. The argument in favor of this policy, which ran counter to sixty years of established tax programs, was based on the Laffer Curve, an economic model developed by Arthur Laffer. Laffer argued in favor of what came to be known as "trickle-down" economics: the notion that those with the most money to spend—the wealthy—should be given major tax breaks and encouraged to buy products, invest their resources, and otherwise use their wealth. This was expected, in turn, to stimulate production and investment and thereby promote economic growth. Then every American would benefit. This idea was central to Reagan's first economic package, which was passed in the first year of his presidency.

The other major component of Reagan's optimistic, simple campaign was support for massive increases in defense spending. The U.S. military had been declining in size, numbers of weapons, amount of training, and other factors since the end of its involvement in the Vietnam War (1973). In 1980 Reagan argued that it was because of these cuts that the United States' safety was being challenged. Thus he insisted that substantial increases in military spending were required to make the military strong, create a 600-ship navy, and build and deploy new generations of weapons, including nuclear weapons. This policy was also part of the accomplishments of the first year of the Reagan presidency.

Yet at this moment of great triumph the Reagan program set up the dominant problem of the next seventeen years: huge budget deficits. Cutting taxes reduced the revenue government needed to fund existing programs; in addition, the large increases in defense spending put significant demands on decreased resources. The Laffer model did not, at least in the short term, lead to sufficient economic growth to offset declining tax revenues. Reagan claimed that he had hoped to balance the budget through cuts in such social programs as welfare, transportation, and the regulation of business. However, Democrats, who held the majority of seats in both the House of Representatives and the Senate, never supported such cuts, and as a practical matter Reagan was unwilling to anger the beneficiaries of social programs and so never pushed for the levels of reductions that would have been required to balance the budget. In response, government was forced to borrow hundreds of billions of dollars to meet its commitments, which set the political context at least until 1998.

The politics of budget deficits shaped Reagan's administration in multiple ways. First, every new program proposal, whether domestic, economic, or military, was scrutinized in terms of its budgetary implications. Second, Reagan turned to matters of foreign policy—negotiating new treaties, engaging in covert operations, selectively using U.S. military force, and so on—as an arena in which he could establish his legacy.

In domestic and economic policy, only one substantive development occurred in the remainder of Reagan's term. While Reagan advanced many proposals, some of which are covered in this volume, most were either small in scope (enterprise zones, block grant programs, immigration reform) or, like welfare reform, would only be accomplished fully by a later president. In general, Reagan's domestic agenda was comparatively small.

Starting in 1986, Reagan sponsored a significant tax code revision that led to reduced tax rates even as it eliminated many of the loopholes through which many Americans had avoided paying taxes. It was intended to be "revenue neutral," meaning that at the end of the program, the government would collect no more taxes than it had under the previous plan. This accomplishment did create a markedly new tax code for the United States, and while it has been amended many times in the subsequent years, its core philosophy that no one should be able to use loopholes to avoid paying taxes remains the dominant tax strategy of the U.S. government.

It was in the area of foreign policy that Reagan made his most dramatic moves, which constitutes much of his legacy. The twin anchors of his foreign policy were the Reagan Doctrine and the development of nuclear arms control agreements with the Soviet Union.

The Reagan Doctrine, announced in 1983, was appealingly simple. Reagan argued that rather than continuing a dangerous nuclear standoff with the Soviet Union, the United States should adopt a strategy of actively undermining Communist regimes. Key dimensions of this policy were aid to anti-Communist forces in countries like Afghanistan, Grenada, and Nicaragua; defense buildups; the purchase of new nuclear weapons systems like the Trident submarine, the MX missile, and smaller missiles intended for use in Europe; and Star Wars, the Strategic Defense Initiative (SDI), which would provide a shield against incoming Soviet missiles. Cumulatively, the intent of these policies was to undermine the Soviet Union and make it financially and politically impossible for the Soviets to continue the Cold War.

Somewhat surprisingly, given the nature of his rhetoric (Reagan once referred to the Soviet Union as an "Evil Empire"), Reagan also initiated a series of negotiations that led to significant reductions in the numbers and types of nuclear weapons possessed by the United States and the Soviet Union. Thus, even as he worked to undermine Soviet influence through the Reagan Doctrine, he began talks to negotiate the Strategic Arms Reduction Treaty (START) and the Intermediate Nuclear Forces (INF). Indeed, in one striking moment at a private meeting with Soviet leader Mikhail Gorbachev in Rejkavik, Iceland, Reagan proposed the elimination of *all* strategic nuclear weapons from both nations' arsenals. While this radical proposal was quickly dismissed, the net effect of these negotiations was to initiate, for the first time, a reduction in nuclear forces for both of the world's great nuclear superpowers. Where once the Soviet Union and the United States each had over 25,000 warheads capable of reaching the other's shores, by the year 2000 that number was down to 2,500 each, and negotiations continue for further reductions.

Assessing Reagan's legacy is a difficult task. It is more than a matter of counting which proposals Reagan favored and which he opposed, adding up whether he had more successes or more failures, and deciding if he was a successful president or not. His impact was greater, and more subtle, than such an analysis would admit. For example, very few people are neutral regarding Reagan's presidency. For some people, he is a saint who reformed the economy and saved the world; for others, he is an indifferent ideologue who cared only for the wealthy and was willing to let the poor starve. To some degree, both views are valid. First, as has been noted before, the long-term impact of the budget deficits that exploded under Reagan's watch has been profound. The deficit had the effect of tying the hands of each subsequent president. Whatever George Bush or Bill Clinton might have wanted to do, whatever policies and programs they might have wanted to develop, they had to work in the political and economic context established by Reagan. The Reagan economic plan, then, clearly affected the United States for an extended time, regardless of one's opinion about whether the impact was positive or negative.

Second, the foreign policy effects of Reagan's administration were significant. While it is an example of political thoughtlessness to claim that Reagan's policies caused the collapse of the Soviet Union—the idea that seventy years of Soviet corruption and repression had nothing to do with the nation's collapse is indefensible—the Reagan Doctrine, the military buildup, and the development of a new set of policies regarding nuclear forces did shape the capacity and doctrine of the United States in foreign affairs. For example, it is clear that the Persian Gulf War, fought under President Bush, was won as quickly and as easily as it was because of the defense increases that accompanied Reagan's administration. Similarly, continuing reductions in nuclear weapons are an accomplishment built on the foundation laid by Reagan.

Yet, other dimensions of U.S. foreign policy under Ronald Reagan have come back to haunt the United States and its citizens. As part of the Cold War theory that the Soviets had to be challenged everywhere, the United States regularly supported repressive regimes that abused their citizens. The U.S. approach was that, as long as the government was anti-Communist, it deserved American support. This had the effect of linking the United States with repressive and violent governments around the world. Subsequently, many people came to detest and distrust the United States because of its support for authoritarian governments. Alternatively, the United States trained and equipped guerrilla forces around the world that were engaged in anti-Communist wars. Some of these groups, like the one run by Saudi Arabian billionaire Osama bin Laden, who the United States helped to build an anti-Soviet army in Afghanistan, have now turned their knowledge against the United States and its citizens. It was bin Laden's group that is alleged to have bombed U.S. embassies in Kenya and Tanzania in 1998. Cumulatively, then, Reagan left a profound, but mixed, legacy in foreign affairs.

Third, and perhaps most important, Reagan inspired a new generation of political leaders who have gone on to shape political life long after their mentor left office. Reagan articulated a conservative political philosophy that promoted hard work, individual responsibility, and the elimination of federal regulations on business. In this ideology, government is regarded as a burden on business and a threat to individual liberty. Thus, minimum levels of government ought to be encouraged to maximize freedom. However, in matters of private behavior, such as sexual preference, abortion, and drug usage, conservatives argue, government regulation is appropriate. This philosophy, and the articulate way in which Reagan advanced it, inspired many future leaders and shaped their political agendas. Indeed, the Republican takeover of the House of Representatives and Senate in 1994 is a direct consequence of Reagan's administration: the new Republicans who came to office in 1994 were almost all Reagan conservatives, and all recent Republican candidates for president have claimed to be Reagan's true successor. Cumulatively, then, for both good and bad, the period under study here, the presidents of the 1980s and 1990s, is, ultimately, the Reagan era.

DOMESTIC AND ECONOMIC POLICY

THE FIRST REAGAN ECONOMIC PROGRAM (JULY 1981)

Tax policy is a central component of economic policy. By influencing how much money individuals have to spend, and by shaping incentives for business investment, tax law can affect economic growth. Tax policy is also a major political issue since businesses and individuals can try to influence the law in ways that favor their interests. Thus, tax policy is rarely made for purely economic reasons. It is an area in which ideology and interests interact aggressively.

In his first economic plan, which was announced in the context of high unemployment, high interest rates, high inflation, and high frustration, Reagan proposed a radical solution: major tax cuts. Reagan believed that big tax cuts would stimulate economic growth since people would have more money in their pockets. They would use this money to purchase items or make investments, which would then stimulate new production, new employment, and the updating of out-of-date equipment. He also believed that reducing government's income would force it to cut unnecessary programs—at least those he opposed. Finally, he insisted that the tax cut was a pro-family policy because it would increase the resources parents had to use in raising their children.

Critics of the Reagan policy, including Congressmen Richard Gephardt (D-MO) and Ted Weiss (D-NY), made two significant points. First, they noted that major tax cuts would require either massive spending reductions or government borrowing. Both were painful, and Reagan had tried to avoid the pain by not clearly stating his plans. Second, since wealthy people pay more taxes than do the poor, major tax cuts inevitably save affluent individuals far more money than less affluent individuals. Reagan's tax plan, then, was regarded as a program aimed at helping the rich at the expense of the poor.

The short-term effects of Reagan's proposals were dramatic. His plan won support in Congress, and both parts of the Reagan proposal—tax cuts and increased defense spending—were adopted. Other spending was not significantly reduced. Almost immediately, the United States began to run substantial budget deficits, deficits that continued to grow to over $300 billion per year in Bush's presidency. However, the economy also began to grow in this period, suggesting that Reagan's plans did help the nation recover from the recession it was enduring when he took office.

For the longer term, the United States entered a period of major deficits that lasted for the next seventeen years. Taxes were raised during Reagan's, Bush's, and Clinton's administrations, and social and defense spending were cut. Furthermore, new program spending was substantially limited by the realities of the budget crisis: in the face of huge deficits, it was very hard to justify new expenditures. Thus, Reagan was able to influence government well after he left office because the consequences of his 1981 tax policy left the government with limited resources. It was only after 1998, when the United States entered a period of budget surplus after years of economic growth, that it became possible for new programs to be developed in a comparatively easy manner. Whether this occurred because of Reagan's economic plan or despite it remains a point of major debate in the political system.

REAGAN'S ADDRESS TO THE NATION ON FEDERAL TAX REDUCTION LEGISLATION

July 27, 1981

It's been nearly 6 months since I first reported to you on the state of the nation's economy. I'm afraid my message that night was grim and disturbing. I remember telling you we were in the worst economic mess since the Great Depression. Prices were continuing to spiral upward, unemployment was reaching intolerable levels, and all because government was too big and spent too much of our money.

. . .

For 19 out of the last 20 years, the Federal Government has spent more than it took in. There will be another large deficit in this present year which ends September 30th, but with our program in place, it won't be quite as big as it might have been. And starting next year, the deficits will get smaller until in just a few years the budget can be balanced. And we hope we can begin whittling at that almost $1 trillion debt that hangs over the future of our children.

. . .

Time won't allow me to explain every detail. But our bill includes just about everything to help the economy. We reduce the marriage penalty, that unfair tax that has a working husband and wife pay more tax than if they were single. We increase the exemption on the inheritance or estate tax to $600,000, so that farmers and family-owned businesses don't have to sell the farm or store in the event of death just to pay the taxes.

Most important, we wipe out the tax entirely for a surviving spouse. No longer, for example, will a widow have to sell the family source of income to pay a tax on her husband's death.

. . .

Our bipartisan tax bill targets three-quarters of its tax relief to middle-income wage earners who presently pay almost three-quarters of the total income tax. It also then indexes the tax brackets to ensure that you can keep that tax reduction in the years ahead. There also is, as I said, estate tax relief that will keep family farms and family-owned businesses in the family, and there are provisions for personal retirement plans and individual savings accounts.

Because our bipartisan bill is so clearly drawn and broadly based, it provides the kind of predictability and certainty that the financial segments of our society need to make investment decisions that stimulate productivity and make our economy grow. Even more important, if the tax cut goes to you, the American people, in the third year, that money returned to you won't be available to the Congress to spend, and that, in my view, is what this whole controversy comes down to. Are you entitled to the fruits of your own labor or does government have some presumptive right to spend and spend and spend?

. . .

During recent months many of you have asked what can you do to help make America strong again. I urge you again to contact your Senators and Congressmen. Tell them of your support for this bipartisan proposal. Tell them you believe this is an unequalled opportunity to help return America to prosperity and make government again the servant of the people.

In a few days the Congress will stand at the fork of two roads. One road is all too familiar to us. It leads ultimately to higher taxes. It merely brings us full circle back to the source of our economic problems, where the government decides that it knows better than you what should be done with your earnings and, in fact, how you should conduct your life. The other road promises to renew the American spirit. It's a road of hope and opportunity. It places the direction of your life back in your hands where it belongs.

I've not taken your time this evening merely to ask you to trust me. Instead, I ask you to trust yourselves. That's what America is all about. Our struggle for nationhood, our unrelenting fight for freedom, our very existence—these have all rested on the assurance that you must be free to shape your life as you are best able to, that no one can stop you from reaching higher or take from you the creativity that has made America the envy of mankind.

Public Papers of the President: Ronald Reagan. July 27, 1981: 664–668.

CRITICISM OF PRESIDENT REAGAN'S ECONOMIC PROPOSALS

February 19, 1981

Mr. Richard Gephardt (D-MO). Mr. Speaker, the President's speech last night was an extremely clear statement of his economic game plan. Most Members agree, as I do, that spending restraint, regulatory reform and a tighter monetary policy are in order and consistent with our need to fight an underlying 10 percent inflation rate and unemployment at the same time. The specifics and fairness of those three proposals will undoubtedly be debated and discussed but I sense a great deal of support for carrying out the President's overall goals. On tax policy it is harder to agree. The flaw there is not with the concept but the means. If the tax cut can be reshaped—to be conditioned on the spending cuts, to be made fair to middle-income Americans, and if its size and composition can be modified and moderated so that we do not simply replace Government programs with personal consumption—then a tax reduction will spur economic growth without higher deficits, higher interest rates and higher inflation.

The Congressional Record. February 19, 1981: H 2487.

February 19, 1981

Mr. Ted Weiss (D-NY). Mr. Speaker, Ronald Reagan's proposal to slash taxes, increase defense spending, and balance the budget, all at the same time was derided barely a year ago as "voodoo economics" by that prominent Republican statesman, George Bush. Last night that very proposal, together with massive cutbacks in programs for America's neediest individuals and communities, was placed before the Congress and the American people. Pretending to be evenhanded, the President's program would devastate low- and middle-income Americans while providing in classic Republican fashion great tax benefits for big business and the wealthiest individuals in our society.

Sounding a clarion call to repeal the social advances of the 20th century, the President proclaimed that the Government's taxing power "must not be used to regulate the economy or bring about social change."

True as this Republican administration seems to be to its tradition, I hope that we as Democrats will be also true to ourselves, and that the budget and the tax programs we adopt will be for the benefit of all Americans, not just for the privileged few.

The Congressional Record. February 19, 1981: H 2489.

AIR TRAFFIC CONTROLLERS STRIKE (AUGUST 1981)

In August 1981, the Professional Air Traffic Controllers Organization (PATCO) called a strike in support of their demands for higher wages and better working conditions. This violated a U.S. law that denies some federal employees the right to strike on the grounds that some functions, including air traffic control, police, and fire service, are so essential to the operation of government that the people who serve in these jobs cannot leave them in an employment dispute. Thus, unlike workers engaged in private business, who if they strike cause only inconveniences for others, workers in government agencies are believed to be so important to the public order and safety that they cannot be permitted to strike. The PATCO strike brought the importance of such jobs to the forefront and also stimulated a debate about the rights of employees both in government and in private business.

In response to the PATCO strike, President Reagan fired all the striking workers for violating federal law. As the accompanying reading makes clear, he declared the work of these employees to be central to public safety, and he insisted that their demands were unreasonable. Furthermore, he argued that, even if their demands had been reasonable, he would have fired the air traffic controllers for violating the law and risking the safety of the flying public and the economic livelihood of businesses that rely on air service.

Those who argued against the firing, including Congressman Bruce Vento (D-MN) and *St. Paul Dispatch* columnist William Sumner, argued that government employees ought to have the same rights as all other workers, including the right to strike. They also noted that the air traffic control system was seriously understaffed as a consequence of Reagan's decision and put the flying public at increased risk. Finally, they argued that Reagan's decision and further order that no controller who went on strike could ever be rehired was a vindictive policy intended to prove only who was "boss."

In the short term, the air traffic controller firings were fully implemented. In the interim between the firing and the training of a new generation of air traffic controllers, supervisors and military personnel were used to direct air travel in the United States. While air traffic was limited as a result of the reduced capacity of the control system, no major problems were reported. The principle that some government employees perform such essential functions that they cannot go on strike stands as the law of the land today.

Over the longer term, the PATCO strike did not hinder the growth of airline travel in the United States. Both the numbers of daily flights and the total number of passengers flown per year have jumped dramatically in the United States since the time of the air traffic controller strike. In fact, the air traffic system is essentially full: there is almost no remaining space in which airplanes can land at the busiest U.S. airports. Partly in response to this pressure, many former air traffic controllers were rehired in the 1990s. However, neither PATCO nor the members of any other federal workers union have gone on strike since 1981.

REAGAN'S STATEMENT AND A QUESTION-AND-ANSWER SESSION WITH REPORTERS ON THE AIR TRAFFIC CONTROLLERS STRIKE

August 3, 1981

The President. This morning at 7 A.M. the union representing those who man America's air traffic control facilities called a strike. This was the culmination of 7 months of negotiations between the Federal Aviation Administration and the union. At one point in these negotiations agreement was reached and signed by both sides, granting a $40 million increase in salaries and benefits. This is twice what other government employees can expect. It was granted in recognition of the difficulties inherent in the work these people perform. Now, however, the union demands are 17 times what had been agreed to—$681 million. This would impose a tax burden on their fellow citizens which is unacceptable.

I would like to thank the supervisors and controllers who are on the job today, helping to get the nation's air system operating safely. In the New York area, for example, four supervisors were scheduled to report for work, and 17 additionally volunteered. At National Airport a traffic controller told a newsperson he had resigned from the union and reported to work because, "How can I ask my kids to obey the law if I don't?" This is a great tribute to America.

Let me make one thing plain. I respect the right of workers in the private sector to strike. Indeed, as president of my own union, I led the first strike ever called by that union. I guess I'm maybe the first one to ever hold this office who is a lifetime member of an AFL-CIO union. But we cannot compare labor-management relations in the private sector with government. Government cannot close down the assembly line. It has to provide without interruption the protective services which are government's reason for being.

It was in recognition of this that the Congress passed a law forbidding strikes by government employees against the public safety. Let me read the solemn oath taken by each of these employees, a sworn affidavit, when they accepted their jobs: "I am not participating in any strike against the Government of the United States or any agency thereof, and I will not so participate while an employee of the Government of the United States or any agency thereof."

It is for this reason that I must tell those who fail to report for duty this morning they are in violation of the law, and if they do not report for work within 48 hours, they have forfeited their jobs and will be terminated.

Public Papers of the President: Ronald Reagan. August 3, 1981: 687–690.

RECONCILIATION IS NEEDED IN THE AIR TRAFFIC CONTROLLER DISPUTE

November 19, 1981

Mr. Bruce Vento (D-MN). Mr. Speaker, can America afford the inconvenience, expense, and the potential compromising of air traffic safety brought about by the Reagan administration's continued vindictiveness in dealing with the fired air traffic controllers? We as Members of Congress have an obligation to search for and seek out answers to the problems that face our society, yet the problem of dealing with the consequences of firing the striking air traffic controllers has evaded thoughtful consideration from this body.

The actions leading to the present situation have been well aired and need not be repeated. What must be stressed, is the fact that a problem exists that is magnified in human as well as economic terms. The careers and family lives of thousands of air traffic controllers have been ruined, all for the sake of driving home the point that PATCO went on strike illegally. It may be easy to say that in this showdown, the administration won and PATCO lost, but in the end we find that no one is a winner and everyone is a loser. The Government, the air traffic controllers, the public, and the economy are all suffering in this situation.

I bring to the attention of my colleagues, a recent column by William Sumner which appeared in the *St. Paul Dispatch.* I share Mr. Sumner's sentiments that it is time to bury the vindictiveness that has plagued the air traffic controller situation. The article follows:

[From the *St. Paul Dispatch*, Nov. 2, 1981]
IT'S TIME TO BURY VINDICTIVENESS AND REHIRE THE CONTROLLERS
(By William Sumner)

I suppose there are some, including the president, who get some sort of personal satisfaction over the conquest of a cocky union that was going to ground America. A cocky union, and voluble union leaders who attempted to win the impossible on the evening TV news. They defied the law and the president and it looks as though the punishment is to be permanent.

Legal maneuvers continue, but they seem half-hearted. The professional air controllers (PATCO) appear to be finished.

The administration is savoring the victory. PATCO may be down, goes the thinking, but we can still kick it.

. . .

I don't think Reagan got any mandate and I don't think he got a mandate for this, nor, for that matter, for going to vindictive, childish lengths with the air controllers.

I don't think we have to re-hash the strike issues which propelled the controllers' union out of the towers on August 3. They were well paid and had been given an offer that still seems generous. They struck illegally when no one would give them the moon. The 10,000 or so controllers now directing traffic appear likely soon to be enjoying the benefits the PATCO negotiators had won and which were rejected by the union.

The Federal Aviation Administration wants to bring the number of controllers up to 14,000, slightly under the number at work before the strike began. I don't know what this means in terms of training new personnel, for military controllers are still at work in the towers in unspecified numbers. Training continues apace. But the controllers now working are still working beyond 40 hours a week and are said to be in need of rest. To accomplish this, the numbers of flights will be cut down further, by 5 percent. Flights are now up to 83 percent of normal and it seems to be too much.

So there are practical reasons for amnesty even if one leaned toward getting even. PATCO broke the law, but we seem to be more generous toward felons than would be the spirit in evidence here. We need controllers. Why not put up signs saying, "Air Controllers Wanted," and give the erstwhile strikers a crack at the jobs? Why not indeed? We want that pound of flesh. The members of the now decertified union can't take any federal job, as a matter of fact.

Meanwhile, many strikers are ruined. They were used to good salaries and, no doubt, a lot of them had mortgages to match. They have proficiency in a specialized field and many have been reduced to taking unskilled jobs in attempts to feed their families. Mind you, they didn't hold up anyone, or take bribes or shoot anybody, but, in Reagan's mind, they are in the same category as child molesters. Or so it seems.

Sure, they were cocky to the point of being insufferable and they broke the government's no-strike law. But I'll bet that most just went along, as so often happens, conned by their leaders and faintly intimidated along with it. Case by case, as individuals, they should be considered for the new jobs. They are needed, needed almost as much as Reagan needs a stirring dose of humanity.

The Congressional Record. November 19, 1981: E 28489.

ENTERPRISE ZONES (MARCH 1982)

Enterprise zones, geographic areas in poor communities that enjoy reduced taxes and other incentives to promote economic growth, are a common way for conservatives to support programs that help the poor and underprivileged while reducing expenditures on policies like welfare and job training. As a practical matter, high levels of poverty, reliance on welfare, and other social problems are often present in inner cities. In part, this is because economic changes in the 1960s and 1970s encouraged many businesses to relocate to the suburbs far away from inner-city residents. These residents lost their jobs because they could not afford to buy cars to get to the suburbs and public transportation was often unreliable or nonexistent. How to reduce welfare, drug abuse, and other problems in the absence of good jobs thus became a central question of political life. A conservative answer to this question was enterprise zones.

Reagan promoted the concept of enterprise zones to reduce welfare and promote economic growth. In his vision, tax breaks aimed at companies who chose to invest in depressed areas would encourage corporations to build factories, hire workers, and turn welfare recipients into taxpayers in the inner cities. Companies would also be able to avoid some environmental and workplace regulations in return for risking an inner-city investment. Providing incentives to private business was, Reagan felt, a more effective way than government programs to achieve social improvements.

Critics of the enterprise zone concept, such as Congressman Ted Weiss (D-NY), pointed out that the problems in the inner cities were caused by factors other than just a lack of jobs; therefore, promoting job growth would not solve all the issues there. Indeed, such proposals had been tried in the past to little avail. Furthermore, accidental harms to the community might be caused by an enterprise zone business: what if, for example, a business spilled chemicals into the local water supply and was not held accountable since it was exempt from certain regulations? Finally, critics argued that support for poor citizens required federal involvement; relying on the private sector was inherently flawed.

The specific enterprise zone policy being advanced in this reading failed. The Democratic-controlled House of Representatives was able to muster enough votes to defeat Reagan's proposal. However, the general concept has been refined, implemented, and expanded to include economically stressed areas outside the inner cities. Enterprise zones and other incentive programs are popular with the businesses and communities that receive the benefit. However, many such programs have been established in wealthy areas, and social problems like poverty have not been cured. Furthermore, such programs are most effective in those areas, like suburban communities, which have large, well-educated labor forces with transportation. They have been less effective in the poor, inner-city areas they were originally intended to help.

Far more significant in altering the conditions of the inner cities in the 1980s and 1990s has been the booming economy of the last decade. As a result of low national unemployment rates, employers have sought out employees from all racial and demographic groups. This economic boom has been associated with a substantial drop in crime rates for acts like murder, drug abuse, and robbery—all conditions that overwhelmingly affect the kinds of inner-city areas Reagan's enterprise zones proposal was intended to help. Accordingly, while conditions in the inner cities have improved substantially in the last two decades, this improvement has had nothing to do with Reagan's enterprise zones proposal.

REAGAN'S MESSAGE TO THE CONGRESS TRANSMITTING PROPOSED ENTERPRISE ZONE LEGISLATION

March 23, 1982

In my January 26 State of the Union message, I indicated that we would propose legislation for a new effort to revive the decaying areas of America's inner cities and rural towns. We have now completed work on this new effort and it is embodied in the proposed "Enterprise Zone Tax Act." Therefore, I am requesting today that the bill be referred to the appropriate committees and I urge its early enactment.

The Concept of Enterprise Zones

The Enterprise Zone concept is based on utilizing the market to solve urban problems, relying primarily on private sector institutions. The idea is to create a productive, free market environment in economically-depressed areas by reducing taxes, regulations and other government burdens on economic activity. The removal of these burdens will create and expand economic opportunity within the zone areas, allowing private sector firms and entrepreneurs to create jobs—particularly for disadvantaged workers—and expand economic activity.

Enterprise Zones are based on an entirely fresh approach for promoting economic growth in the inner cities. The old approach relied on heavy government subsidies and central planning. A prime example was the Model Cities Program of the 1960's, which concentrated government programs, subsidies and regulations in specific, depressed urban areas. The Enterprise Zone approach would remove government barriers freeing individuals to create, produce and earn their own wages and profits. In its basic thrust, Enterprise Zones are the direct opposite of the Model Cities Program of the 1960's.

Enterprise Zones will not require appropriations at the Federal level, except for necessary administrative expenses. States and cities will still have the option of allocating discretionary Federal funds for their Enterprise Zones if they desire, or to appropriate additional funds of their own for such zones.

Enterprise Zones must be more than just a Federal initiative. State and local contributions to these zones will be critically important in the selection of the zones, and probably determine whether individual zones succeed or fail. In the spirit of our new policy of Federalism, State and local governments will have broad flexibility to develop the contributions to their zones most suitable to local conditions and preferences.

The Elements of Enterprise Zones

The Enterprise Zone program includes four basic elements:

First, tax reduction at the Federal, State and local levels to lessen this obvious burden on economic activity.

Second, regulatory relief at the Federal, State and local levels to reduce burdens which can be equally costly.

Third, new efforts to improve local services, including experimentation with private alternatives to provide those services. Eliminating inefficiencies of monopolized government services and increasing reliance on the private sector are key parts of the overall Enterprise Zone theme. Experience has shown that these efforts can save taxpayers substantial sums while significantly improving services at the same time.

Finally, involvement in the program by neighborhood organizations. These organizations can contribute much to the improvement of Enterprise Zone neighborhoods. They can also help to ensure that local residents participate in the economic success of the zones.

By combining all these elements we will create the right environment to help revive our Nation's economically-depressed areas.

. . .

More than government expenditures and subsidies, residents of economically-depressed areas need opportunities. This is the focus of the Enterprise Zone program. The program will identify and remove government barriers to entrepreneurs who can create jobs and economic growth. It will spark the latent talents and abilities already in existence in our Nation's most depressed areas. This bold, new concept deserves to be given a chance to work. As I said in my State of the Union Address, some will say our mission is to save free enterprise, but, I say that with your help, we must free enterprise so that together we can save America.

Public Papers of the President: Ronald Reagan. March 23, 1982: 352–355.

CRITICAL OBSERVATIONS ON THE ENTERPRISE ZONE PROPOSAL

March 23, 1982

Mr. Ted Weiss (D-NY). It is my view that the Federal Government has an absolute responsibility to assist the economically distressed areas of our cities. The people living in these areas are subjected to massive unemployment rates, surrounding physical deterioration and a high incidence of crime. Their human predicament is one without a helping hand, without a future and without hope. Yet, the poverty which overwhelms them is not the fault of these individuals nor of the cities in which they live. It is a national problem and requires a national solution. In approaching that solution, however, I believe we cannot depend solely on untried proposals like enterprise zones while existing Federal programs which have proven effective are senselessly cut or eliminated.

The main idea in the administration's enterprise zone proposal is to reduce regulatory and tax burdens in these distressed areas, thereby establishing a favorable investment climate to stimulate economic growth and community revitalization. But the urban problems we face in these areas are much greater than a mere regulatory and tax burden. Several academic studies have concluded that the regulatory and tax relief proposed will not be a significant incentive in the private sector's decisions where to locate. Availability of capital, access to markets and skilled labor, an improved infrastructure and better local services have all been cited as more important to business than relative burdens. All these factors must be addressed if we want to stimulate economic development in distressed areas. But the enterprise zone proposal only focuses on one very small aspect of the problem. Clearly, we cannot expect it to work on its own.

Proponents of the concept believe that the enterprise zones will be highly successful in revitalizing these depressed neighborhoods and creating jobs. But the experience in Puerto Rico has already taught us a significant lesson about the limitations of using tax incentives to stimulate economic growth. Operation Bootstrap, America's first enterprise zone experiment, was begun in 1950. Major tax and regulatory relief was provided and the island's cheap and largely unskilled labor force was promoted to induce business to locate there. It did, and economic growth resulted for some time, but economic development did not. To quote Edward Humberger, president of the Community Development Collaborative, of Washington, D.C.:

> Operation Bootstrap's first enterprises were large sugar plantations which displaced the small farm economy. Prior to their development, fully 93 percent of the land was arable and the agricultural economy was moderately diversified. By 1977, however, only 40 percent was still arable and Puerto Rico had become a new importer of $800 million in foodstuffs annually. The second industrial transfusion brought the textile and shoe industries to the island—but they began leaving when labor in Taiwan and Central America became cheaper. Next came the petrochemical industry, which created few jobs, and the pharmaceutical industry, which did not need much unskilled labor. Like an addict, the economy's next transfusion of investment rests on the recent discovery of nickel and copper deposits which will be extracted by the large oil companies.

The hard lesson we learn from Puerto Rico's enterprise zone experiment is that communities and regions need balanced economic growth and development. Operation Bootstrap's tax incentive program did not develop a self-reliant and diversified economy. Long-term viability requires a measure of community involvement, local ownership, and a skilled mature labor force, not a colonial dependence on outside capital. Economic development, not just growth, must be the goal of every revitalization effort.

. . .

Community revitalization in depressed areas will require public as well as private funds. The cities will need money to plan what appropriate development would be, will need money to improve the infrastructure to make areas viable for business' needs, will need job training funds to provide skills for unemployed residents, will need money to provide housing for the displaced, and will need money to provide effective monitoring and evaluation of any program implemented. Where are the municipalities to come up with the resources to do these things? And where will small businesses get sufficient seed capital to begin new enterprises in these areas?

. . .

In summary, we must not allow the debate over the enterprise zone proposal to blind us to the fact that it addresses only a very small part of the problem. If it becomes the sole program for urban development, many people will suffer. Failure of such a program would weaken the tax base of the city while further adding to its welfare burden. While no one can provide guarantees of success of any efforts to revitalize distressed areas, we should demand that the odds not be against the possibility of success.

The Congressional Record. March 23, 1982: E 5210–5212.

THE 1986 TAX REFORM ACT (MAY 1985)

Tax policy is a central component of economic policy. By influencing how much money individuals have to spend, and by shaping incentives for business investment, tax law can affect economic growth. Tax policy is also a major political issue since businesses and individuals try to influence the law in ways that favor their interests. Thus, tax policy is rarely made for purely "economic" reasons. It is an area in which ideology and interests aggressively interact.

As a conservative, Reagan favored reducing taxes as much as possible. This, he argued, would have two beneficial effects: it would reduce taxes on business, thereby encouraging innovation; and it would cut the amount of money coming to government, thereby forcing it to consider eliminating programs, especially those Reagan opposed. In 1986 his administration pushed forward a radical tax policy that would cut tax rates by a significant degree as well as eliminate many of the loopholes many wealthy businesses and individuals had used to avoid paying taxes. He advanced this policy as a pro-family, anti–special interest measure that would allow families to keep more of their wages while eliminating the breaks special interest groups had used to their benefit. He also claimed that the policy would be "revenue-neutral," meaning that the government would collect no more or less taxes than it did under current law. This argument was intended to calm the fears of those who feared that taxes would increase or that reduced revenues for the federal government would increase the deficit.

Like Congressman Don Bonker (D-WA), opponents of the 1986 tax reform made several arguments. They noted that, in contrast with the many increasing-with-income tax rates that were part of current tax law, the new plan would offer only three tax rates for *all* taxpayers. This, they complained, violated the concept of progressivity—the idea that more affluent people ought to pay more in taxes than poorer people—which had been at the heart of U.S. tax policy during the twentieth century. They also feared that the bill hid a major tax cut that would increase the deficit. Concerns emerged that a radical change in tax law would upset the shaky U.S. economy: many people and corporations had made decisions in light of the current law, and if it were changed, their investments might go bad. Finally, they worried that the change would do nothing to encourage Americans to save and invest more, an important practice to ensure long-term economic growth.

Reagan's proposed tax reform was enacted into law in 1986. Its passage was something of a political miracle: every interest group in Washington, D.C., attempted to insert benefits for itself into the code. However, what emerged was a relatively loophole-free policy that radically reduced tax rates and caused most wealthy people and corporations to pay, rather than shelter, their taxes. It also turned out to be revenue neutral and did not influence the budget deficit. Nor did it cause the major disruptions in the economy feared by some.

Within a few years, however, new loopholes were established in the code, and new tax rates have been added over time. The basic premise of the 1986 reform, that exceptions should be limited and most people should pay a flat rate, has survived, but the 2000 tax code has been substantially revised from Reagan's early efforts. Accordingly, his plan demonstrates a primary rule of politics: it ain't over 'til it's over —and it's never over. Indeed, the president elected in 2000, Texas Governor George Bush, has promoted a flatter tax modeled on the Reagan approach—a sign of how much has changed since the 1986 reform.

REAGAN'S REMARKS ON TAX REFORM TO CONCERNED CITIZENS

May 29, 1985

I don't know if you happened to be watching TV last night, but the networks were kind enough to give me a few minutes to speak about a subject that's very close to my heart and close to your wallets. I'm talking about our historical—or historic proposal to completely overhaul that old jalopy of our tax system, replace it with a fairer, simpler, sleeker, more compassionate model—an all-American tax plan providing new freedom, fairness, and hope for all.

Short of sending the IRS, the Internal Revenue Service, on a permanent holiday, this historic reform will give the long-suffering American taxpayers the most relief they've had since, well, at least since our historic 23-percent tax cut of 1981.

. . .

Our proposal is not a tax increase, and it will not increase the deficit. It will mean lower taxes for a majority of Americans, with expanded opportunities to save and invest. We want to do away with the trials and tribulations of filling out your tax forms for as many people as possible. Eventually, as many as half of all the taxpayers won't have to worry about 1040 Forms. They won't have to fill out any tax form at all. We're thinking of calling this one the zero form.

We're replacing the present steeply graded system of 14 different tax rates with a flatter, simpler, 3-step design that will allow you to keep more of each individual dollar that you earn. That means you'll get to save more of that raise that you earned, or if you go out there and work extra hard, you know that you're doing it for yourself and your family, not just to line the pockets of the Federal Government. It's our belief that the tax system should no longer be an obstacle course on the road to success.

What does America's tax plan mean for the average family? . . . Of those who file and pay taxes, 7 in 10 will pay at a maximum rate of 15 percent, and fully 97 percent of all taxpayers will pay no more than 25 cents on the very last dollar they earn. Only 3 percent of America's families will have to pay at the highest rate, which will be 35 percent.

. . .

Our plan will also mean an historic correction of a problem we've let go on too long—the increasing tax burden on low- and fixed-income Americans that's been knocking the bottom rungs off the ladder of opportunity. A compassionate, pro-family opportunity society should give a break as well to those Americans struggling to get by and move up. And that's exactly what we intend to do.

. . .

We're also going to make some other chances to help families—or changes, I should say, not chances. Right now our tax system discriminates against homemakers, making IRA's fully available only to spouses who work outside the home. We're going to change that. Believe me, the work of the homemaker deserves to be treated with as much dignity and worth as that of any other worker. Well, it's a pretty harebrained social policy that punishes spouses who decide to stay home and take care of the children. So, now every husband and wife will each have full access to an IRA tax-deductible savings account up to $4,000 a couple every year.

. . .

It's been remarked that there are three stages of reaction to a new idea like our tax proposal. First stage is: "It's crazy. It'll never work. Don't waste my time." The second: "It's possible, but it's not worth doing." And finally: "I've always said it was a good idea. I'm glad I thought of it." Well, we're rapidly sweeping up on that third stage.

Even those in this town who are still reluctant are being lifted up and carried forward by the momentum of public support for a fundamental change in our tax laws. And once called impossible, tax fairness and simplification are now all but inevitable.

. . .

I'm going to paraphrase a statement by Admiral Farragut—cleaned up just a little: Blast the torpedos! Full speed ahead! For too long we've lived with a tax system that is a blot, a stain on the shining mantle of our democratic government. We've quietly tolerated a tax code which we know is an outrage, one riddled through with special privileges and inequities that violates our most fundamental American values of justice and fair play.

As I said last night—and I bet a lot of you here today would agree with me—in its very spirit and substance our tax system could only be described as un-American. Well, there are two things we can do about it. We can either declare April 15th a day of national mourning—or we can change the system. And I don't think Americans can recognize an injustice without trying to change it.

Now, that's how this great country got started. Our forefathers rebelled against the injustice of oppressive taxation. In place of King George's despotism, they created a government of, by, and for the people—a new democratic nation in which all men were created equal.

Today we're undertaking another great adventure in freedom—a second American revolution, a peaceful revolution of hope and opportunity. And one of its first orders of business is to toss our present moldy tax code overboard and get a new one.

. . .

But for the sake of our traditions and for the sake of our present well-being and future happiness, we must take this next vital step toward freedom. It'll be good for our economy; it'll be good for individuals; it will be fairer and more just. But most of all, it will help strengthen America's most important institution—the family. As I said last night, this is the single, strongest, pro-family initiative in postwar history.

The family is the moral core of our society, the repository of our values, and the preserver of our traditions. The family's like a tree with its roots in the experience of past generations and its branches reaching boldly out into the future. Our families are the safe haven where we're taught charity, generosity, and love and from which spring our most cherished concepts of human dignity and the worth of each individual life. It's there that we learn to nourish the young and care for the elderly.

. . .

You know, every once in a while I've heard people say we don't have any heroes anymore. They haven't looked around their own neighborhood. You see them getting up, sending the kids off to school, going to work every morning, supporting their church and their charity and all the good things in this society. You bet they're heroes. It's through their sweat, toil, and tears that the foundations of our society are built, and America's tax plan will simply give them a little help.

We've come too far down the road of progress to turn back now. I don't believe that having tasted the success of these last 4 years, we still shrink from the challenge to make that success complete. Together we can make 1985 one of the milestone years in history, a date that future generations will look back on as marking a crucial step in the steady ascent of human freedom. We can do it. And if you help, we'll do it this year.

Public Papers of the President: Ronald Reagan. May 29, 1985: 686–689.

CRITICISM OF THE TAX REFORM ACT OF 1986

August 8, 1986

Mr. Don Bonker (D-WA). Like most of my colleagues, I aspire [to] a tax system that is just. That the present Tax Code is appallingly flawed is no longer doubted. It blatantly invites abuse, particularly by the wealthy; its notorious loopholes and tax shelters legitimatize cheating; the fact that Fortune 500 corporations and many of the Nation's super-rich pay no taxes is an insult to those who pay their fair share.

Over the years, Congress has loaded up the Tax Code with a variety of preferences and shelters. It is time to remove them and put fairness back into the system. That is why the tax reform bill was so appealing. Among other things, the bill removes 6 million working poor from the tax rolls. Many of the special preferences for individuals and corporations will be eliminated, and speculation would no longer influence business and investment decisions. A tough minimum tax rate would be added for corporations whose attorneys have managed to pare their share of the tax burden down from 40 percent in 1950 to only 8 percent today.

For individuals, the bill increases the standard deduction and nearly doubles the personal exemption, further easing the burden on lower- and middle-income taxpayers. These are major reforms that address the most egregious problems in the present code and go a long way toward restoring fairness. Any legislation that contains these provisions is worthy of serious consideration.

But the legislation unfortunately includes provisions that give disproportionate benefits to the wealthy and could imperil our Nation's fragile economy.

By narrowing the tax schedule to two rates, we lose the progressivity that has characterized our tax system over the years. At one time the very wealthy paid over 90 percent on their income. Then the maximum rate was cut to 50 percent in 1981, and now it will be 28 percent. Under the new law, the average tax cut for individuals who earn over $200,000 per year will be $3,385 compared with an average cut of only $225 for individuals who earn between $20,000 and $30,000.

The corporate tax rate will be dropped to 34 percent, down from the current 40 percent rate. While removal of the investment tax credit and other preferences will offset the lowest rate, there is no guarantee that these firms will pay more, as the bill's sponsors promise. One corporate attorney told me, "We have a neutral position on the bill: We pay no taxes under the current system and we don't intend to under the new system."

I am also troubled by what an overhaul of the Tax Code will do to an already shaky economy. And despite the assurances of its sponsors, there is no guarantee that the tax bill will be revenue neutral.

. . .

Here are what I can best describe as the major fault lines in the Tax Reform Act of 1986 which prompted me to vote against it in the House of Representatives.

From a national economic perspective, this bill possibly will reduce Federal tax receipts, increase the deficit, and intensify the pressure upon Congress to slash important programs which have already been cut to the bone over the past 5 years. The bill provides some $120 billion in tax reductions over the next 6 years, but will that amount be offset by higher taxes on corporations? At a time when we have a $200 billion Federal deficit, I am skeptical that the bill will remain revenue neutral, given the plethora of attorneys and accountants whose sophisticated bookkeeping methods enable large corporations and the wealthy to avoid taxes. A downturn in the economy or a small percentage error in the estimates will affect revenues, and in turn threaten many important Federal programs.

Furthermore, this tax package could damage U.S. competitiveness at a time when skyrocketing trade deficits threaten our economic well-being. With a fragile domestic recovery that is sustained by an enormous external debt, this is not the time to be overhauling our Tax Code and posing uncertainties for the future. How will the new tax affect our competitive position in the world economy and the escalating trade deficit? What kind of message are we sending to investment planners, businesses, and the suppliers of venture capital? Will consumer spending of the extra disposable income go to purchasing more imports, thus adding to the trade deficit?

The bill also does nothing to improve our Nation's savings. In fact, it wipes out existing provisions designed to promote savings, investment, and capital formation. Our savings rate is the lowest in the industrialized world—one-half or one-third of the savings rate in West Germany and Japan—and this bill may result in continued stagnant savings and investment, increased consumer spending, higher debt, and a corresponding increase in interest rates. In the end, we must rely on more foreign capital and an ever-mounting external debt to finance U.S. growth as well as our escalating public and private debts.

. . .

Mr. Speaker, I have followed this particular legislation during its many lives over the past 2 years and want to commend those on the various committees who have labored long and hard to bring this bill to fruition. They were able to win many long-overdue reforms and make the Tax Code more fair in many areas. On balance, however, after considering the effects of this bill upon our Nation's competitiveness and growth, its potential impact upon the deficit and Federal programs, and the severe problems it posed for my own State, I had to reluctantly cast my vote against this measure.

The Congressional Record. August 8, 1986: E 3434–3435.

BALANCING THE BUDGET (OCTOBER 1985)

Budget deficits were a central component of the American political experience at the end of the twentieth century. Budget deficits complicate political life in a number of ways. First, while it is relatively easy for the United States to borrow money, that money has to be paid back—with interest. Thus, money borrowed today limits the amount of money that will be available for use in the future, and the more the nation borrows, the more intense this problem becomes. Second, while the nation can reduce borrowing by cutting spending, such cuts inevitably hurt programs that benefit many people. The nation might also raise taxes to increase its revenue. Either of these choices is likely to cause political anger which can cost elected politicians their jobs. Third, how much money the federal government spends influences how the economy grows—which itself influences things like how much income tax it collects, since people who are thrown out of work as a result of the government's spending (or lack of spending) do not pay taxes and instead draw unemployment insurance. Dealing with deficits, then, is a significant problem for any president.

Reagan preferred a policy of balancing the budget by cutting spending, mostly in the area of domestic and social programs like welfare, education, housing, and other programs he thought the federal government should not be involved in. He insisted that defense spending ought to be increased, however. First calling for a constitutional amendment requiring a balanced budget (it failed), Reagan then supported a bill known as Gramm-Rudman (for its sponsors) which linked program cuts to specific target dates for reducing the budget deficit. In this way, he and other supporters of budget cuts hoped to avoid political punishment: they could claim that the cuts in popular programs were the result of a law over which they had no control.

Opponents of broad-brush approaches like the balanced budget amendment and Gramm-Rudman made several points in supporting their case. Like Senator Gary Hart (D-CO), they argued that the Constitution laid out Congress' responsibility in the budget process, and while this responsibility did not always lead to smooth budget making, it was inappropriate to alter the Constitution just because the process was "ugly." Furthermore, they raised the fear that a small group of people could force cuts in popular programs since the various proposals required "supermajorities" of more than 50 percent to alter the targets. Thus conservatives could substantially eliminate social and domestic programs they did not like despite the fact that these programs were generally popular and conservatives could never eliminate them by a majority vote.

A version of Gramm-Rudman known as Gramm-Rudman-Hollings did pass in 1986, but it did little to alter the course of budget deficits. Its targets were generally ignored as political leaders voted to extend the deadlines to avoid making difficult political choices. By the early 1990s the U.S. budget deficit had expanded to over $300 billion per year. These deficits hurt the U.S. economy, limited spending for programs popular with the American people, and influenced President George Bush's failed reelection campaign in 1992.

Ultimately, however, through a combination of tax increases, program cuts, and economic growth, the United States began generating surpluses in the late 1990s. It is unclear whether Reagan's economic proposals influenced this outcome: conservatives generally say they did; liberals generally insist they did not. In any case, neither Gramm-Rudman nor a balanced budget amendment had anything to do with influencing the rise of budget surpluses. Instead, limited fiscal responsibility in Washington, combined with astonishing economic growth, has led to the current surplus. Additionally, issues like the balanced budget amendment and Gramm-Rudman are politically dead.

REAGAN'S RADIO ADDRESS TO THE NATION ON THE BUDGET DEFICIT

October 5, 1985

Today I'd like to talk to you about . . . a dramatic new legislative proposal. . . .

... Yesterday I gave my enthusiastic support to what might well become historic legislation—the Balanced Budget and Emergency Deficit Control Act of 1985—introduced by Senator Phil Gramm of Texas and Senator Warren Rudman of New Hampshire. This legislation will impose the discipline our government has so long lacked to control its insatiable appetite to spend. Under this proposal the Federal Government, by law, would be required to lock in a deficit reduction path leading to a balanced budget. This would be achieved without raising taxes, without jeopardizing our defenses, and without breaking our commitments on Social Security. The proposal would establish a maximum allowable deficit ceiling, beginning with the current level of $180 billion, and then mandate that this deficit be reduced—by equal amounts each year—until we reach a balanced budget in calendar year 1990. Moreover, I personally believe in, and I've asked Congress to put in place, a balanced budget amendment to the Constitution to take effect in 1991. By doing this, we could make sure that our progress would not be lost.

The importance of the proposal to eliminate deficit spending can hardly be overstated. For decades Federal spending has been growing virtually out of control. It took 173 years, from the establishment of our government in 1789 to the Kennedy administration in 1962, for the annual budget of the United States to reach $100 billion. It took only the next 9 years for the budget to double to 200 billion, and in the 14 years since, it has more than quadrupled to over 900 billion. Not surprisingly, as the Government has been spending like a drunken sailor, it's taken our country deeper and deeper into the red. Indeed, today the Federal deficit amounts to more than $211 billion.

Now, this deficit has not—and I repeat, not—developed because of our tax cut. On the contrary, government revenues have actually been rising rapidly since we cut tax rates—42 percent since we started, but spending has increased by 60 percent. But overall, since our tax cut, government has still spent more than it has taken in. It sort of reminds me of that old definition of a baby—an enormous appetite at one end and no sense of responsibility at the other. Well, with the passage of the bill I endorsed yesterday, the Government of the United States can show that, at long last, we are growing up, and we're gaining that sense of responsibility. The Senate is debating this proposal today, and I strongly urge them to approve it before the debt limit authority expires on Monday.

Let me add here a personal caveat: While spending control is vital to the economic well-being of this nation, the highest priority of any American Government is preservation of the national security. The maintenance of a national defense second to none, indeed, the only legitimate justification for running a large annual deficit—as we ran every year of

World War II—is preservation of the Nation, itself. When the spending cuts are made by this administration, as they must be made, the security of this country, its allies, and its friends will not be put at risk. The Congress has agreed, and next year I will propose those amounts already accepted as necessary for keeping the peace.

Public Papers of the President: Ronald Reagan. October 5, 1985: 1195–1196.

DEBATE ON THE BALANCED BUDGET AMENDMENT

March 25, 1986

Mr. Gary Hart (D-CO). Mr. President, each of us in this Chamber took office with an oath to uphold and defend the Constitution. That pledge obligates us to defend not just the letter of our national charter but also its intent. We are obligated to be constitutional conservatives; to conserve the spirit the framers breathed into the Constitution; to alter its principles and its purpose not at all.

I oppose Senate Joint Resolution 225, the so-called balanced budget amendment, because it defies that spirit.

Set aside the economic arguments against this resolution, as persuasive as they are. Put aside whether exact budgetary balance is the best fiscal strategy in all circumstances. Never mind that today's ruinous deficits were created by the same President who is this amendment's leading advocate. My objection is simply that this amendment violates the fundamental principles that have sustained for nearly 200 years what Madison called our "paramount Constitution."

First, this amendment is inconsistent with the Constitution's purpose. That purpose is not to dictate the hourly management of our Government but to enshrine the larger, underlying ideals which must guide it and guide this Nation.

. . .

. . . Consider all the questions of economics, accounting, budgeting, and statistics which this amendment begs. What constitutes total outlays and receipts? Should we rely on year-end totals or estimates? Whose estimates? Do those of the Congressional Budget Office overrule the Office of Management and Budget? We need to answer each of these questions and many more besides in detail to make the amendment workable. An alternative version of this amendment, Senate Joint Resolution 13, tried to grapple with just a few of these questions and, by doing so, more than doubled the number of words it proposed to add to our Constitution.

As we resolved each of these complex issues through Congress or the courts, the effect of this amendment would be to straitjacket our Constitution into an inflexible doctrine—despite changes in economic conditions or public opinion—until the end of our Nation's days. . . .

. . .

Second, the proposed amendment is directly at odds with the Constitution's doctrine of the separation of powers. It would require the abdication of legislative authority to either the executive, the judiciary, or both.

This becomes clear as we consider how the amendment would be enforced. What if Congress violated the amendment by passing an unbalanced peacetime budget? One possibility is the President would block certain Federal expenditures. The Supreme Court ruled a decade ago that such an "impoundment" process violated the Constitution's letter, and—even with this amendment—it would violate the Constitution's spirit still.

The other possibility is that the courts would be asked to rule on the constitutionality of an unbalanced budget. Suddenly, it would be up to our judges to say whether estimates of receipts and outlays were accurate; whether we must cut the budget across-the-board, or only change certain spending programs and taxes.

. . .

Third, the amendment would ride roughshod over the central constitutional principle of majority rule. The Constitution hallows this principle by carefully circumscribing the occasions that require "supermajorities." It limits these to matters of highest importance, such as impeachment, ratification of treaties, overriding vetoes, Presidential succession, and the expulsion of a Member of Congress.

The proposed amendment, by contrast, would impose the highest order of supermajority—three-fifths of the whole number of both Houses of Congress—on the lowest order of fiscal detail. War could be declared by simple majority; a 1 percent increase in unemployment benefits would require greater scrutiny.

The result would be tyranny by minority. Indeed, the amendment would enable Senators representing only 10 percent of America's population to control all budget and tax policies for all Americans. . . .

Fourth, the proposal violates what constitutional scholar Laurence Tribe identifies as one of the key tests of appropriateness for amendments: Whether it is an effective and essential last resort. It is certainly not effective. The amendment could easily be circumvented through at least six major loopholes, including the use of tax expenditures, off-budget spending authority, regulatory authority, and phony economic forecasts.

Nor is this proposal an essential last resort. Its proponents claim we need the amendment to remedy the tendency of well-organized interest groups to secure Federal spending beyond what the broader public supports. But we have yet to try a simpler cure to that malady: Strict limits on campaign contributions by the "PAC's" [political action committees] that lobby for these vocal interest groups. Indeed, a good "first resort" would be for some of the amendment's sponsors to drop their longheld opposition to such limits on PAC's.

Ultimately, this amendment would erode Government of, by, and for the people. Those who long for the kind of responsible governance the Constitution envisioned should consider just one point: Even if Congress were to approve the amendment today, it would still await ratification by 38 States—a process that would take 2 years at a bare minimum. Thus, Congress would not need to balance the budget until at least fiscal year 1991. . . .

. . .

From 1789 to 1981, no constitutional amendment was necessary to keep deficit spending from getting seriously out of hand. All it took was firm public and official disapproval of such spending when it was not required by economic or military circumstances. To restore that attitude today, all we need are a President with the courage to submit a balanced budget, a Congress with the courage to cut spending and restore revenues, and a public understanding that the fault for runaway deficits hardly lies in the most magnificent Constitution humankind has ever known.

The Congressional Record. March 25, 1986: S 3301–3302.

IMMIGRATION REFORM (NOVEMBER 1986)

Immigration has been a central issue in the United States since its founding. With the exception of Native Americans, everyone in the United States is descended from immigrants. Immigration is nonetheless not always viewed in a positive way. When potential immigrants are from ethnic and racial minorities or when the economic conditions of the United States put recent immigrants in competition for low-paying jobs with U.S. citizens, inevitably pressure is put on the federal government to limit immigration. By the 1980s, both of these "negative" conditions existed: economic times were tough, and hundreds of thousands of often illegal immigrants were entering the United States from Latin and South America.

President Reagan supported an immigration reform proposal that placed sanctions on employers who hired illegal immigrants. It also required that employers determine whether an individual applying for a job had a legal right to work in the United States. His hope was that, by reducing or eliminating the economic incentives to come to the United States, illegal immigration would be cut at the source: if there were no jobs in the United States, people simply would not come.

Opponents like Congressman Matthew Martinez (D-CA) made several counterpoints to Reagan's proposal. First, they noted that control of immigration was a federal issue that should not be enforced by employers. Second, they argued that given that most illegal immigrants were Latino, the net effect of the proposal would be to encourage discrimination against all Latino applicants regardless of their legal status. Finally, they pointed out that people were leaving their home countries because of the difficult political and economic conditions there; simply cutting off access to jobs in the United States would not address the fundamental problems driving illegal immigration.

Reagan's immigration reform proposal became law in 1985. In the short term many of the concerns raised by critics proved true: employers were often reluctant to hire even U.S. citizens of Latino descent for fear of exposing themselves to federal investigation. In addition, illegal immigration to the United States did not slow at all since the economic and political conditions in the immigrants' home countries continued to push them toward the United States. Several more reform proposals have been enacted, including a provision of the welfare reform law passed under President Clinton which denies access to these services, even to legal immigrants.

Given the remarkable economic opportunities and political stability in the United States, however, nothing has prevented people from coming to the United States. By 2000 illegal immigration was still common, but, with the exception of the states and communities most directly affected by it, typically states in the American Southwest, illegal immigration is not a major political issue at this writing. Many communities are so desperate for labor, especially labor for low-paying, unskilled jobs, that they do not care where workers come from. This attitude will no doubt change in poor economic conditions.

REAGAN'S STATEMENT ON SIGNING THE IMMIGRATION REFORM AND CONTROL ACT OF 1986

November 6, 1986

The Immigration Reform and Control Act of 1986 is the most comprehensive reform of our immigration laws since 1952. In the past 35 years our nation has been increasingly affected by illegal immigration. This legislation takes a major step toward meeting this challenge to our sovereignty. At the same time, it preserves and enhances the Nation's heritage of legal immigration. . . .

In 1981 this administration asked the Congress to pass a comprehensive legislative package, including employer sanctions, other measures to increase enforcement of the immigration laws, and legalization. The act provides these three essential components. The employer sanctions program is the keystone and major element. It will remove the incentive for illegal immigration by eliminating the job opportunities which draw illegal aliens here. We have consistently supported a legalization program which is both generous to the alien and fair to the countless thousands of people throughout the world who seek legally to come to America. The legalization provisions in this act will go far to improve the lives of a class of individuals who now must hide in the shadows, without access to many of the benefits of a free and open society. Very soon many of these men and women will be able to step into the sunlight and, ultimately, if they choose, they may become Americans.

. . .

Distance has not discouraged illegal immigration to the United States from all around the globe. The problem of illegal immigration should not, therefore, be seen as a problem between the United States and its neighbors. Our objective is only to establish a reasonable, fair, orderly, and secure system of immigration into this country and not to discriminate in any way against particular nations or people.

Public Papers of the President: Ronald Reagan. November 6, 1986: 1522–1524.

REMARKS BY REPRESENTATIVE MATTHEW G. MARTINEZ BEFORE CENTER FOR MIGRATION STUDIES NINTH ANNUAL NATIONAL LEGAL CONFERENCE ON IMMIGRATION AND REFUGEE POLICY

May 5, 1986

Mr. Matthew Martinez (D-CA). I would like to thank the Center for Migration Studies for asking me to speak to you today on this extremely important subject. Once again, powerful forces are going to try to push through the House of Representatives an immigration bill that encourages America to turn against its Hispanic population. Once again, it is up to us to stand up to, and defeat, this dangerous and backsliding legislation.

Like the Simpson-Mazzoli bill before it, the Simpson-Rodino bill is fueled mainly by political pressure to "do something" about immigration policy. It is true that America's immigration policy needs a close re-examination and overhaul—and has needed it for 20 years. But the frenzy in Congress triggered by public demand is a momentum that has not had much rational guidance, as last session's House debate over Simpson-Mazzoli and this session's Senate debate over Simpson-Rodino will attest. Each has resulted in a bill that is insufficiently debated and not properly amended. Unless Members of Congress concentrate less this year on public posturing and more on the tough and intricate issues surrounding immigration policy, we are going to face another year without immigration policy, we are going to face another year without immigration reform.

The first thing we can do to make immigration reform work this year is to realize that it is not going to work with this bill as it stands. With a few cosmetic changes, this legislation is essentially the same as Simpson-Mazzoli, which proved unacceptable. Why are these bills unacceptable?

The first reason is that they seek to control illegal immigration using employer sanctions. This approach seeks to shift the burden of enforcing immigration laws from the Federal Government—where it belongs, to private citizens—where it does not. The obvious effect will be that employers who are afraid of hiring illegal immigrants will discriminate against "foreign looking" people, especially Hispanics. Either that, or businesses will take the risk of keeping illegal immigrants in their employment, but doing so in a clandestine way that makes working conditions for these people even worse than they already are.

My District community would be hard hit by this legislation. With over 284,000 people of Hispanic heritage—the second highest concentration of Hispanics within a single district in the State of California—and with an unemployment 3 to 4% higher than the national average, we do not need laws that make it even harder than it already is for Hispanics to find jobs and to receive equal and fair treatment by employers. The sanctions contained in the Simpson-Rodino bill would also put employers in a kind of double jeopardy. First, employers would be held responsible for the verification of employees' citizenship status, which places them in a position of having to obtain and validate the proper identification documents. And they would also be targets of discrimination charges and fines for perceived discriminatory hiring practices. There is a better way to curtail the hiring of illegal aliens. It is already the law.

The point is that employer sanctions have failed on the state scale, and remain untested on a national scale. An authoritative study published in the *Stanford Journal of International Law* in the summer of 1983, along with numerous other documents, amply confirms this fact. At the same time, wide-scale discrimination against Hispanics is now a vivid reality in our society. The Los Angeles County Commission on Human Relations recently reported that "hostile attitudes toward immigrants and refugees . . . are widespread among the general public, that numerous forms of employment discrimination and exploitations are a major problem for immigrants and refugees," and that "the Immigration and Naturalization Service has targeted Latinos and Asians in workplace raids, resulting in discriminatory treatment of Latino and Asian immigrants and refugees and numerous Latinos and Asians who are American citizens." If this is the current situation in Los Angeles County, what can we expect if employer sanctions are enacted?

. . .

We must take a look at the real reasons immigrants are flooding our country. As long as the tremendous economic disparity exists between the United States and our Latin American neighbors, we cannot conceivably stabilize immigration. Legally or illegally, they will come. Wouldn't you? We must encourage more bilateral aid and joint economic development programs with our neighbors to the south, such as Mexico. This is happening now on the government level, but it must happen on the private level also. Mexico must also be encouraged to liberalize its foreign investment laws, and make the climate more hospitable to American business. We must demand more short- and long-term cooperation from the Mexican and Central and South American governments in solving our immigration problem.

The heart and soul of our nation's immigration policy has always shone on the Statue of Liberty:

> Give me your tired, your poor,
>   Your huddled masses yearning to breathe free,
> The wretched refuse of your teeming shore,
>   Send these, the homeless, tempest-tossed,
>   to me:
> I lift my lamp beside the golden door.

These are trying times, and many would respond by closing the golden door. We must guard it diligently and wisely, but never close it. For the day we do is the day we blow out the lamp of freedom, justice and opportunity that has made us a beacon to the world.

The Congressional Record. May 5, 1986: E 1501–1502.

WELFARE REFORM (FEBRUARY 1987)

Welfare is one of the central, and most controversial, policies of the United States. In a nation of vast resources, wealth, and excess, it seems unfair and unreasonable that anyone would be hungry and desperate. Yet, at the same time, Americans believe that people ought to work for their living; government support seems improper and subject to abuse if individuals remain recipients for their entire lives.

Reagan supported a welfare reform proposal which provided basic benefits even while it cut costs and provided incentives, such as support for education and job training, to encourage people to take steps to get themselves off the welfare rolls. The core of his argument was based on the classic conservative premise that economic incentives could be shaped to push people into preferred behaviors; thus, if the system encouraged people to get an education, they would, having received that education, get good jobs and leave the welfare system. In addition, he noted that the massive budget deficits currently being experienced by the United States required cost control measures.

Opponents came from both the left and the right. Liberals feared that reducing support would promote homelessness, starvation, and frustration in a period of economic downturn in which even better-educated people struggled to find jobs. Conservatives generally thought that welfare ought to be ended as such, and that in any case more pressure should be placed on recipients to exploit opportunities like education and then to get out of the system. Elements of both of these arguments can be found in the statement made by Congresswoman Margaret Roukema (R-NJ).

Reagan's proposal was signed into law in 1988. It did very little to change welfare rolls in the short term because, as the U.S. economy slid into recession in the early 1990s, millions of people lost their jobs and needed to receive welfare to make ends meet. Additionally, many welfare recipients were young mothers, and it is difficult to reduce welfare dependence unless employers, or government, or some other group provides quality day care for working mothers. Nothing in Reagan's legislation provided this service; accordingly, even those mothers wanting jobs faced problems since jobs were scarce and day care was rare.

The Reagan reforms did serve as a foundation from which a subsequent welfare reform law was passed in the Clinton administration. This later law essentially ended modern welfare in as much as it placed cumulative time limits on how long individuals could draw from the system—no matter how bad times get, people can draw welfare only for limited periods throughout their lives. The Clinton proposal also included job training and day-care incentive programs to encourage welfare-to-work. So far, as employment opportunities have grown throughout the economic boom of the 1990s, most of those who were affected by welfare reform have found jobs. It remains to be seen what the impact will be when the economy goes into a decline.

REAGAN'S REMARKS AT A WHITE HOUSE BRIEFING FOR SUPPORTERS OF WELFARE

February 9, 1987

America's welfare system has been a longstanding concern with us. But too frequently that concern has been interpreted as merely a desire to prevent waste or fraud or stop welfare abuse. Well now, don't get me wrong—those are worthy and important objectives. Protecting the taxpayers' investment in Federal spending is a worthy objective—especially since we want our Federal welfare spending to go to the people who really need it, the poor themselves, and not to people who already live comfortably. And all the economic progress that we've made, for example, has relied on trying to control Federal spending. When we took office, huge Federal programs with built-in yearly spending increases were just reaching maturation.

So, first we had to take steps to slow down the Federal spending juggernaut. We cut the rate of spending increase. And then, finally, this year we're managing to get the Federal Government to actually spend less in real terms than it spent the year before. Talk about the Earth shaking!

. . .

Back in 1982, in a speech to a black political organization, I raised some of the questions discussed by the scholarly work of Charles Murray in the *Public Interest*. At the time this wasn't exactly fashionable, but since then things have been changing. Slowly a new bipartisan consensus on America's welfare system has developed—a consensus that holds what only a few could say a short time ago: that it is our welfare system that is one of the most serious obstacles to progress for the poor. The evidence is in, and the history is clear: Twenty years ago, with the best of intentions, the Federal Government began a program that it hoped would wipe out poverty in America. Today the Federal Government and State governments, with 8 major welfare programs and more than 50 smaller ones, spends more than $130 billion to pursue this objective. And now, with less than half of this money, we could give every poor man, woman, and child enough to lift them above the poverty line. But believe me, it isn't just the arithmetic that doesn't make sense. During the past few years, we've seen serious questions raised—in scholarly works like Mr. Murray's book *Losing Ground*, which showed poverty actually went up as the Federal Government spent more to eliminate it, to major network television specials featuring grim personal testimonials about the Federal welfare system. And the issue here is really compassion.

How compassionate is a welfare system that discourages families that are economically self-reliant, that takes 6,000 pages of Federal regulations to explain, and is so complex it confuses and demoralizes the poor? How compassionate is a system that robs the poor of the tools to break the cycle of dependency? Well, the emerging consensus on welfare is finally agreeing with us that the Federal welfare system has become a poverty trap, a trap that is wreaking havoc on the very support system the poor need most to lift themselves up and out of destitution—the family. This growing bipartisan consensus holds that our current welfare system is not only a failure but counterproductive—the institutionalization of ghetto life where, as Bill Moyers put it in his special on this subject last year: "Mothers are children, fathers don't count, and the street is the strongest school."

. . .

We have to fight the impulse of many to believe that one policy change or reform, written and implemented here in Washington, can solve the problem of poverty and welfare dependency. We know from 20 years' painful experience that it cannot. In seeking solutions we, as a nation, need to draw upon the practical genius of the thousands of community leaders and individuals who deal with that problem every day. The Federal Government should retain its current financing role, but it cannot provide all the answers. We need to reevaluate our entire antipoverty strategy—a reevaluation that will provide us with new approaches and initiatives, initiatives that will have as their goal the defense and strengthening of the family as the key to a strategic assault on poverty. . . .

And today I just want to seek your active support, to ask you to join together with many millions of other Americans in this critical domestic initiative. We know the answers are out there—in our 50 States, in our cities and neighborhoods, and in the minds and hearts of the thousands of self-help leaders who are ready with hundreds of antipoverty ideas— if only our complex welfare system will allow them greater freedom to succeed. They can show us how to make work more rewarding than welfare; how to provide incentives for dignity, instead of incentives for dependency. And I'm certain that we can, as a nation, move forward and together on this issue. I've said a great many times, instead of citing at the end of each year how many people were being maintained on welfare—if the program was really correct, every year they would be saying how many people we had been able to remove from welfare and restore to a position of independence. Now, all of us care about the poor, all of us want to see the tragedy that is poverty ended. So, let's get to work. Now, I realize there's going to be some crabbing, and there's going to be some of the same kind of press that, well, I've been getting kind of used to in the last few weeks.

Public Papers of the President: Ronald Reagan. February 9, 1987: 115–118.

CONGRESSIONAL DEBATE ON WELFARE REFORM

December 16, 1987

Mrs. Margaret Roukema (R-NJ). Mr. Chairman, I come to this issue of welfare reform as a member of the Education and Labor Committee and as one of the congressional leaders of child support enforcement reform. I also served for 4 years as vice chairman of the Select Committee on Hunger.

Through our hearings and studies on the problems of hunger and education in this country, it has become apparent that our current welfare system is broken and needs to be fixed. It is inconsistent with the economic realities of contemporary society. That's why a bipartisan consensus has developed in support of restructuring our welfare system.

And I tell you today that welfare reform could have and should have been the crowning achievement—a legislative watershed—of the 100th Congress. It was to be the landmark legislation for the millions of women and children who must now suffer a lifetime of impoverishment.

Unfortunately this bill, H.R. 1720, does not fulfill the promise of reform. It should be defeated.

I cannot stand here and say the Republican substitute is the total answer to the welfare conundrum. It has some serious flaws—the funding is inadequate although the incentives to the States stand on firm principles.

. . .

My assessment is that in a number of areas, this bill, if enacted will trigger the law of perverse effects. There exists the potential that this bill will make it more attractive to go on welfare and stay on welfare.

How? Let me give you but two examples.

H.R. 1720 provides that a welfare mother does not have to have training or take on a job if she has a child 3 years or younger. Contrast that with the facts of today's work force:

Today there are 51 million women who work. Latest figures show that more than 50 percent of working mothers have children under age 1! And yet, this bill holds up a different standard, a standard that is totally inconsistent with the economic and social realities of contemporary America.

Imagine this: A welfare mother could actually continue to have a child every 2 years and never have to work at all. That's wrong. And not only will that mother not have to work, but her children, born into impoverishment, will have little hope for their own futures. And the cycle of poverty and dependency continues.

I ask: How much longer do you think the two-worker couple will tolerate the welfare state and its cost to them in taxes to support that welfare mother? How much longer must children suffer a lifetime of despair? The answer is that they should not have to.

Another key provision of this bill permits an AFDC [Aid to Families with Dependent Children] recipient attending a postsecondary institution full time to be exempted from any work requirement. College attendance would qualify the welfare recipient to receive welfare and AFDC benefits, including child care, transportation and Medicaid. There is no requirement for even part-time work.

While college study is laudable and could open up the opportunity for a higher paying job, it would seem apparent that welfare recipients who are skilled enough to gain admission to attend a college are more likely already to possess the skills necessary to obtain some level of employment.

But the reason this provision is egregious is that hundreds of thousands of people are currently working their way through school. The Bureau of Labor Statistics recently compiled data which show that of 1.5 million students enrolled in postsecondary institutions, 593,000 are working, while an additional 90,000 are seeking employment.

This means that one-fourth of the class of 1985 worked at least part-time while making their way through school. Yet this bill does not require an AFDC recipient to engage in a job search, if attending a full-time baccaluareate program. We expect of some what we do not even ask of others!

Question. Are we not creating a de facto higher education entitlement program here?

The welfare system should be a short-term transitional program to restore individuals to self-sufficiency. But, when disincentives to work outweigh the incentives, we undermine the program itself and waste the opportunity to help restore welfare families to personal and financial independence.

As the number of two-worker families increases, the key to welfare reform is to maintain a balance of equity between adequate welfare benefits and strong incentives to work. If benefits are not adequate we may have children and families without enough to live on. If benefits are too generous, however, there is a strong disincentive for the low-income working families.

An equal balance must be found between benefits on the one hand and work, education, and training programs on the other. Congress has a golden opportunity to bring reform to the welfare system and yet we are letting this opportunity slip right through our hands.

We must create legislation that will help break the cycle of dependency and give welfare recipients the opportunity and incentive to work, without creating a disincentive for the hard working two-parent family struggling to make ends meet.

I urge defeat of this bill.

The Congressional Record. December 16, 1987: H 11515–11516.

THE NOMINATION OF ROBERT BORK TO THE U.S. SUPREME COURT (SEPTEMBER 1987)

The opportunity to appoint a new justice to the U.S. Supreme Court is one of the great, enduring wishes of every president. Supreme Court justices serve for life, assuming they are not impeached and removed (none ever has been), and almost always remain in office for years, even decades, after the president who appointed them has left office. Thus, if a president can appoint like-minded people to the Supreme Court, the president's political philosophy can influence the nation far beyond his time in office.

When Ronald Reagan nominated Robert Bork to the Supreme Court in 1987, he nominated one of the most conservative people ever designated to serve in that office. A strict constructionist, Bork did not believe some rights like the right to privacy existed because the Constitution does not expressly state the existence of this right. Since the right to privacy touches on a host of other issues, like religious freedom, abortion rights, and even rights of patients to keep their medical records secret, strict constructionism has profound implications for American political life. Knowing that these attitudes were controversial, Reagan defended his nominee on the grounds of his qualifications. Like other presidents before and since who nominated controversial individuals to the Supreme Court, Reagan insisted that the Senate, which must confirm all judicial nominees, should judge only Bork's qualifications: since Bork was well qualified, he ought to be confirmed.

Senator Ted Kennedy (D-MA), perhaps the most vocal of Bork's many critics, argued that the "qualification" defense was constitutionally inadequate. The Constitution, Kennedy noted, requires that the Senate confirm appointments. It does not specify *how* it is to make its judgments. Moreover, as is seen in the excerpt of one his speeches opposing Bork's confirmation, Kennedy, like other opponents, argued that Bork's ideology—his opposition to the right to privacy, civil rights in general, and abortion rights, as well as other issues—disqualified him from office. On the merits, then, Kennedy argued that Bork did not belong on the Supreme Court.

Bork was rejected by the Senate by a vote of 42 to 58. Reagan's next nominee, Harvard law professor Douglas Ginsburg, withdrew his name when it was learned that he had used marijuana with some of his law students. Ultimately, Anthony Kennedy (no relation to the senator from Massachusetts) was confirmed in 1988. This established two trends that continue to this day: close Senate consideration of controversial nominees (see the nomination of Clarence Thomas to the Supreme Court during the Bush presidency) and the appointment of noncontroversial individuals to the Court. Thus, over time, neither strongly conservative nor strongly liberal individuals have been nominated or confirmed to the Court, and today the Court is balanced toward the middle of most controversial issues. Given the closeness of the 2000 presidential and congressional elections, this pattern of centrist-leaning justices being appointed to the Supreme Court seems likely to continue.

REAGAN'S REMARKS AT A WHITE HOUSE BRIEFING ON THE NOMINATION OF ROBERT H. BORK TO BE AN ASSOCIATE JUSTICE OF THE SUPREME COURT OF THE UNITED STATES

September 30, 1987

Americans who are committed to a Supreme Court with the highest standards speak with one voice. Judge Bork is not the conservative or liberal nominee; he is America's nominee to the United States Supreme Court. And just like my other nominees to the Court, he's not going to promote my political views; he's going to apply a superb legal mind to the task of interpreting the Constitution and the laws of the United States. The support for him reveals the fact that he is superbly qualified, an individual of unsurpassed integrity, and a principled advocate of judicial restraint. We will not be satisfied with allowing special interests to determine the qualifications to serve on our country's highest court.

. . .

. . . more relevant than a political label are the qualifications of the nominee, and all of us better understand the significance of that point. Our history commands that the nomination of a Supreme Court Justice by a President and the act of confirmation by the United States Senate be carried out with the highest level of statesmanship. Whether President, Senator, or concerned citizen, when we enter the halls of justice and select the next steward of our Constitution, Americans traditionally leave outside their partisan leanings and the narrow special interests. Each of us owes a sacred debt to our ancestors, who established the rule of law in this Republic, and to the citizens of the future, to whom we entrust our nation's destiny. In a special way, this duty now falls upon the United States Senate as it nears a crossroad, a crossroad of conscience, as it prepares to decide on the confirmation of Robert Bork. Let us insist that the Senate not give in to noisy, strident pressures and that elected officials not be swayed by a deliberate campaign of disinformation and distortion.

. . .

. . . A President, whether Republican or Democrat, liberal or conservative, seeks out the best qualified person who generally shares the President's judicial philosophy. The Senate then decides whether the nominee meets the qualifications to serve. This way, over the years, the Supreme Court becomes composed of the best minds reflecting varied but accepted judicial philosophies. Now is not the time to change the standard, to break that tradition. And I know you join me in calling for statesmanship, not partisanship, in the confirmation of Robert Bork to the Supreme Court.

. . .

Beyond his scholarship and judicial qualifications, there's nothing more significant for his confirmation than the war on crime. Last week, Fred Foreman, representing the Nation's district attorneys, observed that there is a large group in this country made up of women, minorities, the weak, and the aged. Although not well-organized, he reckoned they were in Judge Bork's corner, because they are the victims of crime. And I guess he ought to know; he and the thousands of young prosecutors around the country are the ones who have to vindicate the rights of the victims and send the criminals to jail. Now, both as Solicitor General and as judge, Robert Bork has been a principled champion in the fight against crime, and that's the kind of Justice honest citizens deserve to have on the Court.

. . .

Judge Bork has argued for more reasonable interpretations of criminal procedures that assure both justice and the prompt conviction of criminals rather than allowing dangerous criminals to go free on unjustified technicalities. He has not hesitated to overturn convictions where genuine constitutional rights have been violated. He has consistently rendered judgment in a clear-eyed manner with the aim of protecting the rights of the innocent. And that's what justice should be all about— protecting our rights as Americans. And that's why 400,000 law enforcement officers have thrown their support behind Judge Bork, the battle against crime, and for the rule of law. Criminals terrorize the streets in too many of America's cities.

It's time to decide whether our children and our children's children deserve an America in which the concern is for their safety and not just the protection of the criminal. I saw a surprising statistic the other day. Nearly one-third of the Supreme Court's cases involve matters of criminal justice. The next Justice on that Court better be ready to deal with that challenge; the next Justice better be Robert Bork.

Public Papers of the President: Ronald Reagan. September 30, 1987: 1103–1106.

OPPOSITION TO THE NOMINATION OF ROBERT BORK

October 21, 1987

Mr. Ted Kennedy (D-MA). Mr. President, it is no secret that I oppose the nomination of Judge Bork to the Supreme Court. I stated my opposition the day the nomination was announced—and I'm proud of it.

Although I strongly oppose Judge Bork, I have often supported conservative Supreme Court nominees by conservative Republican Presidents. I voted for the nominations of Chief Justice Burger, Justice Blackmum and Justice Powell by President Nixon. I voted for the nomination of Justice Stevens by President Ford. And I voted for the nominations of Justice O'Connor and Justice Scalia by President Reagan. In fact, President Reagan has named over 300 judges to the Federal bench during the past 7 years, and I have supported all but eight.

But from the beginning, it was clear that the nomination of Judge Bork was more than the usual nomination—which is why it has attracted more than the usual controversy and attention. Virtually everyone, no matter where they are on the issue, recognizes that the Supreme Court is at a turning point, and that whoever fills this vacancy may play a large role in setting the Court's direction for a decade or even longer to come.

Rarely have we had such a combination of circumstance. The Supreme Court is closely divided—and the President has consciously sought to bend it to his will. The Justice who resigned defied any ideological category and he held the decisive balance on many critical issues—and the Justice who was nominated tilted so consistently toward one narrow ideological point of view.

No one disputes the President's right to try to force that tilt on the Supreme Court—and no one should dispute the right of the Senate to try to stop him. That's what advice and consent means in the Constitution. That was the original intent of the Founding Fathers, as that is the meaning of the constitutional role of the Senate today.

At the outset, the advocates of the nomination implicitly conceded that they had a hard case to make. They tried to discredit Judge Bork's opposition, on the foolish ground that all the Senate can or should do on a nomination is read the resume and FBI report—and if the nominee is smart enough, and has stayed out of trouble, the Senate is compelled to confirm him. Ideology shouldn't count, they said, and often it hasn't. But what is sauce for the goose is sauce for the gander. President Reagan obviously took Robert Bork's ideology into account in making the nomination, and the Senate has every right to take it into account in acting on the nomination.

This debate has been a timely lesson, in this bicentennial year of the Constitution, of our commitment to the rule of law, to the principle of equal justice for all Americans, and to the fundamental role of the Supreme Court in protecting the basic rights of every citizen.

In choosing Robert Bork, President Reagan selected a nominee who is unique in his fulminating opposition to fundamental constitutional principles as they are broadly understood in our society. He has expressed that opposition time and again in a long line of attacks on landmark Supreme Court decisions protecting civil rights, the rights of women, the right to privacy, and other individual rights and liberties. Judge Bork may be President Reagan's ideal ideological choice for the Supreme Court, but that ideology is not acceptable to Congress and the country, and it is not acceptable in a Justice of the Nation's highest court.

In analyzing the record of Judge Bork's long professional career, and in his testimony before the Senate Judiciary Committee, a number of themes have emerged:

Judge Bork is antagonistic to the role of the law and the courts in fundamental areas such as ensuring racial justice, protecting the rights of women, and preserving the right of privacy for individuals against oppressive intrusions by the Government.

Judge Bork is a true believer in concentrated power, whether it is big government in the form of unrestrained executive power, or big business in the form of corporations virtually unrestrained by antitrust laws and health and safety regulation.

Judge Bork is not only an enemy of the individual in confrontations with the Government, but he is equally an enemy of Congress in confrontations with the President or when the will of Congress is in conflict with his ideology.

Judge Bork has little respect for precedent. His habit of intemperate statements—some made this year, on the very eve of his nomination—suggests how eager Judge Bork is to rewrite the meaning of the Constitution. His numerous confirmation conversions, implying a newfound respect for precedent, are hardly reassuring.

Judge Bork's hostility toward individuals is nowhere clearer than in his attitude toward civil rights. People of great courage in this country endured great risks over the past three decades in the struggle against race discrimination in America. In the 1960's, while we sought to end segregated lunch counters and "Whites Only" want ads, Robert Bork stridently opposed legislation to end racial discrimination in public accommodations and employment.

Nor can Judge Bork's intemperate opposition be passed off as the understandable aberrations of a provocative professor confounded by the swiftly moving events of a quarter century ago. In 1964, a Senator or a scholar did not have to be a liberal to weigh the issue and judge it rightly. The Civil Rights Act of that year was an historic product of mainstream America, Republican as well as Democrat. It was overwhelmingly endorsed by constitutional experts and swiftly and unanimously sustained by the Supreme Court. And Judge Bork's mentor and colleague at Yale, one of the most respected advocates of conservative legal philosophy and judicial restraint, Alexander Bickel, was a forceful voice in favor of Federal action against discrimination, but Robert Bork disagreed—he said that the historic public accommodations legislation was based on a principle of "unsurpassed ugliness"—when most Americans thought that phrase better described Jim Crow.

. . .

No person nominated to the Supreme Court in this century—or the last—has demonstrated a belief in so broad and unrestricted a view of Presidential power, even when it is exercised illegally. Nothing could be further from the original intent of the Founding Fathers—the last thing they intended at Philadelphia in 1787 was to create a President with the powers of George III.

. . .

It is preposterous—and hypocritical—for the White House to complain that politics suddenly intruded to mar the confirmation process. For much of 1986, President Reagan himself barnstormed the country, calling for the election of Republican Senators who would confirm his judicial nominees. President Reagan failed in that campaign, and his failure there was a harbinger of the American people's rejection of Judge Bork.

It is ridiculous—and untrue—for the supporters of Judge Bork to suggest that politics has been confined to only one side of the current debate. From the day the nomination was announced, my Senate office was inundated by an unprecedented tidal wave of mail. I received over 129,000 letters of support for Judge Bork from across the country, and an even larger number of preprinted postcards expressing such support. And I was hardly a likely target of their affections. Who does President Reagan think was orchestrating that massive political campaign throughout America for Judge Bork—the tooth fairy?

It is equally ridiculous for Judge Bork and the White House to make the dire assertions we have all heard in recent days that the politics of this debate have somehow endangered the independence of the judiciary. As the constitutional scholar he is, Judge Bork himself should certainly know better. As Justice Oliver Wendell Holmes once said, "The

Supreme Court is a quiet place, but it is the quiet at the center of the storm." This stormy confirmation debate and the repudiation of Judge Bork may have shaken the foundations of right-wing ideology in America, but it is only a passing gentle breeze in the long and often much more turbulent history of the Supreme Court in our society. Judge Bork himself was a far greater threat to the role of the Supreme Court than anything that happened in this debate. The simple truth is his nomination collided with the Constitution and with democracy in America, and the Supreme Court and the country have emerged the stronger for it.

. . .

The question is not, and never has been, loyalty to party but to the Constitution; not special interests but the national interest; not the person who would be Justice but the future of justice itself.

. . .

That is the standard by which Robert Bork must be measured—the standard by which any nominee for the Supreme Court should be judged, and the standard which the American people have always set for our highest court. And by that standard, Robert Bork's record does not paint the portrait of a man who should have the last word on what justice means in America.

The Congressional Record. October 21, 1987: S 14698–14701.

HOUSING AND COMMUNITY DEVELOPMENT (FEBRUARY 1988)

The question of what role the federal government should play in the lives of its citizens is at the center of domestic policy debates. Government support for affordable housing, which has been a centerpiece of federal policy since the 1960s, is a common source of contention between conservatives and liberals. Conservatives believe that such programs encourage people to remain dependent on welfare; liberals believe that housing is a basic need that must be provided if people are to succeed in life. Accordingly, housing policy debates expose a fundamental tension in American politics.

Reagan, a conservative, was inherently opposed to federal housing subsidies. However, powerful members of Congress supported these programs, and Reagan chose to compromise with them in order to maintain positive relations with these members for future issues. The policy he promoted attempted to provide maximum levels of choice for both individuals and communities in developing and utilizing federal housing support. The program created enterprise zones (special tax districts in which businesses received tax breaks for developing operations in poor areas), vouchers (government-subsidized checks individuals could spend on housing wherever they could find it), and support for investigations into allegations that various housing providers were refusing to allow minorities into their properties in violation of federal law.

Most pro-subsidy forces were generally satisfied by Reagan's compromise plan. Some critics, however, felt that these proposals did not go far enough to provide housing to all Americans. Others felt they went too far. Reagan's harshest critics, including Senator William Armstrong (R-CO), were conservatives. They argued that federal housing subsidies would increase the budget deficit, that they were unnecessary because enough housing was available, and that, without an incentive to work hard (like the need to pay for housing), people would remain dependent on welfare.

Reagan's program became law in 1988. Since then, there has been a proliferation of enterprise zones and other special programs intended to promote economic development in poor areas. A large amount of housing has been built with federal tax incentives, which requires making apartments accessible to poor people of all races and ethnicities. However, as liberals suspected, these programs have been manipulated to some extent for the benefit of local elites: since the local and state communities control how these dollars are invested (a conservative preference), the funds are often redirected in ways preferred by the community's powerful politicians and business leaders. Homelessness has declined as a result both of these programs and the booming economy of the 1990s.

REAGAN'S REMARKS ON SIGNING THE HOUSING AND COMMUNITY DEVELOPMENT ACT OF 1987

February 5, 1988

I am pleased today to sign this bill, S. 825, the Housing and Community Development Act of 1987. This comprehensive legislation represents both compromise and cooperation between the administration, the Senate, and the House. Through a concerted effort, the legislation was transformed from a budget buster that would have reversed hard-won housing policy reforms into a rational, cost-effective bill that is fiscally responsible.

. . .

A key feature of this housing bill is the permanent authorization of the housing voucher program that we first proposed in 1982. The housing voucher program exemplifies our commitment to community development through public-private partnerships. Vouchers gave families the dignity of choice—the opportunity to choose the type and location of their housing and the ability to be near family and friends and schools and churches or jobs. This legislation puts the private market to work in supplying rental housing by enabling the government to help needy families with vouchers so they can afford to rent housing of their own choosing. This legislation is a big step toward our housing goal of a home for every American family.

In just the last year, our voucher program has helped 100,000 low-income families find housing of their own choosing. We know flexible housing vouchers serve needy families better at substantially less taxpayer cost. And I'm also pleased that this bill authorizes the availability of vouchers to rural areas, but it's very disappointing that the Congress refused to appropriate the funding for a rural housing voucher program this year.

· · ·

S. 825 provides training and technical support for the establishment of new resident management groups and allows them to reinvest savings from resident management to establish small business enterprises. The resident management enterprises of low-income residents have effectively combated crime and poverty and created new pride through self-management in cities around the country.

This bill also adopts our proposal for modernization of public housing and gives us new tools to combat fraud and abuse in housing and FHA [Federal Housing Administration] insurance programs. It also includes authority for the designation of enterprise zones—part of an initiative that we proposed in 1981. I'm also gratified by another provision of this bill which authorizes HUD [Department of Housing and Urban Development] to fund local, private organizations that are working to end housing discrimination. Too often—one case is too many—families and individuals seeking to buy or rent homes still confront bigotry and discrimination. Well, the fair housing initiative program section of this bill will help ensure that such racism will not be tolerated.

· · ·

. . . This is a sound compromise. This bill helps keep a lid on new spending while preserving our key housing reforms. It also includes features that will help ensure that our country can efficiently and effectively meet the challenge of America's changing housing needs. In an earlier day, American pioneers would gather together and help newcomers build their homes. That same spirit of good will and cooperation is what made the passage of this bill possible.

Public Papers of the President: Ronald Reagan. February 4, 1988: 176–178.

HOUSING AND COMMUNITY DEVELOPMENT ACT OF 1987
CONFERENCE REPORT

November 13, 1987

Mr. William Armstrong (R-CO). Mr. President, the symbol of America is the eagle; that is our national emblem. The symbol of America is not the ostrich; but, by gosh, if we vote for this conference report, it should be the ostrich.

I know that the easiest thing for Senators to do is to come to the floor and say: "Well, the fix is in. It is all done. The train is leaving. The boat is about to sail. There is a bipartisan agreement here. The managers have been working on this a long time. What can I do? I am only one; Why should I vote against it, if it is going to pass anyway? It's not my fault or responsibility."

Well, it is our responsibility. It is our responsibility, one Senator at a time. To us has been entrusted the decision of how we will vote. It does matter whether this passes or not, whether the President vetoes it or not, whether his veto is sustained or not. It does matter. This is not a free vote.

Psychologists have known for a long time that one of the most enduring features of human nature is a reluctance—indeed, an intransigent unwillingness—to look at unpleasant facts. But I think we should look at them.

I think it has been clearly established, not only in the debate last night but also over a long period of time, that this legislation is harmful to our country. It is harmful to the budget deficit. It is harmful to the markets that are looking to Congress for some reassurance about the future of the economy. It is harmful to local housing authorities which are calling for reform of these programs. It is harmful to those who have objected to certain new amendments which were included in this conference report, included without the benefit of hearings.

. . .

The first fact is that there is no convincing showing of need for this program. We have about 5 million units of subsidized housing in this country. I do not think there is any showing that it is an insufficient number.

I do not deny that there are people who need help with housing who cannot get it. The problem is that most of this housing—and I use the word "most" advisedly—has been made available to people who are not poor, who are either wealthy or near wealthy or in the middle class. At a time when we have housing-poor people, people who are housing indigents, who cannot get support, we have people who are much better off who are occupying the vast majority of the subsidized units. About 600,000 of these units become available every year; and if we started reallocating those systematically to those truly in need, we would not have to authorize additional new units.

Second, I think we have clearly established that this bill is not timely. We are trying to find some ways to reduce deficits.

· · ·

The response of the proponents of this legislation is, by gosh, it is not fair to blame housing legislation for the national budget crisis, but, of course, nobody was doing that. There is not any Senator who has come to the floor and said that the reason that we got this astronomical problem is because of housing legislation. What we have said is that the cumulated extravagance of the housing legislation is part of the problem. And it just so happens it is the part of it we are addressing today. This is the part that today we have a chance to do something about.

Nor can we be unmindful of the fact that over and above the actual contributions to the securitized public debt there is a quarter of a trillion dollars, $250 billion of unfunded liabilities for which no provisions have been made right now.

If we never adopt another housing authorization or appropriation bill we are going to have to pay off over $250 billion to which we are already committed. That is in addition to the stated explicit national debt of something in excess of $2 trillion.

Mr. President, we have shown and I think conclusively that the figures which are used by the proponents to support this are at the very best, under the most charitable characterization open to serious doubt. They say it is $15 billion in authorization. The OMB [Office of Management and Budget] believes it is $18.7 billion. And so you can take your choice of who you really believe. . . .

· · ·

I am convinced that this is bad legislation, that it should be vetoed by the President. The indication we have is that it will be vetoed. They have sent their coded message over from the administration to the effect that the President's senior advisers are opposed to this legislation and will recommend a veto. My hope is we will be able to show this morning enough strength to sustain such a veto if the President is inclined to veto the bill.

The Congressional Record. November 13, 1987: S 16250–16252.

MILITARY AND FOREIGN POLICY

ARMS CONTROL AND THE MX MISSILE (JULY 1983)

Given the enormous number and awesome destructive capacity of modern nuclear weapons, their acquisition, deployment, and potential use have been a controversial issue throughout the post–World War II era. By the mid-1980s, the United States and the Soviet Union each had at least 25,000 nuclear warheads in their arsenals. Scientific advances of the period made it possible to build even more powerful warheads which could be targeted with greater levels of accuracy. Most significant among these advances was the development of MIRV technology, the ability to put Multiple, Individually Targeted Re-Entry Vehicles (warheads)—MIRVs—on a single missile. Because one missile could carry ten or more warheads, the size of the U.S. arsenal could be dramatically expanded so that ever-more precise targets could be destroyed. A new arms race was about to begin with both the United States and the Soviet Union working to retrofit their existing missiles with the new technology.

President Reagan advocated developing and deploying a new generation of MIRV-capable missiles in the U.S. stockpile. As part of his foreign policy, he pushed Congress to fund two major, new missile systems: the MX "Peacekeeper" ground-based missile and its equivalent, deployed on a new generation of submarines called Trident. These missiles would, Reagan argued, enhance the deterrent capability of U.S. nuclear forces. If the Soviets launched an attack and destroyed many U.S. missiles, each of the remaining weapons could launch a devastating attack on the Soviet homeland. In addition, the enhanced targeting capabilities of these new missiles meant that they could be aimed at smaller, military-only targets rather than major cities. In combination with negotiations, these missiles were expected to strengthen U.S. security.

Opponents of the MX and Trident systems, represented here by Congressman Patrick Leahy (D-VT), argued that the purchase of these new weapons would violate previous arms control agreements with the Soviets and could encourage a new arms race. In particular, they argued that it would violate the SALT II (Strategic Arms Limitation Talks) Treaty which, while never ratified by the Senate, had served as the basis for U.S.–Soviet negotiations for the past several years. In addition, they rejected the idea that more weapons increased national security; once a threshold number was reached, opponents believed, any increase just gave a nation the capacity to destroy rubble again and again. New weapons were not good—they were dangerous.

Ultimately, a small number of MX missiles were purchased and deployed. Mass protests broke out in both Europe and the United States, and political tensions increased during the period. No nuclear war ever broke out between the United States and the Soviet Union, however, and in time, most of the U.S. and Soviet missiles have been destroyed as required in arms-reduction agreements signed after the Soviet Union collapsed in 1991. The Trident was purchased, however, and over ten have been built; each holds at least twenty missiles with at least ten MIRVs. At any given moment, at least half the fleet is at sea acting as the essentially invulnerable component of the United States' deterrent threat.

REAGAN'S RADIO ADDRESS TO THE NATION ON ARMS CONTROL AND REDUCTION

July 16, 1983

Today I want to talk to you about peace. Back in June of 1963, President John F. Kennedy delivered an arms control speech that is still remembered for its eloquence and vision. He told the graduating seniors at American University: "I speak of peace, therefore, as the necessary, rational end of rational men. I realize that the pursuit of peace is not as dramatic as the pursuit of war and, frequently, the words of the pursuer fall on deaf ears. But we have no more urgent task."

Twenty years have passed since those words were spoken, and they've been a troubled era, overshadowed by the dangers of nuclear weapons. We've seen the world's inventory of nuclear weapons steadily expand. Despite many sincere attempts to control the growth of nuclear arsenals, those arsenals have continued to grow. That's the bad news.

The good news is that now, at last, there is hope that we can finally begin to reverse this trend. . . .

Remember, our MX Peacekeeper missile program calls for the deployment of 100 missiles. The level ultimately deployed, however, will clearly be influenced by the outcome in Geneva. If an agreement is reached which calls for deep reductions—which is, of course, our goal—the number of missiles could certainly be adjusted downward.

As the Scowcroft commission rightly pointed out, the MX Peacekeeper missile is an essential part of a comprehensive modernization and arms control program to ensure deterrence today and in the future. We're building the MX Peacekeeper to strengthen deterrence. But it also provides vital negotiating incentives and leverage in Geneva.

. . .

My message . . . is that I have no higher priority than reducing and ultimately removing the threat of nuclear war and seeking the stability necessary for true peace. To achieve that objective, we must reduce the nuclear arsenals of both the United States and the Soviet Union. We must achieve greater stability; that is, we must be sure that we obtain genuine arms reductions, not merely agreements that permit a growth in nuclear arsenals or agreements that proclaim good intentions without the teeth necessary to verify and enforce compliance.

Our current goal must be the reduction of nuclear arsenals. And I for one believe we must never depart from the ultimate goal of banning them from the face of the Earth. That's why we presented ambitious but realistic proposals, and that's why I have been and continue to be willing to consider any serious Soviet counteroffer. And that's why I've made our original proposal more flexible and why I continue to seek new ideas for achieving an arms reduction breakthrough.

Public Papers of the President: Ronald Reagan. July 16, 1983: 1041–1043.

OPPOSITION TO THE SALT II TREATY

December 13, 1985

Mr. Patrick Leahy (D-UT). Mr. President, as the 1st session of the 99th Congress draws to its weary close, I ask the Members to reflect on a very important fact: Had the SALT II Treaty been ratified, it would have expired on December 31 of this year. However, instead of having a legally binding treaty, the United States has been following a policy of informal observance of the main provisions of SALT II, so long as the Soviet Union showed equal restraint. That is a policy I and others in this body have advocated and, under considerable political pressure from the administration to leave it a free hand, fought to preserve.

. . . To put it bluntly, Mr. President, 1984 was an election year, and many people wished to have a cost-free arms control vote. I say cost-free because, as was well understood in the executive branch and in Congress, the "no-undercut" policy required nothing of the United States in terms of dismantlements to that point, while forcing the Soviet Union to make significant cuts in sea-launched ballistic missiles to remain within the applicable SALT limits. Nevertheless, as I vividly recall, our amendment was bitterly criticized by some in this body, and fought until the last moment by the administration. Only when it became crystal clear that the Bumpers-Leahy-Chafee-Heinz amendment would pass comfortably did the administration drop its resistance.

This year proved a more difficult test for the mutual restraint policy. In August, the seventh U.S. Trident submarine, the U.S.S. *Alaska*, went to sea trials. Had the United States not initiated compensating reductions in other multiple warhead ballistic missiles, we would have breached a key SALT II ceiling. Again, the same bipartisan coalition pressed the Senate to declare its support for the "no-undercut" or mutual restraint policy, in order to avoid a total collapse of restraints on strategic offensive systems. On June 5, by a 90 to 5 vote, the Senate adopted our resolution. This was the second time the Senate voted overwhelmingly that the United States should continue the SALT II ceilings. Mr. President, I would like to recall for my colleagues the key language of that amendment:

The United States should, through December 31, 1986, continue to refrain from undercutting the provisions of existing strategic offensive arms agreements to the extent that the Soviet Union refrains from undercutting those provisions, or until a new strategic offensive arms agreement is concluded; and provided, however, nothing in this section shall be construed as prohibiting the U.S. from carrying out other proportionate responses to Soviet undercutting of strategic arms provisions.

. . .

Mr. President, we are all familiar with President Reagan's characterization of the SALT II Treaty as "fatally flawed" when he was campaigning against then–President Carter. Once in office, however, and facing the responsibility for U.S. security, President Reagan found, just as the Joint Chiefs of Staff had testified in 1979, that the SALT II Treaty limits favored the United States. More was required of the Soviet Union to comply with the SALT ceilings than was required of the United States. The deal was a good one for the United States, and it made no sense to scrap it. So, campaign rhetoric forgotten and real responsibility on his shoulders, the President decided to protect the national interest. I applaud him for it, even though I believe it would have been far better had he used his tremendous political base in 1981 to have asked the Senate to approve ratification of the SALT Treaty. This would have gained for the United States even more advantage, as the Soviets would have had to take a net reduction in strategic missiles of some 250 launchers to reach the new ceiling of 2,250. Perhaps even more importantly, the way would have been cleared for immediate initiation of SALT III negotiations. I do not think it inconceivable that, had SALT II been ratified in 1981; we could be on the threshold of deep reductions in SALT III at this very moment.

. . .

Mr. President, one of the peculiar characteristics of being American is to have an abiding faith in technology's ability to solve problems. Technology has served us well, and contributed to the highest living standard in the world. But we also have a tendency to think technology can solve the nuclear threat. The President's conviction, and I believe it is a sincere and well-meant conviction, that star wars can end the nuclear menace is a manifestation of our fascination with technological solutions to a fundamentally political problem. Real disarmament depends on a basic alteration of the political equation between East and West. That will be a long time in coming. In the meantime, it is vital that we do whatever is possible to avoid a nuclear catastrophe. By failing to ratify SALT II and to get on immediately with SALT III, we have disrupted the most hopeful, most meaningful attempt to lower that terrible danger.

President Reagan has chosen a new and different strategy, one which combines an immense nuclear modernization program, a new technological initiative in strategic defense, and an effort to negotiate deep reductions at Geneva. I do not know what his strategy will produce. In frankness, my fear is it will lead only to even more frightful weapons, less security, greater instability, and a growing risk of nuclear holocaust.

The Congressional Record. December 13, 1985: S 17571–17572.

PEACEKEEPING IN LEBANON (OCTOBER 1983)

In 1983 a Marine barracks located in Beirut, Lebanon, was destroyed by a massive car bomb, and more than 200 Marines were killed. The Marines were part of a peacekeeping effort to end a long civil war that had destroyed Beirut. In response to the bombing, questions emerged about whether the United States ought to engage in peacekeeping missions that put U.S. troops at risk when U.S. interests are not directly at stake.

Reagan supported the idea of using American troops in peacekeeping missions. He defended this policy on a number of grounds. First, he articulated the unique role the United States ought to play in the world: as the defender of democracy, it must act. Second, he noted the special significance of the Middle East to the United States because Israel, Lebanon's neighbor, is a close U.S. ally, and because the region contains much of the world's oil supply. Only U.S. participation could reduce the chance of another, devastating Middle East war, Reagan argued.

Congressman Charles Gonzalez (D-TX), like other critics of the peacekeeping effort in Lebanon, made several points in arguing for an end to the operation. Lebanese politics were complicated by issues of religion, history, and culture, each of which was in tension with the other in the middle of a civil war. Inserting U.S. troops into this mix was necessarily to put them in a position of danger. This was even more likely after the United States began to bomb targets in Lebanon (an action it started in the weeks preceding the Beirut attack). In doing this, the United States stopped playing peacekeeper and chose sides in the war. Its troops thus became natural targets for those people being bombed by the United States. Finally, opponents argued that by failing to invoke the War Powers Act—the law that requires presidents to gain congressional approval if troops are going to be in danger for more than sixty days—and engaging the American people in a debate about what the purpose of the operation was, the policy was bound to fail.

Despite substantial congressional opposition, U.S. troops remained in Lebanon for another year, but they were withdrawn when Lebanon's politics continued in chaos. (It was this chaos that became the foundation of the Iran-contra scandal covered in this volume.) U.S. forces neither engaged in continuing operations nor were subjected to any further attacks.

Today, Lebanon is largely controlled by groups loyal to Syria and Iran. More international peacekeeping operations on the part of U.S. troops continue—several are covered in this volume—and indeed have expanded in the aftermath of the end of the Cold War. But the same basic tensions about what U.S. troops should do and why they should do it remain. The United States may have a unique role to play in promoting democracy around the world, but exactly how to do this in a dangerous world filled with people who do not support the United States' self-perceived role is an ever-recurring dilemma.

REAGAN'S ADDRESS TO THE NATION ON EVENTS IN LEBANON

October 27, 1983

Some 2 months ago we were shocked by the brutal massacre of 269 men, women, children, more than 60 of them Americans in the shooting down of a Korean airliner. Now, in these past several days, violence has erupted again, in Lebanon and Grenada.

In Lebanon, we have some 1,600 Marines, part of a multination force that's trying to help the people of Lebanon restore order and stability to that troubled land. Our Marines are assigned to the south of the city of Beirut, near the only airport operating in Lebanon. Just a mile or so to the north is the Italian contingent and not far from them, the French and a company of British soldiers.

This past Sunday, at 22 minutes after 6 Beirut time, with dawn just breaking, a truck, looking like a lot of other vehicles in the city, approached the airport on a busy, main road. There was nothing in its appearance to suggest it was any different than the trucks or cars that were normally seen on or around the airport. But this one was different. At the wheel was a young man on a suicide mission.

The truck carried some 2,000 pounds of explosives, but there was no way our Marine guards could know this. Their first warning that something was wrong came when the truck crashed through a series of barriers, including a chain-link fence and barbed wire entanglements. The guards opened fire, but it was too late. The truck smashed through the doors of the headquarters building in which our Marines were sleeping and instantly exploded. The four-story concrete building collapsed in a pile of rubble.

More than 200 of the sleeping men were killed in that one hideous, insane attack. Many others suffered injury and are hospitalized here or in Europe.

This was not the end of the horror. At almost the same instant, another vehicle on a suicide and murder mission crashed into the headquarters of the French peacekeeping force, an eight-story building, destroying it and killing more than 50 French soldiers.

Prior to this day of horror, there had been several tragedies for our men in the multinational force. Attacks by snipers and mortar fire had taken their toll.

. . . And now many of you are asking: Why should our young men be dying in Lebanon? Why is Lebanon important to us?

Well, it's true, Lebanon is a small country, more than five-and-a-half thousand miles from our shores on the edge of what we call the Middle East. But every President who has occupied this office in recent years has recognized that peace in the Middle East is of vital concern to our nation and, indeed, to our allies in Western Europe and Japan. We've been concerned because the Middle East is a powderkeg; four times in the last 30 years, the Arabs and Israelis have gone to war. And each time, the world has teetered near the edge of catastrophe.

The area is key to the economic and political life of the West. Its strategic importance, its energy resources, the Suez Canal, and the well-being of the nearly 200 million people living there—all are vital to us and to world peace. If that key should fall into the hands of a power or powers hostile to the free world, there would be a direct threat to the United States and to our allies.

We have another reason to be involved. Since 1948 our Nation has recognized and accepted a moral obligation to assure the continued existence of Israel as a nation. Israel shares our democratic values and is a formidable force an invader of the Middle East would have to reckon with.

For several years, Lebanon has been torn by internal strife. Once a prosperous, peaceful nation, its government had become ineffective in controlling the militias that warred on each other. Sixteen months ago, we were watching on our TV screens the shelling and bombing of Beirut which was being used as a fortress by PLO [Palestine Liberation Organization] bands. Hundreds and hundreds of civilians were being killed and wounded in the daily battles.

Syria, which makes no secret of its claim that Lebanon should be a part of a Greater Syria, was occupying a large part of Lebanon. Today, Syria has become a home for 7,000 Soviet advisers and technicians who man a massive amount of Soviet weaponry, including SS-21 ground-to-ground missiles capable of reaching vital areas of Israel.

. . .

In the year that our Marines have been there, Lebanon has made important steps toward stability and order. The physical presence of the Marines lends support to both the Lebanese Government and its army. It allows the hard work of diplomacy to go forward. Indeed, without the peacekeepers from the U.S., France, Italy, and Britain, the efforts to find a peaceful solution in Lebanon would collapse.

. . .

To answer those who ask if we're serving any purpose in being there, let me answer a question with a question. Would the terrorists have launched their suicide attacks against the multinational force if it were not doing its job? The multinational force was attacked precisely because it is doing the job it was sent to do in Beirut. It is accomplishing its mission.

Now then, where do we go from here? What can we do now to help Lebanon gain greater stability so that our Marines can come home? Well, I believe we can take three steps now that will make a difference.

First, we will accelerate the search for peace and stability in that region. Little attention has been paid to the fact that we've had special envoys there working, literally, around the clock to bring the warring factions together. This coming Monday in Geneva, President Gemayel of Lebanon will sit down with other factions from his country to see if national reconciliation can be achieved. He has our firm support. I will soon be announcing a replacement for Bud McFarlane, who was preceded by Phil Habib. Both worked tirelessly and must be credited for much if not most of the progress we've made.

Second, we'll work even more closely with our allies in providing support for the Government of Lebanon and for the rebuilding of a national consensus.

Third, we will ensure that the multinational peace-keeping forces, our Marines, are given the greatest possible protection. Our Commandant of the Marine Corps, General Kelley, returned from Lebanon today and will be advising us on steps we can take to improve security. Vice President [George H.W.] Bush returned just last night from Beirut and gave me a full report of his brief visit.

Beyond our progress in Lebanon, let us remember that our main goal and purpose is to achieve a broader peace in all of the Middle East. The factions and bitterness that we see in Lebanon are just a microcosm of the difficulties that are spread across much of that region. A peace initiative for the entire Middle East, consistent with the Camp David accords and U.N. resolutions 242 and 338, still offers the best hope for bringing peace to the region.

Let me ask those who say we should get out of Lebanon: If we were to leave Lebanon now, what message would that send to those who foment instability and terrorism? If America were to walk away from Lebanon, what chance would there be for a negotiated settlement, producing a unified democratic Lebanon?

If we turned our backs on Lebanon now, what would be the future of Israel? At stake is the fate of only the second Arab country to negotiate a major agreement with Israel. That's another accomplishment of this past year, the May 17th accord signed by Lebanon and Israel.

If terrorism and intimidation succeed, it'll be a devastating blow to the peace process and to Israel's search for genuine security. It won't just be Lebanon sentenced to a future of chaos. Can the United States, or the free world, for that matter, stand by and see the Middle East incorporated into the Soviet bloc? What of Western Europe and Japan's dependence on Middle East oil for the energy to fuel their industries? The Middle East is, as I've said, vital to our national security and economic well-being.

Brave young men have been taken from us. Many others have been grievously wounded. Are we to tell them their sacrifice was wasted? They gave their lives in defense of our national security every bit as much as any man who ever died fighting in a war. We must not strip every ounce of meaning and purpose from their courageous sacrifice.

We're a nation with global responsibilities. We're not somewhere else in the world protecting someone else's interests; we're there protecting our own.

Public Papers of the President: Ronald Reagan. October 27, 1983: 1517–1522.

CRITICISM OF U.S. PEACEKEEPING EFFORTS IN LEBANON

October 27, 1983

Mr. Charles Gonzalez (D-TX). Mr. Speaker, all of us have been through an extraordinary—I would say overwhelming week. We are distracted by the weird invasion of Grenada, a nation consisting of 110,000 souls on an island no bigger than the District of Columbia. Yet despite that sensational event, every glance we make out the window brings the tragedy of Lebanon back to mind. Those half-masted flags, the daily casualty lists, and the information sheets from the Pentagon that tell of the mechanics of how the harvest of dead will be handled, would not let us forget the horror of Lebanon, nor the trap that the United States is in, nor the failure of Congress to meet its responsibilities to question and change a policy that had failed long before disaster struck.

It is not enough to deplore the military blunders that contributed mightily to the tragic killing of so many of our men in Lebanon, for the short and brutal truth is that it was the political policies we endorsed in Congress that were responsible for most of the military errors. For example, the majority that endorsed the War Powers Resolution compromise a few weeks ago never questioned the wisdom of keeping those troops in an open, exposed, low encampment. There were few who bothered to ask about how defensible the position was. The prevailing view was that same vacuous, pollyanna White House statement that back in January said:

(The situation) is not fraught with danger . . . (the Marines) have been there three or four months without any major incident . . . they are not in conflict, not in contact with anybody that could produce a major incident.

About 3 months after that airy dismissal of genuine concern about the safety of the Marines, a suicide bomber destroyed the U.S. Embassy in Beirut, at a loss of 63 lives—mostly Lebanese who worked in the Embassy, but including 17 of our Foreign Service personnel, some of our best and brightest people in public service. Most assuredly, they were not in conflict with anybody, but they got killed anyway, because that is the nature of the fratricide that has been going on in Lebanon since time immemorial. The Embassy bombing was a stark warning that Americans were targets for terrorists, and that in Beirut, to be a person of good will does not mean that you will not become a target for some fanatic who thinks that the sure ticket to Heaven is to blow up innocents who do not belong to your particular sect or faction or militia or splinter group, or who just happen to be in the way of your car bomb. But while we mourned the dead, only a very few of us became concerned enough to wonder about the wisdom of staying in the quagmire of Lebanese politics.

I had opposed putting Americans into Lebanon in the first place. I knew that the military advisers had said it was a bad idea. And I also shared the view of people like George Ball, who warned that putting American troops into a multinational force would draw attacks from extremists of one kind or another, to whom Americans are a symbol. It was like putting iron filings in front of a magnet, and then expecting the magnet not to suck those filings in. I expressed all of this, but in the rush of unwarranted optimism that this would be an operation of a couple of weeks, such questions were treated as not just impertinent, but downright irreverent.

After the Embassy was destroyed, and the Marine mission had dragged on from weeks into 6 months, with no end in sight, I asked myself again: "What is being accomplished?" Is not it time to evaluate this troop commitment and bring the troops home if their presence has not brought about any discernible difference? And I could not find any evidence that the peace talks that were supposed to flow from this multinational force's presence in Beirut had happened, or that there was any prospect of bringing about a government of national unity in Lebanon. It was plain that the longer the stalemate went on, the more unstable the situation would become, the more our Marines would be endangered. I began once more to raise questions.

I asked the chairman of the Committee on Foreign Affairs (Mr. Zablocki) why the War Powers Act did not apply to Lebanon. I cited in detail the committee's own study of the act. And while I got a respectful hearing and a thoughtful response, the answer was essentially, "we don't want to invoke the act until and unless there is some clear crisis." I persisted, and asked what would trigger the committee to consider invoking the act, and the reply was to this effect: "We'll know when it happens." The committee, obviously, did not want to vitiate the act by risking the accusation of crying wolf or risk raising questions that might be brusquely dismissed by confident administration supersalesmen. The possibility of appearing partisan or slightly to one side of respectability was a powerful force to maintain the status quo. The committee was privately concerned about the commitment to Lebanon, but not willing to make its fears openly known, or to raise publicly the fears that were privately felt. On June 16, I offered House Joint Resolution 298, calling for the withdrawal of our forces from Lebanon. That resolution recites exactly how the War Powers Act applies to the force in Lebanon, and it specifically warned how the situation was dangerous and that the dangers would increase as time passed. But there was no action on the resolution, even though no one could refute the arguments that I raised at that time. Complacency was the order of the day, and it was just not respectable to raise uncomfortable questions at a time when the Marines were presumed to be living in perfect safety. In the soft sunshine of early summer, the Embassy bombing almost forgotten, no one wanted to look anything less than optimistic about the future in Lebanon.

The Congressional Record. October 27, 1983: H 29664–29666.

INVASION OF GRENADA (OCTOBER 1983)

In many ways, the U.S. invasion of Grenada was the first example of the Reagan Doctrine in action.

In 1979 Grenada, a former British colony in the Caribbean Sea just north of Venezuela, underwent a coup as a result of which its British-appointed governor was replaced by a revolutionary, Communist government. Grenada's new government invited Cuban workers to the island to help build its infrastructure, in particular to expand its airport to accommodate, it claimed, larger airplanes for greater tourism (tourism is Grenada's most important industry). The government placed the former governor under house arrest and clamped down on civil rights and freedoms.

In 1983 Reagan, without requesting Congressional approval, ordered the U.S. military to invade Grenada, expel its government and the Cubans who supported it, and restore the former administration. He argued for this policy on several grounds. First, he claimed that the Cubans were building a new military base in Grenada for Soviet expansion in the Caribbean. He also noted that Grenada's government had just been overthrown, and, in the absence of a government to protect U.S. citizens living on the island, he insisted that he had to send the troops to ensure the safety of these people. He also claimed an international mandate since a group of nations in the region asked for the United States' assistance in dealing with Grenada.

Opponents of the invasion—in this case, Senator Gary Hart (D-CO)—made a number of points. They noted, for example, that there was no evidence that Americans on the island were in any danger. They also insisted that in sending troops to Grenada President Reagan had placed them "in harm's way" and so was bound to follow the rules established by the War Powers Act of 1973. Passed to counter abuses of the president's power as commander in chief, which occurred during the Vietnam War, the act limits the president's ability to send U.S. troops into dangerous places for an unlimited period of time.

After two weeks of sometimes heavy fighting, U.S. forces were successful. The War Powers Act was never invoked, and U.S. personnel stayed on the island for two years. Some 27,000 medals were handed out to the 8,000 troops who participated in the invasion, although several admirals were eventually court-martialed for selling captured Soviet weapons in private markets. In general, the invasion was regarded as a success for the United States, which desperately needed military good news after the disaster in Lebanon. It also enjoyed broad popular success in the United States.

Since the invasion, the United States has continued its long-standing practice of intervening in the affairs of Caribbean and other Latin and South American nations whenever the United States believes its vital interests are at stake. For example, it sent troops to Haiti in 1993. It has also sent forces to other nations, such as the former Yugoslavia, Rwanda, and Somalia in an effort to stabilize those countries. Finally, U.S. companies, using U.S.–sponsored loans, completed the expansion of Grenada's airport, opening it to the many large, tourist-laden airplanes that land there every day. U.S. military intervention in other countries has, if anything, become more common since the invasion of Grenada.

REAGAN'S ADDRESS TO THE NATION ON EVENTS IN GRENADA

October 27, 1983

Now, I know another part of the world is very much on our minds, a place much closer to our shores: Grenada. The island is only twice the size of the District of Columbia, with a total population of about 110,000 people.

Grenada and a half dozen other Caribbean islands here were, until recently, British colonies. They're now independent states and members of the British Commonwealth. While they respect each other's independence, they also feel a kinship with each other and think of themselves as one people.

In 1979 trouble came to Grenada. Maurice Bishop, a protege of Fidel Castro, staged a military coup and overthrew the government which had been elected under the constitution left to the people by the British. He sought the help of Cuba in building an airport, which he claimed was for tourist trade, but which looked suspiciously suitable for military aircraft, including Soviet-built long-range bombers.

. . .

In this last year or so, Prime Minister Bishop gave indications that he might like better relations with the United States. He even made a trip to our country and met with senior officials of the White House and the State Department. Whether he was serious or not, we'll never know. On October 12th, a small group in his militia seized him and put him under arrest. They were, if anything, more radical and more devoted to Castro's Cuba than he had been.

Several days later, a crowd of citizens appeared before Bishop's home, freed him, and escorted him toward the headquarters of the military council. They were fired upon. A number, including some children, were killed, and Bishop was seized. He and several members of his cabinet were subsequently executed, and a 24-hour shoot-to-kill curfew was put in effect. Grenada was without a government, its only authority exercised by a self-proclaimed band of military men.

There were then about 1,000 of our citizens on Grenada, 800 of them students in St. George's University Medical School. Concerned that they'd be harmed or held as hostages, I ordered a flotilla of ships, then on its way to Lebanon with marines, part of our regular rotation program, to circle south on a course that would put them somewhere in the vicinity of Grenada in case there should be a need to evacuate our people.

Last weekend, I was awakened in the early morning hours and told that six members of the Organization of Eastern Caribbean States, joined by Jamaica and Barbados, had sent an urgent request that we join them in a military operation to restore order and democracy to Grenada. They were proposing this action under the terms of a treaty, a mutual assistance pact that existed among them.

These small, peaceful nations needed our help. Three of them don't have armies at all, and the others have very limited forces. The legitimacy of their request, plus my own concern for our citizens, dictated my decision. I believe our government has a responsibility to go to the aid of its citizens, if their right to life and liberty is threatened. The nightmare of our hostages in Iran must never be repeated.

We knew we had little time and that complete secrecy was vital to ensure both the safety of the young men who would undertake this mission and the Americans they were about to rescue. The Joint Chiefs worked around the clock to come up with a plan. They had little intelligence information about conditions on the island.

We had to assume that several hundred Cubans working on the airport could be military reserves. Well, as it turned out, the number was much larger, and they were a military force. Six hundred of them have been taken prisoner, and we have discovered a complete base with weapons and communications equipment, which makes it clear a Cuban occupation of the island had been planned.

Two hours ago we released the first photos from Grenada. They included pictures of a warehouse of military equipment—one of three we've uncovered so far. This warehouse contained weapons and ammunition stacked almost to the ceiling, enough to supply thousands of terrorists. Grenada, we were told, was a friendly island paradise for tourism. Well, it wasn't. It was a Soviet-Cuban colony, being readied as a major military bastion to export terror and undermine democracy. We got there just in time.

Public Papers of the President: Ronald Reagan. October 27, 1983: 1517–1522.

CONGRESSIONAL OPPOSITION TO INTERVENTION IN GRENADA

October 28, 1983

Mr. Gary Hart (D-CO). Mr. President, in recent times, there has seldom been a week as traumatic as that which this Nation has experienced, the week just ending—we hope it is ending.

So far as we know, at the present time there are Americans still engaged in hostilities, in combat, in this hemisphere, on the island of Grenada. We have suffered casualties there. We hope there will be no more.

We have certainly seen the devastation of upward of 250 young American lives in Lebanon, in one of the most tragic occurrences this Nation has experienced in the last 10 years.

. . .

The amendment puts the Senate on record as stating that the President of the United States is bound by the War Powers Act; that the insertion of troops into an area of hostilities in Grenada falls within the definition under which the act becomes operative; and, finally, as that act provides, requires that all American military personnel be withdrawn from that area of hostilities within the period of 60 days that began upon their insertion of the notification that was filed by the President with Congress that that engagement had begun, unless Congress acts to extend the period of time for American involvement.

One can ask—one might well ask—why an amendment of this sort is necessary if, in fact, there is a law called the War Powers Act.

Mr. President, the amendment is necessary because there is continuing question raised by the administration—the President, the Secretary of State, and other officials—as to whether, one, they believe the act to be constitutional and, two, even if it is, whether they intend to comply with it fully.

. . .

We, the U.S. Senate, find that the War Powers Act is still the law of
the land and is still in full force and effect. It still binds all citizens of
our country up to and including the President of the United States. And
we expect the President, absent a change or repeal in that law, to obey
it.

That law requires simply two things: When Americans are introduced
into an area of hostility, and I do not think any thoughtful person would
question that they are in an area of hostility in Grenada and indeed in
Lebanon, that the President shall report that fact forthwith within 48
hours to Congress, and the procedure for doing that is set out in pretty
great detail in section 4(a) of the War Powers Resolution.

. . .

That is pretty straightforward, Mr. President. The President may not
like it. Indeed, he may even believe it not to be constitutional. But until
the Supreme Court says it is unconstitutional it is the law of the United
States and the President is bound by it.

He has an option. He can come to seek repeal of that law. He has not
done so. I suspect we all know the reason why.

So, Mr. President, it is unfortunate in the aftermath of Watergate to
find ourselves once again in a situation where in Lebanon and Grenada,
or anywhere else, Congress finds it necessary to require the President to
comply with the law of the United States.

One hopes that the President will withdraw all U.S. Armed Forces
from Grenada within 60 days. We have been given no assurance that
will happen.

Indeed, in the letter which the President sent to the President pro tem-
pore and Speaker of the House of Representatives, dated October 25,
1983, in the operative last paragraph of that letter the President says as
follows:

. . . it is not possible at this time to predict the duration of the temporary presence of United States Armed Forces in Grenada, . . .

And further:

Our forces will remain only so long as their presence is required.

Mr. President, that is not what the War Powers Act says. The War
Powers Act says those forces will be withdrawn within 60 days after
introduction or certainly no more than 60 days after the date of this letter,
unless Congress says they may remain.

I can think of no better way, clearer way, more official way of pointing
out to the President that the Senate and Congress intends for this law to
be upheld.

The Congressional Record. October 28, 1983: S 29829–29830.

STRATEGIC DEFENSE INITIATIVE (JULY 1985)

The Strategic Defense Initiative (SDI), or "Star Wars" as it came to be known, was a central component of Reagan's military policy. Initially proposed in 1983, it envisioned the construction of a network of antiballistic missile systems that would be capable of destroying incoming enemy attacks. No enemy would be able to attack the United States, and, if an attack were launched, U.S. nuclear forces would survive to retaliate. Rather than living in fear of nuclear annihilation, then, Americans could feel secure under an antimissile "umbrella."

Reagan argued for SDI on a number of grounds—some of which, ironically, he later rejected in support of new arms-reduction agreements. First, he argued that the Soviet Union could not be trusted to keep any arms-control agreements; rather, they were engaged in an effort to achieve a nuclear superiority with which they could attack and overwhelm the United States. In addition, he insisted that the difficult design of an antimissile system (how to hit a small object hundreds of miles in space which is moving at 15,000 miles per hour) could be solved by American scientists. Finally, he argued that investments in the scientific research necessary to develop the program could have substantial benefits to the U.S. economy.

Reagan's opponents, here represented by Senator William Proxmire (D-WI), argued that SDI was wrong for a number of reasons. For example, the development of such a system would probably violate the 1972 Anti-Ballistic Missile (ABM) Treaty, which forbids the United States and the Soviet Union from deploying antimissile systems. Such a violation of the treaty might be viewed as an aggressive act by the Soviet Union, encouraging war. Further, if they were nervous about the impact of the system, the Soviets might launch a preemptive nuclear strike before SDI was fully developed. SDI was also expected to be enormously expensive, increasing budget deficits or requiring significant cuts in other programs. Finally, SDI violated the logic of deterrence—that no one will attack because both will be destroyed. With SDI, fighting a nuclear war, at least for the United States, would become "thinkable."

In the short term, Congress approved minor funding for SDI research. However, the system was never built. The technical complexities of designing and building the system could not be overcome. Furthermore, Reagan turned his attention away from SDI late in his administration because he was negotiating arms-control agreements with the Soviet Union and did not wish to imply that the Soviets could not be trusted to keep their word on these new treaties. Thus, by the end of his administration, Reagan had largely abandoned SDI.

Ironically, in the long term, SDI reemerged as an issue in the 2000 presidential campaign when proponents of SDI—who claim to be fulfilling Reagan's legacy—encouraged its development on the grounds that it might stop a "rogue" attack on the United States and its allies— that is an attack from a small nation with a minor nuclear weapons force which might lash out at the United States. This has become a defining point separating Democrats and Republicans: most Republicans favor testing and deploying a version of SDI, while most Democrats do not. The Russians continue to argue that such a system violates the 1972 ABM treaty. It is a point of continuing contention in contemporary American politics.

REAGAN'S RADIO ADDRESS TO THE NATION ON THE STRATEGIC DEFENSE INITIATIVE

July 13, 1985

In a television address to the Nation on March 23, 1983, I challenged the scientific community to change the course of history by embarking on a research effort to counter Soviet threats with measures purely defensive—measures to reassure people their security no longer depends alone on threats of mutual nuclear annihilation to deter a Soviet attack, but measures enabling us to intercept and destroy ballistic missiles before they reach our soil or that of our allies. A nonnuclear strategic defense makes good sense. It's better to protect lives than to avenge them. But another reason, equally simple and compelling, persuades us to its merit. As the Book of Luke says: "If a strong man shall keep his court well guarded, he shall live in peace." Well, SDI, our Strategic Defense Initiative, could prove crucial to guarding security and peace for America and her allies.

The strategic challenges we face are far different from those in 1972, when the United States and the Soviet Union signed the SALT I and antiballistic missile treaties. When those treaties were signed, certain assumptions about the Soviets were made that . . . have not proven justified. For example, it was assumed the treaties would lead to a stable balance and, ultimately, to real reductions in strategic arms. But the Soviet Union has never accepted any meaningful and verifiable reductions in offensive nuclear arms—none. It was assumed the treaties were based on acceptance of parity in offensive weapons systems, but the Soviets have continued to race for superiority. As former Secretary of Defense

Harold Brown put it, "When we build, they build. When we stop, they build." It was assumed the Soviets would accept the innocent notion that being mutually vulnerable to attack was in our common interest. They haven't.

The Soviets have repeatedly condemned as provocative our research on defense against their first-strike missiles, while blanketing their own country with the most sophisticated air defense system ever seen to protect against our second-strike bombers. And while we dismantled our lone ABM system 10 years ago, the Soviets have consistently improved the world's only missile defense system deployed around Moscow. They've also developed and deployed the world's only operational killer satellite system and then proceeded to condemn the United States for daring even to test such a weapon.

It was assumed that an effective defense would not be feasible in 1972. But in that very year, Soviet Marshal Grechko testified to the Supreme Soviet: "The treaty on limiting ABM systems imposes no limitations on the performance of research and experimental work aimed at resolving the problem of defending the country against nuclear missile attack." Thus, the Soviets have devoted a huge share of their military budget to a sophisticated strategic defense program which, in resources already allocated, far exceeds what the United States anticipates spending in the current decade.

Finally, it was assumed that the agreements signed would be complied with, but the Soviets are seriously violating them in both offensive and defensive areas. It is the Soviet Union that has violated the 1972 ABM treaty with its construction of a massive radar facility at Krasnoyarsk. Further, the Soviet Union has tested and deployed sophisticated air defense systems which we judge may have capabilities against ballistic missiles.

Given these facts, is it not preposterous for the Soviets, already researching defense technologies for two decades, to now condemn our embryonic SDI program? And as Paul Nitze, one of my chief arms control advisers, pointed out, Soviet hypocrisy is even more glaring when we realize who's taking advantage of our open society to propagandize against our SDI program. A letter to the *New York Times* denouncing SDI was signed by the very Soviet scientists who've been developing the Soviet strategic defense program; other Soviet scientists who signed have spent their entire careers developing offensive weapons. I intend to mention this when I meet with Mr. [Mikhail] Gorbachev in Geneva this November. I will tell him the United States not only has the right to go forward with research for a strategic missile defense, but in light of the scale of their program we'd be the greatest fools on Earth not to do so.

Public Papers of the President: Ronald Reagan. July 13, 1985: 1517–1522.

WHY CONGRESS SHOULD NOT FUND STAR WARS

March 14, 1985

Mr. William Proxmire (D-WI). Mr. President, in the past few weeks the country has been treated to a series of excellent in-depth articles in the *New York Times*, the *Washington Post*, and other papers about the President's determination to press ahead with the fabulously expensive antinuclear missile defense system that has been widely dubbed "star wars." One of the very best analyses appeared in the Sunday, March 10, issue of the *Washington Post*. It was written by Robert Kaiser. I hope as many Members of Congress as possible will take the time to read it. Reading the article would mean 10 minutes well spent, for these reasons: First, the cost of star wars, second, its critical significance for arms control, and third, its potential threat to the nuclear stability that has helped keep the superpower peace for the past 35 years.

The Kaiser article is a frank polemic against star wars. The Reagan administration has asked for some $3.7 billion for research on star wars in the 1986 budget. This Congress will have to act on that request over the next few months. The request represents the first really massive increase in star wars funding. It would increase the appropriations from a 1985 level of $1.5 billion by a whopping 150 percent in a single year. If we approve this funding this year, we will be well on the road to spending the $30 billion the administration is requesting over the next 6 years for star wars research. Those down payments will put us right on the brink of the really big money, the expenditure of hundreds of billions of dollars—perhaps a trillion or more. That prospect will bring on the invasion of Congress by the military-industrial complex lobby with blood in their eyes.

The irony is that star wars is coming on with a soft-soap campaign as the wise road to the end of the arms race and a future of effective defense and arms control. How about it? Listen to Kaiser:

Amid all the intellectual dishonesty now dominating discussion of these issues, perhaps the most dishonest suggestion of all is that somehow, creation of a star wars system would end the arms race. Why? Even the most idealized version of a successful defensive system will leave room for an opponent's inventiveness—especially when you consider that a completed system can never be tested in conditions remotely resembling the one that would prevail, if it were ever actually used.

No, the very best we can expect from star wars is the ability to knock out most of the Soviet missiles launched against us in a war. We could never be so sure of the system as to launch an attack against the Soviets with confidence that they could not retaliate. In other words, the best we could get is a world of enormous technological uncertainty, in which both superpowers would have to calculate that a decision to launch a nuclear war was crazy.

But that is the world we have today. There is no good reason to spend hundreds or thousands of billions of dollars to recreate the status quo on a higher and riskier level of ingenuity.

That is it, Mr. President: star wars will at best give us a nuclear stand-off, which is precisely what we have today. That is at best. But at best, it will cost hundreds of billions of dollars, and it will create greater uncertainty, greater instability, greater complexity, and therefore a greater likelihood that, through accident or the illusion that one side might win, nuclear war would begin.

. . .

Mr. President, if this Congress follows the administration request and provides a 150-percent increase in funding for star wars research, it will be making two mistakes. First, we will be taking a long step toward a massively increased arms race. We will add a defensive race to a stepped-up offensive arms race. The Soviets will have no choice except to increase their offensive and defensive nuclear arms spending. Second, we will take a fateful step down the road to total fiscal irresponsibility. Today's $200 billion budget deficits will seem like piggy bank stuff by comparison.

The Congressional Record. March 14, 1985: S 2882–2883.

ECONOMIC SANCTIONS ON SOUTH AFRICA (SEPTEMBER 1985)

Given that the United States has an image of itself as the world's leading force for democracy, it regularly faces questions regarding the purposes of its relations with other nations. Whether it is a military role in protecting the world's democracies or the way its trade relations can influence other nations, the question of how America should use its power in international affairs is a constant question.

The question of the use of U.S. power is particularly prevalent in issues of trade. Should the United States engage in profitable economic relations with nations whose policies we oppose, or not? The answer the United

States gives is varied: in some cases, trade is promoted; in others, it is opposed. South Africa stands as a useful test case of this trade-based dilemma. In the 1980s, South Africa's long-standing policy of apartheid—the separation of the races and the reserving of advantage and privilege to whites—challenged the United States' claim to be an advocate of human rights and dignity. Yet its pro-West anti-Communist foreign policy made it a valuable ally in the Cold War, and its vast resources and wealth made it a significant trade partner.

Facing significant domestic protest about South Africa's racist policies, Reagan tried to construct a system of mild sanctions that would assuage the protestors' anger but would maintain the active trade and foreign relations between South Africa and the United States that he preferred. He argued that the Sullivan rules, a set of criteria by which South African companies could be judged to determine whether they were practitioners of apartheid, were a sufficient tool to ensure that country would not enforce racist policies in its dealings with the United States. Further, he insisted that open trade and diplomatic relations with the United States would expose South Africans to the benefits of nonracist policies. Thus, democracy would be advanced through trade.

Opponents such as Congressman Howard Wolpe (D-MI) called for divestment from South Africa. They insisted that U.S. trade relations would inevitably support the leading forces in South Africa, and so would cause apartheid to continue. Only the elimination of trade could actually end apartheid.

Ultimately, Reagan's preferences became U.S. policy. The United States never divested itself from South Africa. It also maintained relatively close diplomatic and military ties there. This, ironically, ran counter to Reagan administration policies *banning* trade with nations like Cuba on the grounds that they were not sufficiently capitalist and democratic. Finally, the Sullivan rules, finally adopted by the United States as criteria for evaluating businesses in South Africa, made almost no difference in the quality of life for South Africa's black majority: U.S. companies simply sold their investments in South Africa through a corporate shell game that allowed the U.S. company to continue receiving profits from South African investments while avoiding responsibility for these companies' practices.

After years of extended struggle, apartheid came to an end when South Africans elected a relatively moderate government, and political reforms were enacted. Today, South Africa is governed by its black majority, and the United States maintains close relations. Sanctions, or the lack thereof, were only minor factors in the transformation of that nation. The efforts of domestic South African leaders, both black and white, were responsible for the change.

REAGAN'S REMARKS ON SIGNING THE EXECUTIVE ORDER PROHIBITING TRADE AND CERTAIN OTHER TRANSACTIONS INVOLVING SOUTH AFRICA

September 9, 1985

I want to speak this morning about South Africa and about what America can do to help promote peace and justice in that country so troubled and tormented by racial conflict. The system of apartheid means deliberate, systematic, institutionalized racial discrimination, denying the black majority their God-given rights. America's view of apartheid is simple and straightforward: We believe it's wrong. We condemn it, and we're united in hoping for the day when apartheid will be no more.

Our influence over South African society is limited, but we do have some influence, and the question is how to use it. Many people of good will in this country have differing views. In my view, we must work for peaceful evolution and reform. Our aim cannot be to punish South Africa with economic sanctions that would injure the very people we're trying to help. I believe we must help all those who peacefully oppose apartheid, and we must recognize that the opponents of apartheid, using terrorism and violence, will bring not freedom and salvation, but greater suffering and more opportunities for expanded Soviet influence within South Africa and in the entire region.

What we see in South Africa is a beginning of a process of change. The changes in policy so far are inadequate, but ironically, they've been enough to raise expectations and stimulate demands for more far-reaching, immediate change. It's the growing economic power of the black majority that has put them in a position to insist on political change. South Africa is not a totalitarian society. There is a vigorous opposition press, and every day we see examples of outspoken protest and access to the international media that would never be possible in many parts of Africa or in the Soviet Union, for that matter.

But it is our active engagement, our willingness to try that gives us influence. Yes, we in America, because of what we are and what we stand for, have influence to do good. We also have immense potential to make things worse. Before taking fateful steps, we must ponder the key question: Are we helping to change the system? Or are we punishing the blacks, whom we seek to help? American policy through several administrations has been to use our influence and our leverage against apartheid, not against innocent people who are the victims of apartheid. Being true to our heritage does not mean quitting, but reaching out, expanding our help for black education and community development, calling for political dialog, urging South Africans of all races to seize the opportunity for peaceful accommodation before it's too late.

. . .

I want to encourage ongoing actions by our government and by private Americans to improve the living standards of South Africa's black majority. The Sullivan code, devised by a distinguished black minister from Philadelphia, the Reverend Leon Sullivan, has set the highest standards of labor practices for progressive employers throughout South Africa. I urge all American companies to participate in it, and I'm instructing the American Ambassador to South Africa to make every effort to get companies which have not adopted them—the Sullivan principles—to do so. In addition, my Executive order will ban U.S. Government export assistance to any American firm in South Africa employing more than 25 persons which does not adhere to the comprehensive fair employment principles stated in the order by the end of this year.

. . .

The problems of South Africa were not created overnight and will not be solved overnight, but there is no time to waste. To withdraw from this drama or to fan its flames will serve neither our interests nor those of the South African people. If all Americans join together behind a common program, we can have so much more influence for good.

Public Papers of the President: Ronald Reagan. September 7, 1985: 1054–1057.

PRESIDENT'S EXECUTIVE ORDER ON SOUTH AFRICA FALLS SHORT OF CONGRESSIONAL GOALS

September 10, 1985

Mr. Howard Wolpe (D-MI). Mr. Speaker, by continuing to resist the congressional sanctions legislation and by offering his own far weaker version of sanctions in his Executive order, President Reagan continues to fail to take advantage of an opportunity he now has to both embrace and strengthen the extraordinary bipartisan consensus that exists, within this Congress and across this land of ours that we must make a very direct break with the policies of constructive engagement.

In South Africa itself, the President's Executive order will be understood essentially as a means of trying to resist stronger sanctions. It thereby encourages the Afrikaners, the white minority regime, in their belief that they can in fact hold on indefinitely, that the current American interest in South Africa is only a passing fancy, and that they can maintain their horrendous system of apartheid without real economic cost and without any significant degree of international isolation. The President's executive order is temporizing. His constant remarks by way of an apology for South Africa are only encouraging greater repression, inviting greater violence, and terribly compromising American interests not only in South Africa but throughout the African Continent.

Mr. Speaker, I urge the President to abide by the consensus that exists in this Congress to give his support to the congressional sanctions legislation.

The Congressional Record. September 10, 1985: H 7310–7311.

BOMBING OF LIBYA (APRIL 1986)

In 1986 a bomb was placed in a nightclub frequented by U.S. servicemen in Berlin, Germany. One U.S. soldier was killed. After an investigation, the United States determined that agents from Libya had planted the bomb. In response, President Reagan ordered an air strike against Libya to punish that nation for supporting terrorism.

Reagan's defense of the bombing addresses the anger of a powerful nation capable of projecting force around the world which perceives that it has a unique role in the world as the planet's leading defender of democracy. He ordered the attack as an act of revenge: a death of an American anywhere, warned Reagan, means that the entire military might of the United States will be brought down against those who commit the crime. This is a message of deterrence. But there is another message in Reagan's speech: the United States, as the leader of the free world, has a mission to defend democracy everywhere, and it will do so with all the power it has at its disposal.

Opponents of the bombing, including Senator Claiborne Pell (D-RI) and the Reverend F. Forrester Church, made several arguments against the reprisal raid. First, they argued that military power is as likely to cause more anger and aggression against the United States as it is to deter such attacks. Further, they criticized the raid on the grounds that it had caused what the military calls "collateral"—which means civilian—damage. How can the United States claim the moral high ground, they argued, if it commits acts that kill more innocent people than the original attack did? Finally, while it is not in either of these statements, other criticisms were made that indicated that the United States attacked the wrong target—that Syria, not Libya, had been behind the attack in Berlin.

Despite the fact that one U.S. airplane was destroyed, killing its pilot, the American people generally supported the raid and regarded it as a sign of strength on Reagan's part. Indeed, Reagan's role in directing this raid helped resurrect his reputation as a good leader in the area of foreign policy—a reputation that had been sullied in the Iran-contra scandal.

The success of this raid has encouraged similar assaults—Iraq, Afghanistan, Sudan, and so on—by subsequent presidents. The response bombing of terrorist targets is a guaranteed political winner for U.S. leaders. However, as critics suggest, each attack tends to encourage a new generation of people to hate the United States. It is an endless cycle. In addition, Libya remains an isolated nation believed to sponsor terrorism, as does Syria. And U.S. citizens remain targets of political violence worldwide. Thus, while retributive bombing satisfies American public opinion, it appears to have little impact on solving the problems that stimulate acts of terrorism in the first place.

REAGAN'S ADDRESS TO THE NATION ON THE UNITED STATES AIR STRIKE AGAINST LIBYA

April 14, 1986

At 7 o'clock this evening eastern time air and naval forces of the United States launched a series of strikes against the headquarters, terrorist facilities, and military assets that support Mu'ammar Qadhafi's subversive activities. The attacks were concentrated and carefully targeted to minimize casualties among the Libyan people with whom we have no quarrel. From initial reports, our forces have succeeded in their mission.

Several weeks ago in New Orleans, I warned Colonel Qadhafi we would hold his regime accountable for any new terrorist attacks launched against American citizens. More recently I made it clear we would respond as soon as we determined conclusively who was responsible for such attacks. On April 5th in West Berlin a terrorist bomb exploded in a nightclub frequented by American servicemen. Sergeant Kenneth Ford and a young Turkish woman were killed and 230 others were wounded, among them some 50 American military personnel. This monstrous brutality is but the latest act in Colonel Qadhafi's reign of terror. The evidence is now conclusive that the terrorist bombing of La Belle discotheque was planned and executed under the direct orders of the Libyan regime. On March 25th, more than a week before the attack, orders were sent from Tripoli to the Libyan People's Bureau in East Berlin to conduct a terrorist attack against Americans to cause maximum and indiscriminate casualties. Libya's agents then planted the bomb. On April 4th the People's Bureau alerted Tripoli that the attack would be carried out the following morning. The next day they reported back to Tripoli on the great success of their mission.

Our evidence is direct; it is precise; it is irrefutable. We have solid evidence about other attacks Qadhafi has planned against the United States installations and diplomats and even American tourists. Thanks to close cooperation with our friends, some of these have been prevented. With the help of French authorities, we recently aborted one such attack: a planned massacre, using grenades and small arms, of civilians waiting in line for visas at an American Embassy.

Colonel Qadhafi is not only an enemy of the United States. His record of subversion and aggression against the neighboring States in Africa is well documented and well known. He has ordered the murder of fellow Libyans in countless countries. He has sanctioned acts of terror in Africa, Europe, and the Middle East, as well as the Western Hemisphere. Today we have done what we had to do. If necessary, we shall do it again. It gives me no pleasure to say that, and I wish it were otherwise. Before Qadhafi seized power in 1969, the people of Libya had been friends of the United States. And I'm sure that today most Libyans are ashamed and disgusted that this man has made their country a synonym for barbarism around the world. The Libyan people are a decent people caught in the grip of a tyrant.

To our friends and allies in Europe who cooperated in today's mission, I would only say you have the permanent gratitude of the American people. Europeans who remember history understand better than most that there is no security, no safety, in the appeasement of evil. It must be the core of Western policy that there be no sanctuary for terror. And to sustain such a policy, free men and free nations must unite and work together. Sometimes it is said that by imposing sanctions against Colonel Qadhafi or by striking at his terrorist installations we only magnify the man's importance, that the proper way to deal with him is to ignore him. I do not agree.

· · ·

We believe that this preemptive action against his terrorist installations will not only diminish Colonel Qadhafi's capacity to export terror, it will provide him with incentives and reasons to alter his criminal behavior. I have no illusion that tonight's action will ring down the curtain on Qadhafi's reign of terror. But this mission, violent though it was, can bring closer a safer and more secure world for decent men and women. We will persevere. This afternoon we consulted with the leaders of Congress regarding what we were about to do and why. Tonight I salute the skill and professionalism of the men and women of our Armed Forces who carried out this mission. It's an honor to be your Commander in Chief.

We Americans are slow to anger. We always seek peaceful avenues before resorting to the use of force—and we did. We tried quiet diplomacy, public condemnation, economic sanctions, and demonstrations of military force. None succeeded. Despite our repeated warnings, Qadhafi continued his reckless policy of intimidation, his relentless pursuit of terror. He counted on America to be passive. He counted wrong. I warned that there should be no place on Earth where terrorists can rest and train and practice their deadly skills. I meant it. I said that we would act with others, if possible, and alone if necessary to ensure that terrorists have no sanctuary anywhere. Tonight, we have.

Public Papers of the President: Ronald Reagan. April 14, 1986: 468–469.

A DISSENTING VIEW ON THE LIBYA REPRISAL

May 1, 1986

Mr. Claiborne Pell (D-RI). Mr. President, as elected representatives we have a duty to reflect on what is right as well as on what is popular. By all accounts, the recent bombing of Libya is extremely popular; but some question whether it was right as a response to terrorism.

The Reverend F. Forrester Church, the son of my dear friend and our former colleague Frank Church, recently preached a very moving sermon in New York, asserting that by adopting a policy of an eye for an eye or a baby for a baby we have lost the moral high ground and our "solution" has added to the problem. In fighting the devil, he said, we have chosen the devil's own instruments.

Reverend Church, often invoking the words of his father, has made a valuable contribution to the debate on means and ends in the struggle against terrorism. I commend his sermon to my colleagues, and I ask unanimous consent that it be printed in the RECORD.

. . .

TERRORISM

(A Sermon Preached on April 20, 1986, at All Souls Unitarian Church, by the Rev. Dr. F. Forrester Church)

In some ways this is going to be a very difficult sermon for me to deliver. For one thing, I feel so strongly about what I am going to say, that I am sure to lose my balance here or there. Passion is not a bad thing, but rarely does it contribute to objectivity. Also, I feel most comfortable with my own views, when I can pose to myself and for others an almost but not quite convincing argument against them. As I have said to you before, much of the time I end up fashioning 100% decisions on 60% convictions. Though this is uncomfortable at times, it does have its advantages. One advantage is that almost never am I tempted to despise those who think differently than I do. After all, I myself could very well be one of them.

But today, I am absolutely sure that I am right. And that worries me. It worries me for two reasons. One is that I am not accustomed to feeling this way. And the other is that judging from the public opinion polls, almost no one in this country agrees with me.

Think about it. Never in the recent history of our country has there been so strong a consensus as there apparently is today around the President's decision to bomb Libya in reprisal for the Libyan directed bombing of a West German nightclub, in which one American G.I. was killed. According to the *New York Times*, 77% of Americans favor this decision while just 14% oppose it, even though a majority of those questioned also believe that this action will increase terrorist activity, not diminish it. At the same time, the President's favorable rating on his conducting of our foreign policy has soared this week to an unprecedented 76%. As of yesterday, not one Democratic U.S. Senator had raised his voice in opposition to the bombing. The only questions that have been raised were by Senators Hatfield, Weicker, and Mathias, all members of the President's own party. . . .

. . .

And yet, throughout the week my conviction grew that this action was terribly, terribly wrong. This morning I want to tell you why.

Let me begin with something I said last week in my sermon on "Paranoia and Power."

Jesus taught us that we must not answer evil with evil. And history teaches that we must choose our enemies carefully because we will become like them. Not only that, but when we do, unconscious of the good in our enemies and terrified by their evil, we eventually will become like them at their least attractive. Accordingly, when we react to terrorism with bombs of our own, killing innocent civilians and even children, we too become terrorists.

This past week, we have added a tragic new chapter to the primitive ethics of an eye for an eye and a tooth for a tooth. It could be subtitled "a baby for a baby." One infant is blown out of the side of an airplane, another blown out of her crib by our bombs.

Former President Jimmy Carter said in an interview on Thursday, that if his daughter, Amy, had been killed in this manner, he would devote his life to exacting revenge upon whoever had done it. This is not a part of his Christian theology, but it is certainly understandable from a human point of view. On the other hand, such revenge is a part of the teachings of Islam. Friday, in the streets of Tripoli, angry citizens and religious leaders were calling for a Holy War to be declared against the United States all around the world. Our government claims that we have taken a major step to end terrorism by showing that no terrorist act will go unanswered. This betrays a complete lack of understanding both of the nature of terrorism itself, and of the Islamic faith. What we forget is this. If, as they are often taught, instant bliss is the reward for death in a holy cause, religious zealots—whether terrorist, holy innocent, or both—are delighted to don the martyr's crown. And even if they don't win a free ride to heaven, here on earth their self-proclaimed holy cause will surely be advanced. Tertullian, an early church father, said of Christian martyrs that "the blood of the martyrs is the seed of the church." By creating new martyrs in the nation of Islam, we too seed the dark clouds of terrorism all around the globe.

This, then, is my first major concern. But acting according to fear, frustration, and anger, we have not reduced but rather added to the level of violence in the world. Not only that, but we have become a full partner in that violence. We have also added to the level of terror in the hearts of our European allies.

This is not to say that the President's action and the American people's response, is not powered by deep moral outrage. Of course it is. We are a morally motivated people. We speak a public language that is filled with religious and moral metaphor. We paint our enemies as demonic, and often their actions justify such a title. We also speak of evil empires, and thus create a mythos for Armageddon that pits the powers of good against the powers of evil.

Certainly, there is no question in many of our minds that terrorism is demonic. The question is how do you fight the devil? We have chosen to fight him with his own instruments. And we have chosen as our pretext self-defense. Sometimes, we have no choice, as in World War II in our struggle against [Adolf] Hitler. Then, we answered our allies' call to protect them against German Imperialism and the evils of fascism.

Today, however, our allies, whether rightly or wrongly, are as wary of us as they are of our common enemy. Somehow, we have lost the moral initiative. Because the enemy, in this case Colonel Khadafi [Qadhafi], is so pernicious, we have a hard time perceiving that anything we might do to punish him could be anything but right, regardless of the consequences. But here, the consequences as well as the means of accomplishing them are patently counter-productive. All we have done is further isolate ourselves. In the eyes of our allies, we again have become part of the problem rather than part of the solution.

I don't know what the answer to terrorism is. And it is frustrating not to have a quick-fix, a solution that will surely work. Because of this frustration, to counter our sense of helplessness we are tempted to try anything. I understand that. But when our solution adds to the problem, we surely, even from a pragmatic point of view, without any consideration of the moral issues involved, we surely should forbear. One thing we learned in Vietnam was that we could not successfully wage a conventional war against guerrillas in the jungle. Soon we shall learn that we cannot wage a conventional war against tiny bands of violent zealots either. There is one thing we could do, however, if we had the strength and patience and confidence to do so. We could hold to the moral high ground. We could remember what we were taught as little children, that two wrongs do not make a right, and that good ends do not justify evil means. We could model a different code than that modeled by those we despise.

The Congressional Record. May 1, 1986: S 5136–5138.

IRAN-CONTRA SCANDAL (MARCH 1987)

The Iran-contra scandal was one of the central events in Reagan's presidency. When Congress cut off funding for the contra rebels fighting the Communist Sandinista government of Nicaragua, Reagan sought to find alternative ways to support the contras as part of the Reagan Doctrine. Coincidentally, Iran, which had been a U.S. ally until its revolution in 1979 and was currently engaged in a war with its neighbor Iraq, needed a resupply of high-tech American weapons to continue its struggle. Iran had substantial control over several terrorist groups in Lebanon that had captured American citizens and were holding them hostage. Thus, in return for Iran's promise to help win the release of American hostages in Lebanon, Reagan secretly authorized the sale of weapons to Iran despite the fact that such sales had been banned under law. These sales generated significant profits since the United States and the brokers it used to transfer the weapons charged much more for the weapons than they actually cost. Under the guidance of several senior officials in the Reagan administration, these profits were transferred to various bank accounts where they were used to fund the contra war in Nicaragua. (No evidence ever came forward that Reagan knew of these fund transfers in advance; however, during the scandal, he did sign a letter known as a "finding" authorizing the transfer and backdated it to cover the entire time of the operation.) The scandal was exposed when a newspaper in Beirut, Lebanon, published the details in 1986, although Western media did not pick up on the story until early 1987.

Many issues emerged during the Iran-contra scandal: did Reagan violate the law by supporting an operation to fund the contras? Did the backdating of the finding legitimating the operation constitute an impeachable offense? Did Reagan know about the operation in advance, or was he the dupe of others in his administration? Was the need to fight communism in Central America so great that it justified breaking the law in the best interests of the nation? The readings that follow this introduction manifest many of these questions. Reagan, for example, argued in favor of the weapons sales and use of funds on a number of different grounds. While he acknowledged that the funding of the contras was technically illegal, he insisted that the threat posed by the Communist Sandinista government in Nicaragua justified the violation of the law. Furthermore, he argued that the fate of the hostages in Lebanon, one of whom was the station chief for the Central Intelligence Agency, made the need to deal with Iran imperative. Finally, he claimed that he had been an unwitting dupe of others in his administration: while he admitted responsibility for their actions, he made it clear that he was not aware of them.

Critics of the arms-for-hostages and contra support programs, such as Congresswoman Cardiss Collins (D-IL), argued that the law ending funding for the contras was clear. Moreover, they insisted that the contras, many of whom had served in the army of the dictator overthrown by the Sandinistas, lacked the support of the Nicaraguan people and so were undeserving of support in the first place. In addition, they noted that in selling weapons to the Iranians the president had overstepped his constitutional powers since he had spent money, which only Congress is authorized to do. They called for impeachment hearings against the president, but they never materialized.

The Iran-contra scandal seriously damaged Reagan's presidency. His popularity declined for over a year, and Congress launched a series of investigations. A number of senior administration officials were forced to resign and went to prison. Reagan himself, however, escaped direct blame, and left office as a popular political figure.

The Sandinista government eventually negotiated a peace agreement with the contras but not until after the collapse of the Soviet Union in

1991. The last of the hostages held in Lebanon were not released until Bill Clinton became president in 1993. For many, this scandal constituted the low point of the Reagan presidency. However, the United States continues to support efforts to undermine enemy governments; for example, U.S. tax dollars are used to sponsor groups trying to overthrow Saddam Hussein's government in Iraq. Other operations, less public, surely exist. Accordingly, despite the negative reaction of the American people to Iran-contra, the United States continues to use its powers to promote secret operations against other nations.

REAGAN'S ADDRESS TO THE NATION ON THE IRAN ARMS AND CONTRA AID CONTROVERSY

March 4, 1987

For the past 3 months, I've been silent on the revelations about Iran. And you must have been thinking: "Well, why doesn't he tell us what's happening? Why doesn't he just speak to us as he has in the past when we've faced troubles or tragedies?" Others of you, I guess, were thinking: "What's he doing hiding out in the White House?" Well, the reason I haven't spoken to you before now is this: You deserve the truth. And as frustrating as the waiting has been, I felt it was improper to come to you with sketchy reports, or possibly even erroneous statements, which would then have to be corrected, creating even more doubt and confusion. There's been enough of that. I've paid a price for my silence in terms of your trust and confidence. But I've had to wait, as you have, for the complete story. That's why I appointed Ambassador David Abshini as my Special Counsellor to help get out the thousands of documents to the various investigations. And I appointed a Special Review Board, the Tower board, which took on the chore of pulling the truth together for me and getting to the bottom of things. It has now issued its findings.

I'm often accused of being an optimist, and it's true I had to hunt pretty hard to find any good news in the Board's report. As you know, it's well-stocked with criticisms, which I'll discuss in a moment; but I was very relieved to read this sentence: "[T]he Board is convinced that the President does indeed want the full story to be told." And that will continue to be my pledge to you as the other investigations go forward. . . .

I've studied the Board's report. Its findings are honest, convincing, and highly critical; and I accept them. And tonight I want to share with you my thoughts on these findings and report to you on the actions I'm taking to implement the Board's recommendations. First, let me say I take full responsibility for my own actions and for those of my administration. As angry as I may be about activities undertaken without my knowledge, I am still accountable for those activities. As disappointed as I may be in some who served me, I'm still the one who must answer to the American people for this behavior. And as personally distasteful as I find secret bank accounts and diverted funds—well, as the Navy would say, this happened on my watch.

Let's start with the part that is the most controversial. A few months ago I told the American people I did not trade arms for hostages. My heart and my best intentions still tell me that's true, but the facts and the evidence tell me it is not. As the Tower board reported, what began as a strategic opening to Iran deteriorated, in its implementation, into trading arms for hostages. This runs counter to my own beliefs, to administration policy, and to the original strategy we had in mind. There are reasons why it happened, but no excuses. It was a mistake. I undertook the original Iran initiative in order to develop relations with those who might assume leadership in a post-Khomeini government.

It's clear from the Board's report, however, that I let my personal concern for the hostages spill over into the geopolitical strategy of reaching out to Iran. I asked so many questions about the hostages' welfare that I didn't ask enough about the specifics of the total Iran plan. Let me say to the hostage families: We have not given up. We never will. And I promise you we'll use every legitimate means to free your loved ones from captivity. But I must also caution that those Americans who freely remain in such dangerous areas must know that they're responsible for their own safety.

Now, another major aspect of the Board's findings regards the transfer of funds to the Nicaraguan contras. The Tower board wasn't able to find out what happened to this money, so the facts here will be left to the continuing investigations of the court-appointed Independent Counsel and the two congressional investigating committees. I'm confident the truth will come out about this matter, as well. As I told the Tower board, I didn't know about any diversion of funds to the contras. But as President, I cannot escape responsibility.

Much has been said about my management style, a style that's worked successfully for me during 8 years as Governor of California and for most of my Presidency. The way I work is to identify the problem, find the right individuals to do the job, and then let them go to it. I've found this invariably brings out the best in people. They seem to rise to their full capability, and in the long run you get more done. When it came to managing the NSC [National Security Council] staff, let's face it, my style didn't match its previous track record. I've already begun correcting this. As a start, yesterday I met with the entire professional staff of the National Security Council. I defined for them the values I want to guide the national security policies of this country. I told them that I wanted a policy that was as justifiable and understandable in public as it was in secret. I wanted a policy that reflected the will of the Congress as well as of the White House. And I told them that there'll be no more freelancing by individuals when it comes to our national security.

. . .

Now, what should happen when you make a mistake is this: You take your knocks, you learn your lessons, and then you move on. That's the healthiest way to deal with a problem. This in no way diminishes the importance of the other continuing investigations, but the business of our country and our people must proceed. I've gotten this message from Republicans and Democrats in Congress, from allies around the world, and—if we're reading the signals right—even from the Soviets. And of course, I've heard the message from you, the American people. You know, by the time you reach my age, you've made plenty of mistakes. And if you've lived your life properly—so, you learn. You put things in perspective. You pull your energies together. You change. You go forward.

Public Papers of the President: Ronald Reagan. March 4, 1987: 208–211.

IT'S TIME TO TAKE ANOTHER LOOK AT THE CONTRAS

March 4, 1987

Mrs. Cardiss Collins (D-IL). Mr. Speaker, I called this special meeting in order to underscore the need for a new Central American policy. As the first Member of the 100th Congress to introduce legislation calling for a moratorium on Contra funding, I believe that the time has come to take a new look at the wisdom of supporting the Contras.

The Iran/Contra scandal raises important questions concerning foreign policy and congressional authority. This administration's illegal transfer of funds from Iran is a dangerous intrusion into congressional domain and endangers United States foreign policy worldwide.

The Boland amendment was clear. Congress intended to oversee all Contra funding. In 1985, we approved $27 million in humanitarian aid to the Contras. Last year, $100 million was authorized. No other funds were approved.

By sending more money to the Contras from the Iran-arms slush fund, the administration not only violated the law, but attempted to usurp legislative authority.

Furthermore, the Contras are benefiting from this lawbreaking. If nothing is done, they will receive millions of dollars more than Congress intended, and they don't deserve this windfall.

The President claims that these fighters will bring democracy to Nicaragua, but he never explains how.

The Contras do not have the support of the Nicaraguan people; their leaders are former officers of the Nicaraguan National Guard—the very same men who tortured and killed their own citizens under the dictator Anastasio Somoza, and they operate with total disregard for the international standards of human decency.

In December, the human rights group, America's Watch, documented the Contras' use of land mines which killed and injured many civilians. According to press reports, 1,100 civilians were killed or wounded in the fighting in 1986. It is my belief that soldiers who kill civilians and use terrorist tactics cannot bring democracy to Nicaragua.

. . .

A moratorium on Contra funding will give Congress and the American people time to reassess this support; time to decide if providing money for those who terrorize civilians will further the cause of freedom; time to decide whether giving money to men who steal and run drugs is in the best interest of our Nation; and time to decide whether secret slush funds and sleazy black-bag operations make wise foreign policy.

The Congressional Record. March 4, 1987: H 984.

INTERMEDIATE-RANGE NUCLEAR FORCES TREATY (DECEMBER 1987)

The term "intermediate-range nuclear weapons" refers to delivery systems for nuclear weapons that have insufficient range to make an intercontinental flight to attack an enemy. In general, these are weapons that are attached to missiles with less than a 1,000-mile range, cruise missiles (air- and sea-launched missiles that use jet engines for propulsion), and other delivery systems like artillery.

Intermediate-range nuclear weapons are highly controversial for a number of reasons. First, U.S. allies regard these weapons as undesirable because they are based in allied territories, are likely to be fired at targets either in or near the home countries, and are inevitably targeted by enemies with their own nuclear stockpiles. This is in contrast with intercontinental ballistic missiles which would be fired from the United States (or from its submarines) and thus bring an enemy's retaliation on the United States itself. Second, their advanced basing means that if an enemy attacks and approaches the location where the weapons are based, there may be increased pressure to use the weapons before they are captured, thus causing a nuclear war.

In the early days of his administration, Reagan, as part of his defense buildup, supported the purchase and deployment of a new generation of intermediate-range nuclear weapons called Pershing II. These missiles were deployed in Europe and Asia, causing massive protests in the host countries. Reagan insisted that these weapons were necessary to maintain the United States' nuclear deterrent—if the United States were attacked, it would be able to destroy an enemy with a barrage of nuclear weapons, and since potential enemies knew this, they would never attack the United States.

However, toward the end of his administration, Reagan changed gears and promoted changes in the nuclear policy of the United States. Key among these was the reduction of the numbers and types of nuclear weapons in the arsenals of both the United States and the Soviet Union. He advocated this change in terms of arms reduction, rather than arms control, and noted that there were sufficient guarantees in the structure of the U.S. deterrent to survive the downsizing of its intermediate nuclear forces. Opponents of the change argued that the Soviet Union could not be trusted to keep its part of an arms-reduction agreement, and so would cheat its way to a position of nuclear dominance. Then, they argued, the U.S. deterrent would fail.

The following excerpts come from debate in favor of and in opposition to the Intermediate-Range Nuclear Forces Treaty signed by President Reagan and Soviet President Mikhail Gorbachev on December 8, 1987. After ratification by the U.S. Senate, on May 27, 1988, by a 93 to 5 vote, the elimination of many types of intermediate-range weapons was begun. This move was hailed by the United States' European allies, and it led to an immediate thaw in U.S.–Soviet relations.

In the long term, especially after the collapse of the Soviet Union in 1991, it stimulated a series of agreements that have substantially reduced the number of both intermediate- and intercontinental nuclear weapons. Today, both the United States and Russia have fewer than 12,500 nuclear warheads in their respective arsenals. Reagan's political journey was from Cold Warrior to Peacemaker. In so moving, he set the agenda for the presidents who followed.

REAGAN'S REMARKS ON SIGNING THE INTERMEDIATE-RANGE NUCLEAR FORCES TREATY

December 8, 1987

It was over 6 years ago, November 18, 1981, that I first proposed what would come to be called the zero option. . . . Unlike treaties in the past, it didn't simply codify the status quo or a new arms buildup; it didn't simply talk of controlling an arms race.

For the first time in history, the language of "arms control" was replaced by "arms reduction"—in this case, the complete elimination of an entire class of U.S. and Soviet nuclear missiles. Of course, this required a dramatic shift in thinking, and it took conventional wisdom some time to catch up. Reaction, to say the least, was mixed. To some the zero option was impossibly visionary and unrealistic; to others merely a propaganda ploy. Well, with patience, determination, and commitment, we've made this impossible vision a reality.

. . . strong and fundamental moral differences continue to exist between our nations. But today, on this vital issue, at least, we've seen what can be accomplished when we pull together.

The numbers alone demonstrate the value of this agreement. On the Soviet side, over 1,500 deployed warheads will be removed, and all ground-launched intermediate-range missiles, including the SS-20's, will be destroyed. On our side, our entire complement of Pershing II and ground-launched cruise missiles, with some 400 deployed warheads, will all be destroyed. Additional backup missiles on both sides will also be destroyed.

But the importance of this treaty transcends numbers. . . . The maxim is: *Dovorey no provorey*—trust, but verify.

. . .

This agreement contains the most stringent verification regime in history, including provisions for inspection teams actually residing in each other's territory and several other forms of onsite inspection, as well. This treaty protects the interests of America's friends and allies. It also embodies another important principle: the need for *glasnost*, a greater openness in military programs and forces.

We can only hope that this history-making agreement will not be an end in itself but the beginning of a working relationship that will enable us to tackle the other urgent issues before us: strategic offensive nuclear weapons, the balance of conventional forces in Europe, the destructive and tragic regional conflicts that beset so many parts of our globe, and respect for the human and natural rights God has granted to all men.

Public Papers of the President: Ronald Reagan. December 8, 1987: 1455–1456.

INF TREATY REQUIRES CAUTIOUS EXAMINATION

December 8, 1987

Mr. Larry Pressler (R-SD). Mr. President, the Intermediate Nuclear Forces [INF] Treaty is scheduled to be signed today at the White House. I urge all of our colleagues to withhold support for this agreement until we have had an opportunity to carefully scrutinize it in committee hearings.

We have not yet seen all of the important details in the treaty. However, enough has been revealed publicly to raise serious questions whether it is in the best interest of United States and free world security. Each day this week, I would like to comment on some concerns regarding the direction we seem to be taking in arms control negotiations with the Soviet Union.

It is clear beyond doubt that the Soviets have violated prior or existing agreements with the United States. The latest confirmation of this important fact occurred just last week in the latest annual Presidential report to the Congress on Soviet noncompliance with arms control agreements. That report from the President documents a new instance of Soviet violation of the Anti-Ballistic Missile [ABM] Treaty. The Soviets have installed in the Ukraine two sophisticated radar systems of a type prohibited by the ABM Treaty, except as part of the ABM system circling Moscow.

Mr. President, although I do not yet have a copy of it, I believe that the INF Agreement could well be the Trojan horse which will lead to other arms control agreements next year that might compromise the U.S. strategic position. I say that as a long-term advocate of arms control negotiations, but I am very fearful that the unique set of circumstances in Washington have [*sic*] caused the White House to want this arms control agreement.

. . .

I raise questions about this agreement in the form it is presently written because, first of all, it is not linked to other key issues. No linkage to the way Jews in the Soviet Union are treated; no linkage to Afghanistan or Nicaragua; no linkage to any other Soviet behavior. I fear that a

Strategic Arms Reduction [START] Treaty perhaps already has been agreed to unbeknownst to the U.S. Senate, and the START Treaty will be the true result of the Trojan horse that has entered our city.

Second, I believe very strongly that we should have assurances as to what will be in a START Treaty or what has been agreed to with the Soviets before we commit ourselves on such a treaty.

Third, . . . only 2 weeks ago the President of the United States made a finding that the Soviets have cheated on the ABM Treaty. I shall have some further remarks on that.

Finally, this agreement could result in a higher cost to American taxpayers to replace with conventional forces some of the nuclear forces in Europe.

Let me first touch briefly on the issue of linkage. It is my strongest feeling that the sense of euphoria in this city is tattering over some very great problems here and abroad. I already have mentioned the domestic problems, but regarding linkage, suddenly we are saying that there is no concern for the minorities, for Soviet Jewry, for the various other minorities that have been demonstrating on the streets of Washington. We are embracing a regime that we have called the "evil empire."

Also, we do not know what commitments have been made by this President and this administration regarding a START Treaty which will be much more serious. Therein will lie the threat to the SDI program, and some of our basic security interests here in the continental United States.

On the issue of cheating, I find it most phenomenal that on the very eve of the INF Treaty the President of the United States made a finding that the Soviets were in fact cheating on the ABM Treaty. In fact, the Soviets previously prohibited radars at two other locations far beyond Moscow.

According to the U.S. Arms Control and Disarmament Agency [ACDA], other Soviet violations of arms control agreements include: Deployment of the SS-25 ICBM; exceeding the strategic nuclear delivery vehicle limits of the unratified SALT II Treaty; concealment of ballistic missile test data and the relation between ICBM's and their launchers; chemical, biological and toxic weapons violations; and nuclear testing violations. In total, ACDA has documented violations and probable violations of arms control provisions of at least seven treaties and agreements entered into by the Soviet Union and the United States.

So, Mr. President, this administration has found the Soviets to be in violation of seven agreements, and all this is being swept under the rug in the euphoria of signing this agreement.

The significance of these violations for the INF agreement debate is that we must consider whether this new treaty will be regarded any differently by the Soviet Union. Will it tie our hands but not the Soviets'?

This is a serious matter that will require the best judgment of all Senators. It is not something we can afford to ignore.

Another major area of concern is verification of the INF Treaty. We know that elimination of the Soviet SS-20 missile, if fully carried out, would remove a powerful weapon from the Soviet arsenal. That would seem to be an accomplishment of some great merit.

I saw pictures of some of these SS-20's on TV last night. However, we cannot forget that the SS-20 is a mobile missile. It can be moved almost anywhere its transporter can take it. How do we verify compliance with the INF Treaty's requirements for the elimination of these mobile missiles over a 3-year period? The treaty's verification procedures as discussed in the media may be inadequate to the task of ensuring compliance on this key point. For example, I question how the limited onsite verification at sites defined in the treaty will protect against the potential concealment of mobile SS-20's at locations not identified in the treaty, and there are many areas not identified in the treaty. Apparently, there will be no provisions for broad challenge inspections under this treaty. Do we have a reliable count of the actual number of existing SS-20's? Would it be possible for the Soviet Union to maintain the operational capability of SS-20 missiles concealed in violation of the INF Treaty? ... We cannot risk dismantling our European INF deterrent force if it is impossible to verify that the Soviets have destroyed all of their SS-20's and other missiles covered by the treaty.

. . .

Finally, we cannot ignore Soviet behavior in other areas of international relations. In my view, it is appropriate to link United States approval of this and other arms control agreements to Soviet human rights violations, the invasion of Afghanistan, massive support for the Marxist-Leninist Sandinista regime in Nicaragua, and continuing adherence to a doctrine of world domination.

Mr. President, these are just a few preliminary concerns I have regarding the INF Treaty. Many others in Congress and beyond these Halls share these concerns. We will be subjected to an intensive hard-sell campaign to approve ratification of the treaty as signed. In view of the many questions surrounding this historic agreement, it would be a serious mistake for the Senate to simply rubber stamp its approval on the treaty. The American people and people throughout the free world deserve more consideration than that. So, once again, I urge our colleagues to avoid being stampeded into endorsing the INF Treaty before it has been given the closest, most careful scrutiny by the Foreign Relations Committee and the Senate as a whole.

The Congressional Record. December 8, 1987: S 17409–17410.

RECOMMENDED READINGS

Anderson, Martin. *The Ten Causes of the Reagan Boom, 1982–1997.* Stanford, Calif.: Hoover Institution on War, Revolution and Peace, Stanford University, 1997.

Bainerman, Joel. *The Crimes of a President: New Revelations on Conspiracy & Cover-up in the Bush & Reagan Administrations.* New York: S.P.I. Books, 1992.

"Balking at Bork." *Economist* 305 (1987): 25–26.

Bamberger, Ruth. "Why Common Cause Opposed the Bork Nomination." *PS* [Washington, D.C.] 20 (1987): 876–880.

Bergmann, Barbara. "A Fresh Start on Welfare Reform." *Challenge* 30 (1987): 44–50.

Berman, Richard A. "The Housing Crisis: Responses to New Federalism." *Journal of Housing* 39 (1982): 173.

Bowder, Geoffrey. "Lebanon's Struggle for Survival." *World Today* 39 (1983): 443–49.

Buck, Jeffrey A. "The Politics of Federal Block Grants: From Nixon to Reagan." *Political Science Quarterly* 99 (1984): 247–70.

Busch, Andrew E. "Ronald Reagan and the Defeat of the Soviet Empire." *Presidential Studies Quarterly* 27, no. 3 (1997): 451.

Cannon, William B. "The Tax Reform Legislation: A Step Backward." *Social Policy* 17 (1986): 34–39.

Caraley, Demetrios. "Changing Conceptions of Federalism." *Political Science Quarterly* 101, no. 2 (1986): 289–305.

Chait, Jonathan. "Gipper's Flippers (Elimination of the Federal Deficit Seems to Vindicate Former President Ronald Reagan)." *New Republic* 218, no. 5 (1998): 6.

Cohen, Richard E. "Democrats Trying to Get Act Together to Confront Reagan's Budget Policy." *National Journal* 13, no. 50 (1981): 2198.

Conlan, Timothy J. *New Federalism: Intergovernmental Reform and Political Change from Nixon to Reagan.* Washington, D.C.: Brookings Institution Press, 1998.

Corrigan, Richard. "Old and New Ideas to Cut the Deficit." *National Journal* 19, no. 2 (1987): 85.

Dommel, Paul R., and Michael J. Rich. "The Rich Get Richer: The Attenuation of Targeting Effects of the Community Development Block Grant Program." *Urban Affairs Quarterly* 22 (1987): 552–79.

Fischer, Beth A. *The Reagan Reversal: Foreign Policy and the End of the Cold War.* Columbia: University of Missouri Press, 1997.

———. "Toeing the Hardline? The Reagan Administration and the Ending of the Cold War." *Political Science Quarterly* 112, no. 3 (1997): 477.

FitzGerald, Frances. *Way Out There in the Blue: Reagan, Star Wars, and the End of the Cold War.* New York: Simon & Schuster, 2000.

Friedman, Barry D. *Regulation in the Reagan-Bush Era: The Eruption of Presidential Influence.* Pittsburgh: University of Pittsburgh Press, 1995.

Gent, Maurice. "The Libya Raid: A Provisional Balance-Sheet." *World Today* 42 (1986): 95–96.

Gilboa, Eytan. "The Panama Invasion Revisited: Lessons for the Use of Force in the Post Cold War Era." *Political Science Quarterly* 110 (1995–1996): 539–662. http://www.mtholyoke.edu/acad/intrel/gilboa.htm.

Hodder-Williams, Richard. "The Strange Story of Judge Robert Bork and a Vacancy on the U.S. Supreme Court." *Political Studies* 36 (1988): 613–17.

"Immigration Reform Passes Congress; A Fresh Deck for Illegal Aliens." *U.S. News and World Report,* October 27, 1986, 10.

"INF Treaty: Not So Fast." *Economist* 307 (1988): 20.

"Is the INF Treaty Sound?" *Congressional Digest* 67 (1988): 97–128.

Jackson, William D. "Soviet Reassessment of Ronald Reagan, 1985–1988." *Political Science Quarterly* 113, no. 4 (1998): 617.

Kahn, Robert S. *Other People's Blood: U.S. Immigration Prisons in the Reagan Decade.* Boulder, Colo.: Westview Press, 1996.

Karmin, Monroe W., and Robert Morse. "When National Debt Gets out of Control." *U.S. News & World Report,* June 14, 1982, 71.

Keisling, P. "Money over What Really Mattered: Where the Air Traffic Controllers Went Wrong." *The Washington Monthly,* September 1983, 14.

Kinahan, G. "Ratification of START: Lessons from the INF Treaty." *Journal of Social, Political, and Economic Studies* 14 (1989): 387–414.

Krepon, Michael. "Assessing Strategic Arms Reduction Proposals." *World Politics* 35 (1983): 216–44.

Laham, Nicholas. *The Reagan Presidency and the Politics of Race: In Pursuit of Colorblind Justice and Limited Government.* Westport, Conn.: Praeger, 1998.

Lambeth, Benjamin, and Kevin Lewis. "The Kremlin and SDI." *Foreign Affairs* (Spring 1988): 755.

Lambro, Donald. "The Republican Pork Barrel: Why It's So Hard to Cut the Budget." *Policy Review* 33 (Summer 1985): 54–56.

Lebow, Richard Ned, and Janice Gross Stein. "Reagan and the Cold War." *Atlantic Monthly.* February 1994. http://www.theatlantic.com/politics/foreign/reagrus.htm.

Martz, John D. *United States Policy in Latin America: A Decade of Crisis and Challenge.* Lincoln: University of Nebraska Press, 1995.

Murray, Matthew H. "SALT II: The Diplomatic Option." *Christian Science Monitor,* June 14, 1985, 18.

"The Nine Lives of Immigration Reform." *Economist* 301 (1986): 31–32.

Northrup, Herbert R. "The Rise and Demise of PATCO." *Industrial and Labor Relations Review* 37 (1984): 167–84.

Nunn, Sam. "Next Steps in Lebanon." *New York Times,* November 1, 1983, A27.

O'Connor, Colleen. "Immigration Reform: A Mess on the Border." *Newsweek,* December 22, 1986, 27.

O'Connor, John. "US Social Welfare Policy: The Reagan Record and Legacy." *Journal of Social Policy* 27, no. 1 (1998): 37.

Pell, Claiborne. "Should Congress Adopt the Proposed Three Year Reagan Approach to Federal Tax Reduction? Con." *Congressional Digest* 60 (1981): 171, 173, 175.

Peterson, George E. *The Reagan Block Grants: What Have We Learned?* Washington, D.C.: Urban Institute Press, 1986.

"The Presidency of Ronald Reagan." University of Texas: Ronald Reagan Presidential Library, August 28, 2000. http://www.lbjlib.utexas.edu/reagan/ref/rrpres.htm.

Quandt, William B. *Reagan's Lebanon Policy: Trial and Error.* Washington, D.C.: Brookings Institution, 1984.

Reagan, Ronald. *Speaking My Mind: Selected Speeches.* Norwalk, Conn.: Easton Press, 1990.

"Reagan vs. Clinton: Who's the Economic Champ?" *Business Week,* February 22, 1999, 22.

Round, Michael A. *Grounded: Reagan and the PATCO Crash.* New York: Garland, 1999.

Rubner, Michael. "The Reagan Administration, the 1973 War Powers Resolution and the Invasion of Grenada." *Political Science Quarterly* 100 (1985–1986): 627–47.

Scheffer, David J. "U.S. Law and the Iran-Contra Affair." *American Journal of International Law."* 81 (1987): 696–723.

Schumacher, Edward. "The United States and Libya." *Foreign Affairs* 65 (1986–1987): 329–48.

Secter, Bob. "Africa Sanctions Passed by Senate; Would Bar Bank Loans, Curb Sales of Computers to Oppose Apartheid." *Los Angeles Times,* July 12, 1985, A1.

Shull, Steven A. *A Kinder, Gentler Racism?: The Reagan-Bush Civil Rights Legacy.* Armonk, N.Y.: M.E. Sharpe, 1993.

Sichelman, Law. "The Housing Agenda." *United States Banker,* February 1987, 56.

Sick, Gary. *October Surprise: America's Hostages in Iran and the Election of Ronald Reagan.* New York: Times Books, 1991.

Siljander, Mark D. "Is the Proposed Reagan 'Enterprise Zone' Program a Sound Approach to the Nation's Urban Problems. Pro." *Congressional Digest* 64 (1988): 152.

Stockman, David. "Should Congress Adopt the Proposed Three Year Reagan Approach to Federal Tax Reduction? Pro." *Congressional Digest* 60 (1981): 170, 172, 174.

"The Trouble with Tax Cuts." *Policy Review* 98 (1999–2000) http://www.policyreview.com/dec99/bartlett.html.

Wagner, David. "The Reaganauts Recall the Gipper." *Insight on the News* 13, no. 39 (1997): 16.

Warnke, Paul C. "Can 18,000 Warheads Be Wrong?" *Human Rights* 11 (1983): 14–17.

Williams, Philip. "Europe without the Umbrella." *Washington Quarterly* 10, no. 2 (1987): 36.

Wilson, Christopher. "Sanctions Close In." *New Statesman* 110 (1985): 17–18.

Zdenek, Robert. "Is the Proposed Reagan 'Enterprise Zone' Program a Sound Approach to the Nation's Urban Problems? Con." *Congressional Digest* 64 (1988): 149.

2

GEORGE H. W. BUSH

(1989–1993)

INTRODUCTION

George Bush's brief presidency was a busy one. The collapse of the Soviet Union and the end of the Cold War, military interventions in Panama and the Persian Gulf, an exploding budget crisis, and a series of important domestic policy achievements packed his four years in office with events and issues that are worthy of note and discussion.

Bush was elected in a period of comparative economic growth and stability. The foreign policy accomplishments of the Reagan administration had led to a substantial lessening of tensions between the United States and the Soviet Union, reducing Cold War fears of imminent conflict between the two superpowers. In contrast with the period in which Ronald Reagan was elected, Bush's election came at a time when continuity was favored.

In response to this political context, Bush ran for office promising to maintain the policies and goals of the Reagan administration. As Reagan's vice president, this claim was credible. However, the 1988 presidential campaign was notable for its negativity and personality-based attacks. Bush attacked his opponent, Massachusetts Governor Michael Dukakis (D), for his record on crime, the environment, and other areas. What Bush did not do was offer a positive agenda that clearly stated his goals, intentions, and values. Thus, when he was elected, he could not claim a mandate of support for his programs. Instead, all he could do was rest on Reagan's legacy. When new issues arose, and when problems emerged from Reagan's policies, Bush's presidency became troubled. Since he could not claim that his election had been a validation of his policy proposals, he was forced to respond to the demands of others in the political system. His 1992 loss to Bill Clinton can be considered a result of his inability to articulate and achieve his own set of policies, rather than those borrowed from Reagan.

In foreign affairs, Bush was faced by a series of challenges that were enormous in scope. Of these, the most significant were the end of the Cold War, the democracy movement in China, the invasion of Panama, and the Persian Gulf War, also known as Operation Desert Storm.

The end of the Cold War signaled a momentous change in world affairs. Since the end of World War II, the United States and the Soviet Union had engaged in a vast international competition to establish and maintain supporting relationships with nations around the world. The two superpowers provided military and financial support to sympathetic regimes and worked to undermine governments favorable to the other side. They developed vast storehouses of nuclear and conventional weapons to defend their interests and to deter war. Their foreign policies were oriented to the maintenance of this stalemate: so long as neither side was gaining a substantial advantage in this conflict, neither would risk war.

Starting in 1989, the Cold War began to end as the Iron Curtain separating Eastern and Western Europe (the border between Soviet- and U.S.–allied countries) crumbled. At first, thousands of East Germans moved through Hungary and Czechoslovakia to freedom in West Germany. This movement was enhanced when the wall separating East and West Berlin was torn down in October 1989. Shortly thereafter most of the borders between the Soviet-satellite countries of Eastern Europe and the West were eased, leading to the end of the Communist-led governments in those countries. Finally, in 1991, the Communist government of the Soviet Union itself collapsed when a coup led by military officers bent on restoring Communist authority failed. In its place, a more democratic, elected regime came to power, and the great contest of the Cold War came to a sudden end.

In response to this collapse, several policy alternatives were available to the Bush administration. Many argued that the United States should assist the countries of the former Soviet Union to develop economically, recover politically, and manage their nuclear stockpiles. Others thought that such aid would allow the Soviets to restore themselves to power in a way that allowed them to threaten the United States and its allies. Bush chose the first course, arguing that the only way to ensure democracy in Eastern Europe was to provide economic aid, military liaison, and negotiation for reductions in nuclear forces. Several programs were developed and implemented to assist both the former Soviet Union and its allies make the transition to non-Communist forms of government.

The changes in the former Soviet Union were, of course, a substantial challenge for the Bush administration. Then, in the midst of assisting in the transition from Cold War enemies to political partners, other problems emerged for Bush to address. Particularly important was a protest movement in the world's other great Communist power, the People's Republic of China. In 1989 millions of Chinese students began demanding political change toward democracy. These protests were concentrated in Beijing at Tiananmen Square, a large plaza outside the gates of the Forbidden City, the former imperial palace grounds. When the protests increased, China's leaders sent in the army to crush the rebellion. In a dramatic night of action, thousands of students were arrested and hundreds were killed and wounded. One brave student attempted to stop a tank from entering the square by standing in front of it as it moved; this image was captured on television and beamed worldwide.

The events at Tiananmen Square caused an international uproar. Many people wanted trade and other relations between the United States and China suspended. They argued that economic and diplomatic ties between the United States and China would help Chinese leaders maintain their antidemocratic positions of power. Others believed that trade would promote democracy. In response, Bush practiced both policies: he cut off some economic and diplomatic ties with China but sent his national security advisor, Brent Scowcroft, to China to assure the government that this suspension was temporary and that the United States would not end its relations with China permanently. Normal relations were restored a year later, and by 2000 China was granted permanent favorable trade relations with the United States.

Panama presented yet another problem for the Bush administration. Long a U.S. ally, Panama had received billions of dollars of U.S. economic and military aid. Further, the canal that bisects the country was a U.S. possession, and the United States had always manipulated Panamanian politics to protect U.S. interests. By 1989, however, the leader of Panama, General Manuel Noriega, refused to follow U.S. instructions and allowed Panamanian airports to be used in the transshipment of drugs from South America to the United States. In response, Bush ordered the U.S. military to invade Panama, capture Noriega, and return him to the United States to face trial. This operation, carried out in November and December 1989, led to Noriega's capture and the establishment of a new government in Panama.

The final event in foreign affairs was the Persian Gulf War. In August 1990 Iraq invaded and occupied its neighbor Kuwait. Despite the fact that just before the invasion the United States had said that it had no interest in the long-simmering conflict between Kuwait and Iraq, Bush responded to the Iraqi occupation quickly. He ordered several U.S. divisions to Saudi Arabia and ultimately sent over 500,000 U.S. troops to the region, the largest number of American forces sent to war since the

Vietnam era. He also assembled a large international coalition in support of his actions. In January 1991, this coalition began an air campaign against Iraqi forces in Kuwait and targets in Iraq that lasted for six weeks. At the end of this bombing campaign, ground forces moved into Kuwait and southern Iraq and defeated the remnants of the Iraqi army in four days. The Kuwaiti government was restored, and sanctions were put into place against Iraq in an effort to force it to end its chemical, biological, and nuclear weapons programs. As of 2000, these sanctions remain in place, as does the Iraqi government led by Saddam Hussein.

In addition to the many foreign policy challenges he faced as president, Bush was forced to deal with some of the domestic and economic consequences of the Reagan revolution. By 1990, for example, the annual budget deficit was over $300 billion and rising rapidly. Reagan-era tax cuts, increasing military expenditures, an economic slowdown, and an unwillingness to cut other programs were causing huge shortfalls in government revenues. This problem caused Bush to support a substantial tax increase in 1990. While he later repudiated this policy, claiming that he had been tricked into it by the Democrats who controlled Congress, budget deficits did begin to fall by the end of his term. However, his support of a tax increase cost him political support among conservatives in the Republican Party.

In domestic affairs, Bush was a surprisingly activist president. Thus, despite the fact that he campaigned as a supporter of Reagan's idea that government should do as little as possible so that people could enjoy maximum levels of freedom, several programs were passed in Bush's time in office that have had profound consequences for the nation over time. Of particular consequence were the Americans with Disabilities Act, the Clean Air Act, the Clean Water Act, and the appointment of Clarence Thomas to the U.S. Supreme Court. The Americans with Disabilities Act added "disability" to the status of a protected civil right, meaning that no one could be discriminated against on the basis of a handicap. Accordingly, businesses and public organizations had to develop policies and practices, ranging from wheelchair-accessible restrooms to accommodations for employment, to allow disabled persons to enjoy a mainstream life. The Clean Air and Clean Water acts empowered the Environmental Protection Agency (EPA) and other departments to write and enforce a host of new regulations to ensure the quality of the air and water essential to life. Finally, the appointment of Clarence Thomas to the Supreme Court proved to be a turning point in the history of gender politics.

Assessing the Bush presidency is difficult. He was in office for only four years, yet the events that took place during those years transformed world politics. In general, it is clear that his ability to manage international politics was strong in relation to other recent U.S. presidents.

While many dispute the appropriateness of specific choices he made, very few people doubt that his international diplomatic skills led to the development of a new relationship between the United States and the Soviet Union, including its former allies. It was also a key factor in building the international coalition that fought the Persian Gulf War.

Bush's domestic political skills were not as polished. When he ran for office promising to carry out the Reagan agenda, but not offering any positive ideas of his own, he set himself up for a loss of support when political and economic circumstances led him to alter some of Reagan's blueprints. The clearest proof of this is the fact that he was not reelected in 1992 despite the fact that, at the end of the Persian Gulf War, he enjoyed 91 percent public approval ratings—numbers that no president had ever experienced. The changes he made to Reagan's policies cost him much conservative support, and his failure to address the needs of people being harmed by a lingering recession undermined his general support. It provided the context in which his successor, Bill Clinton, came to office.

DOMESTIC AND ECONOMIC POLICY

THE BUSH ECONOMIC PLAN (FEBRUARY 1989)

As president, George Bush promoted the supply-side economics model popular with conservatives despite the fact that he had referred to it as "voodoo economics" in the 1980 presidential campaign when he was one of Ronald Reagan's Republican primary opponents. In this model, tax cuts and economic incentives are expected to increase government tax revenues since people have more money to buy goods, these purchases stimulate demand, and businesses to hire more employees to meet the increased demand. These new employees also pay taxes, thereby increasing government revenues.

Bush's 1990 budget proposal was a typical supply-side one. A series of tax cuts, particularly in capital gains taxes charged on investments, would stimulate investment and consumption. In addition, the government would freeze spending on certain programs to reduce costs. Such policies would, Bush insisted, promote economic growth, lead to increased tax revenues, and allow families to keep more of their incomes to help in raising their children. He also promised to keep defense spending high, protecting the United States but not harming social programs.

Congressman Donald Pease (D-OH) and *Business Week* columnist Robert Kuttner rejected Bush's plan out of hand. Their central point was that it is generally the wealthy who benefit from income and capital gains tax cuts. This makes sense since it is necessary to have a measure of wealth before one can invest any money, and a person with $1,000,000 in income pays more taxes than someone making $10,000. They further argued that the investing and spending these wealthy beneficiaries of tax cuts engaged in did not "trickle down" through the entire economy, stimulating job growth for everyone. Instead, most people were getting poorer even as the rich were getting richer. More of the same, then, would be unlikely to benefit everyone. Finally, many critics doubted whether it was possible to increase defense spending while at the same time protecting social programs.

Bush was only moderately successful in implementing his economic plan. Members of Congress balked at cutting taxes for more affluent people and jeopardizing the revenue government needed to operate. However, he was successful in controlling some spending, especially in social programs. These changes did not control budget deficits, however, and in the following year Bush approved a series of tax increases. This proposal, which cost him a great deal of political support among conservatives, contributed to his loss in his reelection bid in 1992.

Ironically, while the Bush economic plan cost him short-term political support, the combination of increased taxes and controlled spending he promoted had long-term benefit for the country. In combination with the economic growth of the 1990s, his plan set in motion the developments that led to the budget surpluses of the late 1990s. Thus, in dealing with $300+ billion deficits in 1990, Bush encouraged the conditions that may lead to multi-trillion dollar surpluses in the 2000–2010 period. As has always been true, politics is not always fair.

BUSH'S REMARKS TO THE SOUTH CAROLINA STATE LEGISLATURE IN COLUMBIA

February 15, 1989

Our experience at the national level is clear: Reducing the capital gains rate has resulted in more revenue to the Federal Government, not less. And it spurs investment; and investment means more jobs. And jobs mean more opportunity. And opportunity is the foundation of American progress. And a lower capital gains rate helps our international competitiveness—all of our biggest trading partners, including Japan and West Germany, tax capital gains modestly if at all. Even as you're taking up this issue in South Carolina, my proposal at the Federal level is to cut the capital gains rate down to 15 percent for investments held for 3 years or more.

Now, as you know, last week I proposed a budget plan for the Federal Government. You may have heard about it. It's getting some attention. And I'm pleased to say no one has said that it's DOA. If anyone does, I'll interpret that as: "Defining Opportunity for Americans."

But when it comes to the Washington budget process, so much of the rhetoric is, as you know, a bit extravagant. Once in the heat of budget politics, a former member of this chamber, Goat Leamond, stepped back from the fray to utter the now-immortal words: "When in doubt, run in circles, scream and shout." Washington all over again.

But in Washington, with all the shouting that sometimes occurs, the words don't mean the same things that most people think that they mean. When they talk about budget cuts in Washington, that usually doesn't mean that spending is going down. And this is the key point. It seems to be the obvious meaning, but it's not. It usually means that spending is going up, but at a slower pace. Senator Rudman of New Hampshire said this week: "Washington is the only town where a man making $20,000 can go in and ask his boss for a raise of $10,000, and then when the boss gives him instead a $5,000 raise, the story comes out: 'Man's Salary Cut by $5,000.' "

On the revenue side, I've taken a pledge to the American people, and I'm going to keep it: No new taxes! You see, I believe that is what the people of this State and the people of America voted for as a whole. And the bottom line in the Federal budget is that it's not my money, it's not the Congress' money, it's the American peoples' money.

. . .

My budget is based on a flexible freeze with no tax increases. This budget recognizes that there are three ways government must serve the people: first, by not taking any more of their hard-earned money than is absolutely necessary; secondly, by creating the environment that permits economic growth, new jobs, and greater opportunity; and finally, by doing the very best to help people with the money that is spent by government, caring for those in need, protecting what we hold in common, and serving the people with efficiency and, yes, compassion.

Even in times when reducing the deficit means tough choices, we must still set priorities. And my budget is a realistic plan that does more for education, more for the environment, and more for the space program. And it makes a larger investment in scientific research to help keep America competitive into the next century. It spends more on the Head Start program to help make America strong into the next generation. And there is another $1 billion in outlays to fight drugs, because we cannot let this menace rob our children of their future. And we propose a new child care initiative, targeted at low-income families and designed to give real choice to families. The family unit is vital to the economic fabric of our society. And government must not discourage parental choice and family involvement. And in this budget, we also restore and double the tax deduction for adopting special-needs children. And we commit a billion dollars to deal with the problems of the homeless. And we don't touch Social Security—that's off-limits.

And we keep our defenses strong. Defending America is one task which is an absolute responsibility for the Federal Government. And this budget enables our national defense to keep up with inflation. It's gone down, net terms, for 4 out of the last 4 years. When our young men and women make a commitment to join our Armed Services, they have the right to know that we will give them the tools to defend themselves and to defend America.

. . .

But to do this does require that choices be made, which is what this budget does. And I'm prepared to work with the Congress to make those hard choices. We weren't sent to Washington—any of us up there—to sit on our hands, either to pass the cost of indecision on to working Americans by raising their taxes or to fail to reduce the deficit, which will cause the cuts to be done automatically under the law. And that's why we must make choices that keep the economy growing, preserve our national defense, and allow government adequately and compassionately to perform the services which it should do. And if we do, we can get the job done—but not with business as usual.

. . .

Public Papers of the President: George Bush. February 15, 1989: 137–138.

LET'S NOT GET ALL WORKED UP AGAIN OVER SAVINGS

March 27, 1990

Mr. Donald Pease (D-OH). Mr. Speaker, while all of us are concerned about promoting savings and investment in the United States, we need to stop and think about just what we mean when we throw around those terms. The fact is that there is more than one way to save and invest for our future.

The need for some variety in perspective when evaluating our economy's needs in these vital areas is the thesis of a thought-provoking essay by Robert Kuttner in the April 2, 1990, issue of *Business Week.* I commend Mr. Kuttner's observations to my colleagues.

(BY ROBERT KUTTNER)

The debate about America's savings rate is heating up again. On one side, orthodox economists blame low investment and low productivity growth on low private savings and high public deficits. To restore growth, we must tighten our belts and begin saving more. This camp cuts across party lines and includes liberals such as Harvard economist Benjamin Friedman, author of *Day of Reckoning: The Consequences of American Economic Policy in the 1980's* ("Society pays for eating its seed corn") as well as for conservatives such as investment banker Peter G. Peterson, whose new book *On Borrowed Time* attributes America's woes to a consumption and entitlement binge.

Yet there is a minority view, and it invites attention. University of Pennsylvania professor Fred Block, for one, challenges the way savings rates are calculated. In a new monograph, Block finds that a major source of savings—private contributions to pensions and social insurance funds—are arbitrarily counted in the National Income & Product Accounts as personal income rather than as additions to savings. Using Federal Reserve flow-of-funds data, which track actual money flowing from households into investment instruments, Block calculates an alternative measure of total private savings: In 1987, it equaled $290 billion rather than the official savings statistics of just $104 billion.

Economist Robert Blecker of American University, for another, finds that low rates of measured net private savings in the 1980s were caused mainly by higher rates of economic depreciation of the nation's capital stock, not by depressed thrift in the household sector. In a soon-to-be-released study for the Economic Policy Institute, Blecker also calculates that the greater concentration of income and wealth in America's households, paradoxically, depressed rather than increased the total supply of savings. That's because the increments in paper net worth—inflated real estate and stock portfolios—enabled wealthy households to "spend more out of current income while still increasing their assets." This, in turn, depressed their net new savings.

Alicia Munnell, chief economist of the Boston Federal Reserve Bank, writing in the *New England Economic Review* and building on recent work by Chicago economist David Aschauer, adds the insight that private savings is only one among many influences on productivity and growth. Public capital (infrastructure) and social capital (education and training) are as important to growth as private investment. The orthodox measures of savings and investment leave out public and social capital and miss much of the phenomenon.

In 1987, Munnell reports, the public capital stock equaled $2.3 trillion, compared with $4 trillion in the private sector. The investments of public capital, which Aschauer found correlated highly with productivity growth, have been in grave decline. According to Munnell, the growth in nonmilitary public capital was 5% in most of the 1960s, 3.3% from 1979 to 1973, 1.8% from 1973 to 1979, and just 0.9% in the 1980s.

The unconventional wisdom on the savings question highlights an issue that gets obscured, perhaps intentionally, in these debates: Who benefits, and who pays? People who worry about savings rates have an uncanny knack for obscuring the distribution aspect. In their writing, America becomes one undifferentiated "we." According to Friedman, "We have enjoyed what appears to be a higher and more stable standard of living by selling our [own] and our children's birthright." Here, it is appropriate to quote Tonto's immortal words to the Lone Ranger: "What do you mean, 'we,' paleface?" Friedman's assertion is nonsensical. For as Blecker reports (and most economists concede), the actual consumption of 80% of the population declined during the 1980s. Perhaps Friedman was one of the lucky 20% who went on a binge at the expense of his children, but most Americans have already experienced a decade of substantial belt-tightening. Given what has happened to most people's actual standard of living, the moralistic note that creeps into the austerity side of the debate is singularly churlish and inappropriate.

The new view also has implications about remedy. If the real problem is distributional concentration (Blecker) or starved social capital (Munnell), then President Bush's proposal to cut capital gains taxes and further rein in public spending is doubly counterproductive. The debate has a final and deliciously contrarian twist. Thanks to the triumph of laissez-faire in the 1980's, we have finally reached the nirvana of free global capital flows, in which money can flow from Tokyo or Frankfurt to New York or vice versa. In this Magic Kingdom, money even flows uphill, from the world's poorest countries to Wall Street. But this reality of one financial world, long sought by men such as Peterson, means that it really doesn't matter what America saves as long as world savings are adequate to finance world growth and America attracts investment. To that end, better roads, rails, and trained workers would help, and we won't get those by cutting the capital gains tax.

The Congressional Record. March 27, 1990: E 838.

DRUG CONTROL (SEPTEMBER 1989)

Starting in the 1960s and continuing through the 1980s, the use of illegal drugs became widespread throughout the United States. Where once only a relatively small percentage of Americans used illegal drugs, by the 1980s many Americans had experimented with marijuana, cocaine, heroin, and other drugs. More important, many younger people were experimenting and regularly using illegal drugs, suggesting that drug abuse would be a continuing problem in the United States.

Bush advocated an aggressive drug-control strategy that came to be labeled the "war on drugs." This strategy included interdicting drugs before they entered the United States, harsh penalties like "three strikes and you're out" for convicted drug dealers (a plan in which three convictions for felonies would lead to automatic life sentences in prison without the possibility of parole), and even serious fines and other sanctions for ordinary drug users. The program also included efforts to educate citizens against drug use. Bush argued that such efforts, if combined, would help stop and then reduce the spread of drug use in the United States.

Many critics of Bush's plan, including Congressman Bill Richardson (D-NM) noted that the various remedies being suggested would be very expensive. Prisons, interdiction efforts, and courts cost a great deal of money to operate. Accordingly, it is easy to "talk tough" about drugs, but perhaps it is unrealistic to implement the policies. Other critics pointed out that locking up large numbers of drug users results simply in prisoners who use drugs; Bush's plan lacked substantial money for treatment of drug offenders so that they would not repeat their crimes.

Support for the war on drugs was significant. Most Americans approved of the get tough approach of locking up prisoners and trying to stop drugs before they reached the United States. Indeed, it is almost impossible to imagine a political leader arguing for a softer, treatment-based response to the drug problem. Accordingly, the basic parameters of Bush's plan were adopted: billions were spent building prisons, converting army units into drug interdiction teams, generating education programs for youths, and promoting harsh penalties for convicted drug dealers and users.

However, despite the many billions of dollars invested in the war on drugs, and despite a rate of imprisonment in the United States that is among the highest in the world, in 2000, drug-use rates are again growing in the United States. Drug abuse remains a serious issue in America. Prison populations have exploded, putting significant pressure on the budgets of many states and the federal government as they struggle to fund construction, hiring, and other requirements of the prison system. Most states have backed off the "three strikes and you're out" mechanism of enforcing drug laws on the grounds that it is too harsh for what are many times very minor offenses. Still, there is no meaningful policy to address drug abuse in the United States.

BUSH'S ADDRESS TO THE NATION ON THE NATIONAL DRUG CONTROL STRATEGY

September 5, 1989

Good evening. This is the first time since taking the oath of office that I felt an issue was so important, so threatening, that it warranted talking directly with you, the American people. All of us agree that the gravest domestic threat facing our nation today is drugs. Drugs have strained our faith in our system of justice. Our courts, our prisons, our legal system, are stretched to the breaking point. The social costs of drugs are mounting. In short, drugs are sapping our strength as a nation. Turn on the evening news or pick up the morning paper and you'll see what some Americans know just by stepping out their front door: Our most serious problem today is cocaine, and in particular, crack.

Who's responsible? Let me tell you straight out—everyone who uses drugs, everyone who sells drugs, and everyone who looks the other way.

Tonight, I'll tell you how many Americans are using illegal drugs. I will present to you our national strategy to deal with every aspect of this threat. And I will ask you to get involved in what promises to be a very difficult fight.

This is crack cocaine seized a few days ago by Drug Enforcement agents in a park just across the street from the White House. It could easily have been heroin or PCP. It's as innocent-looking as candy, but it's turning our cities into battle zones, and it's murdering our children. Let there be no mistake: This stuff is poison. Some used to call drugs harmless recreation; they're not. Drugs are a real and terribly dangerous threat to our neighborhoods, our friends, and our families.

. . .

What, then, is our plan? To begin with, I trust the lesson of experience: No single policy will cut it, no matter how glamorous or magical it may sound. To win the war against addictive drugs like crack will take more than just a Federal strategy: It will take a national strategy, one that reaches into every school, every workplace, involving every family.

. . .

Let me address four of the major elements of our strategy. First, we are determined to enforce the law, to make our streets and neighborhoods safe. . . . Americans have a right to safety in and around their homes. And we won't have safe neighborhoods unless we're tough on drug criminals—much tougher than we are now. Sometimes that means tougher penalties, but more often it just means punishment that is swift and certain.

. . .

The second element of our strategy looks beyond our borders, where the cocaine and crack bought on America's streets is grown and processed.

. . .

The third part of our strategy concerns drug treatment. Experts believe that there are 2 million American drug users who may be able to get off drugs with proper treatment, but right now only 40 percent of them are actually getting help. This is simply not good enough. Many people who need treatment won't seek it on their own, and some who do seek it are put on a waiting list. Most programs were set up to deal with heroin addicts, but today the major problem is cocaine users. It's time we expand our treatment systems and do a better job of providing services to those who need them.

. . .

Fourth, we must stop illegal drug use before it starts. Unfortunately, it begins early—for many kids, before their teens. But it doesn't start the way you might think, from a dealer or an addict hanging around a school playground. More often, our kids first get their drugs free, from friends or even from older brothers or sisters. Peer pressure spreads drug use; peer pressure can help stop it. I am proposing a quarter-of-a-billion-dollar increase in Federal funds for school and community prevention programs that help young people and adults reject enticements to try drugs. And I'm proposing something else. Every school, college, and university, and every workplace must adopt tough but fair policies about drug use by students and employees. And those that will not adopt such policies will not get Federal funds—period!

. . .

If we fight this war as a divided nation, then the war is lost. But if we face this evil as a nation united, this will be nothing but a handful of useless chemicals. Victory—victory over drugs—is our cause, a just cause. And with your help, we are going to win.

Public Papers of the President: George Bush. September 5, 1989: 1136–1140.

CRITICISM OF BUSH'S NATIONAL DRUG CONTROL STRATEGY

September 13, 1989

Mr. Bill Richardson (D-NM). Mr. Speaker, the President's national drug control strategy has been out on the street just over a week now. While we in the Congress have had a chance to formulate our own views on the plan—let us not overlook our constituents' views.

I had a chance recently to speak with someone back home who is on the front lines of the war on drugs—a prosecuting attorney from a Republican county. This conservative DA says he welcomes the President's drug plan, as we all do, but he said flatly, we need more resources.

And that's the bottom line—lack of money.

If we want our cops to catch the drug pushers and users, we need more police and that costs money. If we want prosecutors to successfully convict these criminals, our DA's need additional help—manpower, and that costs money. If we want more judges to sentence the criminals, that costs money. And if we want more prison cells to put these criminals away for a long time, that too is going to cost a lot more money than what President Bush is proposing.

I'm afraid the same can be said about the resources committed by the President for drug prevention, treatment, and education programs. They are all underfunded and inadequate.

The President says he is committed to fighting this war—that's all well and good. But unfortunately, the President's national drug control strategy clearly shows he's not willing to adequately arm his troops.

The Congressional Record. September 13, 1989: H 5602.

AMERICANS WITH DISABILITIES ACT (JULY 1990)

The Americans with Disabilities Act (ADA) is the most sweeping piece of federal civil rights legislation signed into law since the 1960s. It requires that businesses, government agencies, telecommunications services, and any organization that interacts with the public make reasonable accommodations for people with disabilities. Such accommodations could range from making restrooms wheelchair accessible to providing sign language interpreters at public meetings. Its intent was to enable people with disabilities to participate in life as fully as possible.

President Bush supported the ADA as a civil right. Just as people should not be denied the right to vote on the basis of the gender or race, Bush argued, people with disabilities should not be prevented from enjoying the benefits of government services, telecommunications, or even just dining out in a restaurant. Bush argued that the ADA, like laws prohibiting discrimination against African Americans, women, and others, would lead to increased opportunities for the millions of Americans affected by various forms of disabilities.

Congressman Dan Burton (R-IN) and other opponents of the ADA had to express their opposition while not appearing to condemn millions of people to isolation and a lack of access to public goods and services. In general, they argued that the ADA would be extremely costly to businesses, buildings, agencies, schools, and other institutions that had to retrofit their facilities to accommodate disabled people. In addition, they argued that the ADA would set off a new spate of lawsuits on the part of those who wished to use the ADA for their own purposes. They argued that the intent of the law was good, but they were concerned about the burden it might place on private businesses.

The ADA became law in 1990. It has led to a sweeping transformation in the amount of access disabled persons have to public goods and services. It has also been extremely expensive. The fear that many nuisance lawsuits would be based on the ADA has largely not come to pass—courts have tended to dismiss suits that are "unreasonable," a flexible category covering claims that seem to be aimed at manipulating the law for inappropriate causes. Instead, millions of Americans who were formerly denied access to many public facilities and opportunities for employment have been integrated into mainstream society. It is, arguably, one of the greatest civil rights successes in U.S. history.

BUSH'S REMARKS ON SIGNING THE AMERICANS WITH DISABILITIES ACT OF 1990

July 26, 1990

Three weeks ago we celebrated our nation's Independence Day. Today we're here to rejoice in and celebrate another "independence day," one that is long overdue. With today's signing of the landmark Americans with Disabilities Act, every man, woman, and child with a disability can now pass through once-closed doors into a bright new era of equality, independence, and freedom. As I look around at all these joyous faces, I remember clearly how many years of dedicated commitment have gone into making this historic new civil rights act a reality. It's been the work of a true coalition, a strong and inspiring coalition of people who have shared both a dream and a passionate determination to make that dream come true. It's been a coalition in the finest spirit—a joining of Democrats and Republicans, of the legislative and the executive branches, of Federal and State agencies, of public officials and private citizens, of people with disabilities and without.

This historic act is the world's first comprehensive declaration of equality for people with disabilities—the first. Its passage has made the United States the international leader on this human rights issue. Already, leaders of several other countries, including Sweden, Japan, the Soviet Union, and all 12 members of the EEC, have announced that they hope to enact now similar legislation.

Our success with this act proves that we are keeping faith with the spirit of our courageous forefathers who wrote in the Declaration of Independence: "We hold these truths to be self-evident, that all men are created equal, that they are endowed by their Creator with certain unalienable rights." These words have been our guide for more than two centuries as we've labored to form our more perfect union. But tragically, for too many Americans, the blessings of liberty have been limited or even denied. The Civil Rights Act of '64 took a bold step towards righting that wrong. But the stark fact remained that people with disabilities were still victims of segregation and discrimination, and this was intolerable. Today's legislation brings us closer to that day when no Americans will ever again be deprived of their basic guarantee of life, liberty, and the pursuit of happiness.

This act is powerful in its simplicity. It will ensure that people with disabilities are given the basic guarantees for which they have worked so long and so hard: independence, freedom of choice, control of their lives, the opportunity to blend fully and equally into the rich mosaic of the American mainstream. Legally, it will provide our disabled community with a powerful expansion of protections and then basic civil rights. It will guarantee fair and just access to the fruits of American life which we all must be able to enjoy. And then, specifically, first the ADA ensures that employers covered by the act cannot discriminate against qualified individuals with disabilities. Second, the ADA ensures access to public accommodations such as restaurants, hotels, shopping centers, and offices. And third, the ADA ensures expanded access to transportation services. And fourth, the ADA ensures equivalent telephone services for people with speech or hearing impediments.

. . .

Our problems are large, but our unified heart is larger. Our challenges are great, but our will is greater. And in our America, the most generous, optimistic nation on the face of the Earth, we must not and will not rest until every man and woman with a dream has the means to achieve it.

Public Papers of the President: George Bush. July 26, 1990: 1067–1070.

AMERICANS WITH DISABILITIES ACT RESULTS IN ENORMOUS FINANCIAL BURDEN

June 17, 1992

Mr. Dan Burton (R-IN). Mr. Speaker, I want to alert you and my other colleagues to yet another example of the costly consequences of excessive congressional and Federal regulation.

I was recently contacted by Jerry Reighley, president of the Lawrence Parks Board of Recreation in Lawrence, IN, in my district, regarding the enormous financial burden placed upon them in order to comply with the Americans with Disabilities Act [ADA]. For the city of Lawrence's eight parks to comply with the minimum requirements of the ADA by 1993, it will cost the city $250,000. They obviously do not have these extra resources currently available. As a result, Lawrence will be susceptible to the possibility of lawsuits to determine if they are considered liable for their lack of adherence with the law. In addition, this quarter of a million dollars reflect only one aspect of the cost of compliance with the ADA for the taxpayers of Lawrence. The $250,000 does not include the expenses to be incurred by the other sectors of local, county, and State governments, let alone the entire private sector, in complying with the ADA.

No one, especially me, is against including disabled Americans into all facets of life. We should strive to incorporate everyone as much as possible, and I am not arguing here against the noble goal. However, the ADA was a poorly drafted attempt to do it. This law is a boon to lawyers and a boondoggle to taxpayers and the private sector. The ADA's nebulous mandate for reasonable accommodations places a tremendous open-ended liability on society, and its undue hardship exemption is a tenuous defense whose legitimacy only thousands of court cases will decide.

When the ADA was originally debated and passed, congressional Democrats refused again and again to allow Republican amendments that would help small businesses and local governments pay for the law's requirements or that would lessen the scope of the law. Such amendments were called "killer amendments" by the Democrats because they exposed the true financial and regulatory costs of this Government intrusion. As Federal deficits have mounted, Congress has continued to pass expensive legislation but has repeatedly shifted the costs onto local governments and the private sector. It's a safe bet that if the Federal Government cannot afford these far-reaching mandates, neither can States, counties, or small businesses. This must stop.

Therefore, those who control this body must act to correct the dilemmas faced by Lawrence and others. If the Democrat leadership continues in their indifference, the ADA's burdens will force most of America's businesses and local government entities to become law breakers or to face serious economic distress or to spend their few resources to prove they do not have the resources to comply with the law. Congress must wake up to these realities.

As the old adage wisely observes, "the road to hell is paved with good intentions." We must have more than good intentions in writing laws. We should help America's disabled, but the fiscal sanity and rationale that go into the everyday decision-making process of American families and businesses must be introduced into this body's actions as well. If the Nation is going to be forced to abide by the ADA's stringent requirements, I hope the leadership will hear the cries of the electorate and drop its resistance to assisting Lawrence and the thousands of cities and businesses across the country in similar situations who want to comply with the ADA but simply cannot afford to.

The Congressional Record. June 17, 1992: E 1878–1879.

FAMILY AND MEDICAL LEAVE ACT (JUNE 1990)

In the 1950s it was common for families to have only one wage earner. Typically, the man worked for a paycheck while the woman raised the children at home. By the 1990s, however, this was no longer the case. Generally, both parents worked or families were headed by single parents. This put increased pressures on the workplace because, in contrast with the 1950s when the stay-at-home spouse was available to take care of sick children, in the 1990s one or the other of the family's two wage earners had to miss work to care for a child. Similarly, the illness of one wage earner had a profound impact on the family's ability to buy food, medical insurance, housing, and other needs. Such dilemmas caused some people to support policies that would require employers to allow workers to stay at home with a sick child or to sustain an employee who was ill without firing the worker.

President Bush opposed one such proposal, the Family and Medical Leave Act of 1990. Bush argued that, if businesses were forced to keep workers who were unproductive, for whatever reason, those businesses would be less competitive in the world market. As a consequence, the entire business might be put at risk. In addition, Bush argued that a federally mandated program would make it impossible for businesses to adjust programs to their workers' needs. As a consequence, he vetoed the Family and Medical Leave Act of 1990.

In 1989, before it was passed in 1990 and sent to President Bush, Congresswoman Marge Roukema (R-NJ) and other supporters of the act argued that, in the 1990s, it was unrealistic to expect parents to behave like parents in the 1950s. Increased cost of living, the rise in one-parent families, most of which were led by women, and changes in the business world had all caused women to enter the paid workforce in greater numbers than ever before. Accordingly, policy at both the federal and business levels needed to change to accommodate the new reality of the working world.

Bush vetoed the Family and Medical Leave act, and Congress failed to overturn Bush's veto. Thus, it did not pass. However, the question of what kinds of benefits businesses ought to provide workers became a central issue of the 1992 presidential campaign. Many female voters were upset by Bush's veto, and when Bush's opponent, Bill Clinton, argued in favor of such an act, he drew much of his support from those who agreed with him. This was particularly significant since the 1992 election was the first in American history in which more women voted than men, and women supported Clinton by a substantial margin. Bush's opposition to the 1990 Family and Medical Leave Act played a role in his defeat in 1992.

As president, Bill Clinton signed a family and medical leave act which is in force today. Given the very low levels of unemployment in the United States in 2001, many businesses in fact are exceeding the requirements of this law in order to retain their workers. Accordingly, the complaints of many business and political leaders that the act would be too expensive to implement have not proved true. Additionally, millions of parents have benefited from the act to care for sick children and newborns, or to deal with family emergencies.

BUSH'S MESSAGE TO THE HOUSE OF REPRESENTATIVES RETURNING WITHOUT APPROVAL THE FAMILY AND MEDICAL LEAVE ACT OF 1990

June 29, 1990

To the House of Representatives:

I am returning herewith without my approval H.R. 770, the "Family and Medical Leave Act of 1990." This bill would mandate that public and private employers with 50 or more employees, and the Federal Government, provide their employees with leave under specified circumstances.

In vetoing this legislation with its rigid, federally imposed requirements, I want to emphasize my belief that time off for a child's birth or adoption or for family illness is an important benefit for employers to offer employees. I strongly object, however, to the Federal Government mandating leave policies for America's employers and work force. H.R. 770 would do just that.

America faces its stiffest economic competition in history. If our Nation's employers are to succeed in an increasingly complex and competitive global marketplace, they must have the flexibility to meet both this challenge and the needs of their employees. We must ensure that Federal policies do not stifle the creation of new jobs, nor result in the elimination of existing jobs. The Administration is committed to policies that create jobs throughout the economy—serving the most fundamental need of working families.

The strong American labor market of the past decade is a sign of how effectively our current labor policies work. Between 1980 and 1989, the United States created more than 18 million new jobs. In contrast, within European countries, where mandated benefits are more extensive and labor markets less flexible, job growth has been weak. Between 1980 and 1989, all of Europe generated only 5 million new jobs. As a Nation, we must continue the policies that have been so effective in fostering the creation of jobs throughout our economy. H.R. 770 is fundamentally at odds with this crucial objective.

H.R. 770 ignores the realities of today's work place and the diverse needs of workers. Some employees may believe that shorter paid leave is more important than the lengthy, unpaid leave mandated by this legislation. Caring for a sick friend, aunt, or brother might be just as critical to one employee as caring for a child is to another. In other cases, some employees may prefer increased health insurance or pension coverage rather than unpaid family and medical leave.

Choosing among these options traditionally has been within the purview of employer-employee negotiation or the collective bargaining process. By substituting a "one size fits all" Government mandate for innovative individual agreements, this bill ignores the differing family needs and preferences of employees and unduly limits the role of labor-management negotiations.

· · ·

My Administration is strongly committed to policies that recognize that the relationship between work and family must be complementary, and not one that involves conflict. If these policies are to meet the diverse needs of our Nation, they must be carefully, flexibly, and sensitively crafted at the work place by employers and employees, and not through Government mandates imposed by legislation such as H.R. 770.

Public Papers of the President: George Bush. June 29, 1990: 890–891.

REINTRODUCTION OF THE FAMILY AND MEDICAL LEAVE ACT

February 2, 1989

Mrs. Marge Roukema (R-NJ). Mr. Speaker, now, more than ever, the families of America need the protection of a family leave minimum labor standard.

The work force is changing dramatically and these changes have had a profound impact on the American family. The two-worker family is increasingly becoming the norm. The primary provision of the Family and Medical Leave Act—job security—simply guarantees that employees who must take leaves are not fired. This is the job security issue of our day.

And the fact of the matter is that yesterday's family, a working father with a wife who stays home with the children, is no longer the norm.

By and large, in today's family both parents work. Women are entering and reentering the work force with greater frequency than ever before. Today, over 50 million women work outside the home, comprising over 44 percent of our national work force. The vast majority of all mothers hold down jobs outside the home, and increasingly, they are mothers of young children. Fully two-thirds of these working women are single parents. The other third of working women are married to men who earn less than $15,000 per year.

Why are women working in such great numbers today? Clearly, some are professional women on career paths. But the data is clear: the greatest single motivating factor is economic pressure. Simply put, it now takes two wage earners to sustain the same standard of living that one income could provide just 15 years ago. These families are not getting rich. They are getting by.

The cost of the American dream has gone up.

. . .

The time has come to develop a family and medical leave policy that would guarantee that employees who must take leaves of absence because of child birth, a serious illness, or serious illness among family members will not be fired and will have their jobs remain open.

It is the job security issue of our day.

I realize that some business organizations have expressed their philosophical opposition to any family and medical leave legislation claiming that it represents mandated benefits. It does not. It is a minimum standard of protection consistent with the social and economic realities of contemporary society. It is fully consonant with traditional labor laws establishing minimum standards for child labor laws, those against sweat shops, worker health and safety laws, restrictions on overtime, and the minimum wage.

I share the concerns of business, especially small business, that far-reaching family leave legislation could harm productivity and profitability. That's why I have worked so hard to develop a compromise that balances the needs of employees to take leaves and the needs of employers to maintain productivity.

Under its terms, employees would be allowed up to 10 weeks unpaid leave for birth or adoption of a child or to care for a seriously ill child or parent, and up to 15 weeks unpaid leave for their own serious illness. Initially, only employers with at least 50 employees would be covered. After 2 years, a commission would report to Congress about the effect of this legislation on small business. One year later, the benchmark for the number of employees would drop to 35, unless Congress took other action based on the commission report. In order to qualify for leave, employees must have worked for their employer for more than 1 year and for at least 20 hours per week. Finally, the compromise contains a "business necessity" exemption for key personnel.

The compromise embodied in the Family and Medical Leave Act of 1989 strikes the proper balance between the needs of employees to take leave to care for family members and the needs of employers to continue efficient operation.

The Congressional Record. February 2, 1989: E 278–279.

EDUCATION REFORM (MAY 1991)

Education is a perennially popular issue in American politics. Similar to Social Security, almost everyone receives an education benefit from government, and everyone has an opinion about how to make education better. Most legal and financial control of education is held at the state level: states fund schools, establish policies and standards, and manage public education. The federal government plays a lesser role, usually confined to providing grants to assist in funding schools or establishing incentive programs to influence the states to make the choices preferred by the federal government. But since these grants and incentive programs have strings attached—to get the money a state has to follow the federal government's guidelines—federal education policy inevitably leads to contention about how much influence the national government should have over state-based education. At one extreme, some people believe that the states should have total control over their programs. At the other, people argue that national standards are best.

As a conservative, Bush generally believed that state-level controls were best. However, as a practical matter, state-based standards lead to wide differences in the preparation of students both within and among U.S. states. Such inequities caused him to support a plan that would provide incentives to states to provide increased opportunities to at-risk students—students who, by reason of family background, immigrant status, or other factors, tend not to be very successful in the American educational system. In this plan, the federal government would create national standards and would serve as a clearinghouse for information for states. It would also create grants and incentive programs to encourage states to adopt successful ideas. Finally, he advocated a school voucher plan in which students, especially those in poor areas, could enroll in a private school with the government giving the child the value of a public education to use to offset the cost of the private school. Such action, Bush stated, would lead to improvements in education for all Americans.

Opponents of Bush's plan, including Senator Ted Kennedy (D-MA), argued that it was underfunded and insufficient in scope. In Bush's plan, very little new money would be put into education. Thus, poor districts would remain poor, and no real effort would be made to increase opportunities for all students. In addition, the school voucher program was seen to be likely to undermine public schools—tax dollars that had been used to subsidize a public school would be taken away by an unhappy student and given to a private school. It would also inevitably lead to the government's providing funds for use in religious schools, which opponents felt was a violation of the church-state separation which is a major part of American political practice.

Bush's educational plan failed to get through Congress, although a limited voucher program was established by several states. As was the case in so many of Bush's domestic policy agendas, he managed to frustrate both Republicans and Democrats with his plan: Republicans thought it was not radical enough, while Democrats thought it went too far in giving public money to private schools. Accordingly, by the 1992 election, Bush had lost conservative supporters and had made it more difficult to attract liberals.

The trend in national education policy since Bush's loss has been to allow states to experiment, but to provide little in new funding to states. This trend remains the norm. Thus, the federal government does not prevent states from experimenting with limited voucher programs—although the courts have on occasion ruled them unconstitutional on the grounds that giving public money to a private school, if the private school has a religious purpose (as most do), constitutes public support for religion. Similarly, the federal government has allowed states to create charter schools—schools that use public money but are created and controlled by parents and teachers rather than central administrations. Some of these have been very successful; many have failed. Finally, federal money has been used to update classrooms for new technology and to stimulate the hiring of new teachers. No fundamental reform of the system has occurred.

BUSH'S MESSAGE TO THE CONGRESS TRANSMITTING PROPOSED LEGISLATION TO PROMOTE EXCELLENCE IN EDUCATION

May 22, 1991

To the Congress of the United States:

I am pleased to transmit today for your immediate consideration and enactment the "AMERICA 2000 Excellence in Education Act," a bill to help America attain the National Education Goals by the year 2000. I believe that a bold and comprehensive effort, involving all sectors of our society, is needed if we are to implement real educational reforms and reach the National Education Goals by the year 2000. The "AMERICA 2000 Excellence in Education Act" would authorize specific legislative initiatives designed to support such an effort.

Eight years ago, the National Commission on Excellence in Education reported to the Nation that our schools were failing. Since that time, States and localities have enacted a number of school reforms, but these actions have been too slow and too timid. The strategy that I announced on April 18 responds to our need for bold action. It would bring together elected officials, business people, educators, parents, social service providers, civic and religious groups, and, to the greatest extent possible, every American in every community in a crusade to transform our educational system.

. . .

The "AMERICA 2000 Excellence in Education Act" includes the following specific legislative initiatives aimed at fulfilling the principles described below:

- The *New American Schools* program would provide seed money for the start-up of "break-the-mold" schools. These schools would: (1) employ the best that is known about teaching and learning; (2) make use, as appropriate, of the latest technologies; and (3) be tailored to meet the needs and characteristics of individual communities. At least one school would be established in each U.S. Congressional District in communities designated as "AMERICA 2000 Communities."

- The *Merit Schools* program would reward schools that make notable progress toward achievement of the National Education Goals, particularly the goal of ensuring that all students leave grades four, eight, and twelve having demonstrated competence in the core academic subjects. At least 20 percent of each State's funding would be used for awards to schools that have made outstanding progress in mathematics and science education. This program would provide a powerful incentive for all schools to improve their educational performance.

• Attainment of the National Education Goals will depend heavily on the preparation and performance of teachers, principals, and other school leaders. Therefore, three initiatives focus on providing seed money for the training of teachers and school leaders and for the development of alternative teacher and principal certification programs in the States.

—*Governors' Academies for Teachers* would be established in each State. These academies would provide experienced teachers with opportunities for renewal and enhancement of their knowledge and teaching skills in the core academic disciplines of English, mathematics, science, history, and geography. Separate funding would be used by the academies to reward and recognize outstanding teachers of the core subjects.

—*Governors' Academies for School Leaders* would operate in each State to provide current and prospective principals and other school leaders with training in instructional leadership, school-based management, school reform strategies, and other skills necessary for effective educational administration.

—*The Alternative Certification of Teachers and Principals* program would assist States interested in broadening the pool of talent from which to recruit teachers and principals. Funds would assist States to develop and implement, or expand and improve, flexible certification systems. Through these alternative certification systems, talented professionals, and others who have demonstrated subject matter competence or leadership in fields outside of education could become teachers or principals.

. . .

To assist in measuring progress toward the National Education Goals, the bill would make important changes to the authority for the *National Assessment of Educational Progress*. The bill would authorize the collection of State-representative data on English, mathematics, science, history, and geography in grades four, eight, and twelve beginning in 1994. The legislation would also permit the use of National Assessment tests at district and school levels by States that wish to do so.

. . .

I urge the Congress to take prompt and favorable action on this legislation. Taken together, these initiatives, coupled with the rest of the AMERICA 2000 strategy, would spur the actions that are necessary for this country to attain the National Education Goals by the year 2000.

Public Papers of the President: George Bush. May 22, 1991: 1600–1601.

THE DEMOCRATS' POSITION ON EDUCATION

January 28, 1992

Mr. Ted Kennedy (D-MA). Mr. President, when a nation suddenly falls into decline, losing its influence and power, historians probe its policies to determine the cause.

Today, historians are carrying out such analyses on the Soviet Union. But in future years, they may also be exploring the cause of America's decline. How is it, they may ask, that a nation so blessed in its freedoms, so rich in natural resources, so proud of its institutions, suddenly fell into decline? How is it that nations we once sheltered came to overshadow us in vitality and prosperity?

One of the principal causes may well be the failure to devote sufficient attention and resources to the education and training of our citizens. Nations that invest in high-quality education and training will outperform nations that do not make similar investments. The issue is not simply more spending but better spending—focusing our initiatives on efforts that we know will work and can get the job done.

In a recent survey of employers, two-thirds answered negatively when asked about the overall preparation of recent students to hold jobs. That is not surprising, when we consider that roughly 15 percent of the Nation's high school seniors are competent in math according to a recent national analysis. Moreover, in one international study, our 13-year-olds ranked last in ability to solve math problems. We cannot expect to compete in tomorrow's global economy when today's students are already far behind those of other nations.

Education is the lifeblood of our national strength. Whenever the Nation has faced new challenges, one of our first responses has been to redouble our educational efforts.

. . .

But today, when the economy is stalled and our education system is under serious challenge, we seem to have lost our will. We talk about the need for a new commitment to education. We have a President who wants to be called the education President. But when the time comes for action, the administration fails to follow through.

. . .

We must make sure that the doors of higher education are not closed because students cannot afford the costs. The Federal student aid programs have helped millions of students, and those who have received the assistance have gone on to make important contributions to the Nation and to our national well-being.

The President should also endorse new initiatives in job training for the large numbers of high school students who move directly into the labor force. Existing programs should be reviewed and revised and expanded to assure that these students—the Nation's frontline work force of the future—will be well-qualified for their careers. Congress is far ahead of the administration in offering solutions to these problems, and this is an area when leadership is especially urgent.

. . .

Our Democratic proposal to improve American education and reach the national education goals has four parts:

First, we must make Head Start available to every eligible 3-, 4-, and 5-year-old child in the Nation. Expanding Head Start is the single most important step the Federal Government can take to improve American education. The value of Head Start is unquestioned and our commitment to it must be steadfast and unwavering. Legislation pending before the Senate, S. 911, will accomplish this purpose, and I hope the Senate will have a chance to take this measure up very soon.

Second, we must provide funds for restructuring elementary and secondary schools. Unlike the President's plan, which targets resources for too few schools, the Democratic proposal seeks to encourage education reform throughout the Nation. Across America, teachers and administrators are trying innovative ideas to bring the spark back to learning—but too often they cannot fully realize their plans because they lack the necessary funds.

. . .

Third, we must increase college aid for working and middle-income families. Today, more and more families are feeling the burden of the recession, wondering if they can still afford to send their children to college. Yet last year President Bush proposed to restructure Pell grants so that funds are available only to students with family incomes under $10,000. We must move in the opposite direction. Income ceilings and needs-test restrictions must be reformed so that children of working families are not squeezed out of higher education. The Labor Committee has reported out a bill to reauthorize the Higher Education Act that will extend and expand Federal student loan and grant programs, and the Senate will consider this bill in the coming weeks.

Finally, we must develop new programs to support the transition from school to work and to improve the skills of our work force. The majority of young Americans enter the job market without a college degree. Yet all too often, we treat their entry into the work force as an afterthought, as if our educational responsibilities stopped at the schoolhouse door. Democrats are committed to providing Federal support to improve school-to-work transition programs for noncollege-bound youth, and to foster ongoing skill development throughout every worker's career....

. . .

We must not hesitate because of the difficult choices before us. Either we mean what we say about education, or we don't. Let the country decide. Let the American people be the judge.

The Congressional Record. January 28, 1992: S 460.

NOMINATION OF CLARENCE THOMAS TO THE U.S. SUPREME COURT (JULY 1991)

When George Bush nominated Clarence Thomas to the U.S. Supreme Court, he took the opportunity to replace one African American justice, Thurgood Marshall, with another. However, while Marshall was a liberal, Thomas was a conservative. In an attempt to maintain his conservative policies well after he left office, Bush also tried to develop support among African Americans, a constituency that has generally not voted Republican in recent years.

Bush argued for Thomas' approval on grounds common to all presidents in making Supreme Court nominations: qualifications. Bush argued that Thomas' extensive political and judicial experience provided sufficient reasons for anyone to support the nomination. In so doing, Bush downplayed the idea that questions of ideology, character, or past rulings could play an appropriate role in influencing whether people should support his nominee. Since Thomas was qualified, Bush insisted, he should be supported.

Thomas' opponents, who included Congressman Louis Stokes (D-OH) and the Reverend Marvin McMickle, made the argument that Thomas' ideology was a legitimate point of objection. Thus, for them, Thomas' conservative views stood as sufficient grounds for his rejection. Other critics, most notably law professor Anita Hill and women's groups including the National Organization for Women (NOW) accused Thomas of sexually harassing Anita Hill when he was the director of the Equal Employment Opportunity Commission (EEOC). Thomas' conduct in this role was presented as another reason to reject his nomination.

After a contentious nomination hearing, Thomas was approved to serve on the Supreme Court by a 52 to 48 vote. His hearing before the Senate, in the context of the charges made against him, mobilized millions of women to participate in politics. So many women were elected to office in 1992, the year following Thomas' hearing, that it came to be known as the "Year of the Woman." Thomas remains a strongly conservative voice on the Supreme Court.

Since Thomas' confirmation, however, presidents have been reluctant to appoint highly controversial figures to the Supreme Court. The recent pattern has been for presidential staffers to do extensive background research on a candidate—a process known as "vetting"—to identify potentially controversial rulings or allegations in the candidate's past. Anyone with any suspect history is quickly excluded. As a consequence, recent Supreme Court nominees have tended to be moderate people of moderate temperament. The Court retains a moderate, situational majority: some conservative justices vote with the moderates some of the time and some liberal justices vote with the moderates some of the time; the net result is a moderate tone to the Court's rulings.

BUSH'S NEWS CONFERENCE IN KENNEBUNKPORT, MAINE

July 1, 1991

I am very pleased to announce that I will nominate Judge Clarence Thomas to serve as Associate Justice of the United States Supreme Court.

Judge Thomas compiled an excellent record at Holy Cross. He graduated from Yale Law School and served with distinction in the Missouri attorney general's office, in the Reagan-Bush administration, and in my administration. He's a native of Pinpoint, near Savannah, Georgia, where he was raised by his grandparents. His background includes a strong emphasis on education as the key to a better life. And he attended rigorous Catholic schools where he excelled. After spending a year at the Immaculate Conception Seminary in Conception Junction, Missouri, Clarence transferred to Holy Cross College in Worcester, where he supported himself through loans and scholarships and jobs, and graduated with honors in 1971.

After graduation from Yale Law School, he worked for then-Missouri attorney general John Danforth and spent 2½ years litigating cases of all descriptions. In 1977, Judge Thomas practiced law in the private sector, and in 1979, he rejoined Senator Danforth as a legislative assistant in the U.S. Senate. In 1981, President Reagan appointed him Assistant Secretary for Civil Rights in the Department of Education. From 1982 to 1990, he served as President Reagan's Chairman of the Equal Employment Opportunity Commission. And I appointed him to the U.S. Court of Appeals for the District of Columbia in 1990.

I have followed this man's career for some time, and he has excelled in everything that he has attempted. He is a delightful and warm, intelligent person who has great empathy and a wonderful sense of humor. He's also a fiercely independent thinker with an excellent legal mind who believes passionately in equal opportunity for all Americans. He will approach the cases that come before the Court with a commitment to deciding them fairly, as the facts and the law require.

Judge Thomas' life is a model for all Americans, and he's earned the right to sit on this Nation's highest Court. And I am very proud, indeed, to nominate him for this position, and I trust that the Senate will confirm this able man promptly.

. . .

Supreme Court Nominee

Q. Mr. President, how will you answer concerns stemming from Judge Thomas' days as Chairman of the EEOC, that in that post he was somewhat insensitive to the concerns of the elderly and civil rights advocates and that he didn't aggressively pursue their complaints?

The President. Well, obviously, that complaint, if it was even raised in his confirmation hearings for the second highest court in the land, were satisfactorily answered. It is my view that the complaints are unfounded, of course. But I doubt if anybody had strongly felt that, that he would have been confirmed for his present position.

Q. Mr. President, last year you vetoed the civil rights bill, saying it could lead to quotas. Today you've made a nomination that could be easily seen as quota-based. How do you explain this apparent inconsistency?

The President. I don't even see an appearance of inconsistency because what I did is look for the best man. And Clarence Thomas' name was high on the list when the previous nominee went forth, Judge Souter, Mr. Justice Souter now. And so, I don't accept that at all. The fact that he is black and a minority has nothing to do with this in the sense that he is the best qualified at this time. And we had a very thorough screening process then; we had one now that we put into forward gear very fast, but we didn't have to start from square one.

So, Clarence Thomas, seasoned now by more experience on the bench, fits my description of the best man at the right time, or the best person at the right time because women were considered as well.

Q. But do you see how it could be perceived so?

The President. No, I can't see it.

Q. Was race a factor whatsoever, sir, in the selection?

The President. I don't see it at all. The fact that he's a minority—you heard his testimony to the kind of life he's had, and I think that speaks eloquently for itself. But I kept my word to the American people and to the Senate by picking the best man for the job on the merits. And the fact he's minority, so much the better. But that is not the factor, and I would strongly resent any charge that might be forthcoming on quotas when it relates to appointing the best man to the Court. That's the kind of thing I stand for, not opposed to.

. . .

Q. Mr. President, the appointments made by President Reagan and you have put the Court on a conservative road. Is that what you would like to see for the next 10 or 15 years, to reverse some of the more liberal rulings in the past 20 years?

The President. Look, I don't know how Judge Thomas, when he becomes Mr. Justice Thomas, will come down on every issue. And indeed, I didn't discuss specific issues with him. I didn't discuss them with Judge Souter before he became Mr. Justice Souter. But I did look at this: Would he faithfully interpret the Constitution and avoid the tendency to legislate from the Bench? And that's a broad consideration, but that was certainly in his favor in my view. And I don't know whether he'll agree with positions that our administration takes or overthrow decisions or change positions that we think are right. But that doesn't matter. What matters is that he faithfully interpret the Constitution, and I am 100 percent convinced that that's exactly what he'll do.

So, we're not trying to put a philosophical balance on this Court. We're not trying to philosophically affect it. And I said this long ago, long before I became President, that the main consideration in addition to excellence and qualification is this concept of interpreting the Constitution and not legislating from the Federal Bench.

Public Papers of the President: George Bush. July 1, 1991: 801–805.

WHO SAYS BLACKS MUST SUPPORT THOMAS?

July 22, 1991

Mr. Louis Stokes (D-OH). Mr. Speaker, President Bush's decision to nominate Judge Clarence Thomas to the U.S. Supreme Court has provoked a great deal of debate here in the Congress and throughout the Nation. As his confirmation hearings approach, many will examine Thomas' record on affirmative action, civil rights, abortion, and other controversial issues which are certain to come before the Supreme Court.

One question being asked by the White House is why black leaders would be opposed to the nomination of an African-American to the Nation's highest Court. Notable black organizations, including the Congressional Black Caucus and the National Association for the Advancement of Colored People [NAACP], have criticized the nomination of Clarence Thomas.

In an article which appeared in the July 15, 1991 edition of the *Cleveland Plain Dealer*, Rev. Marvin A. McMickle, an outstanding minister and president of the Cleveland Branch of the NAACP, addressed this issue. This thoughtful and incisive article is entitled, "Who Says Blacks Must Support Thomas?"

Mr. Speaker, I am pleased to bring this article to the attention of my colleagues and urge that they take a moment to consider Reverend McMickle's arguments.

(BY REV. MARVIN A. MCMICKLE)

It is, perhaps, time for the local NAACP branch president to say why so many black Americans view the Supreme Court nomination of Clarence Thomas with alarm and concern.

There seems to be some assumption that because Thomas is black, all other blacks in America should welcome the prospect of his presence on the nation's highest court. The fact is, the NAACP national office and I personally view this nomination with cautious pessimism. What is known about the views of Clarence Thomas disturbs me, and what is not known disturbs me even more.

First, however, let me assert my grave concern over the public hysteria created by the criticism of Clarence Thomas by some black persons. Why is it to be assumed that, because he is black, all other blacks should hold their tongues and not express concern about his views and past history? When Robert Bork was nominated, widespread disagreement about his presence on the court was raised by other white Americans, and nobody seemed shocked. Whites are allowed to disagree on matters of policy or ideas, but seem shocked when blacks exercise the same option.

It is one of the lingering effects of racism upon American society that, of course, all black people agree on everything, and one of them would have no need to ever disagree with another. Freedom will not fully come for black Americans until we are as free to hold divergent views among ourselves and to speak freely about those divergent views as is the case for whites, whose views are as divergent as Edward Kennedy and William Sloane Coffin on one side and Jesse Helms and Pat Robertson on the other.

In fact, black America has never been as monolithic as some might think. The modern debate about affirmative action vs. black self-help is reminiscent of the debate 100 years ago between W.E.B. Du Bois and Booker T. Washington over the best approach to black liberation or between Martin Luther King and Malcolm X in the 1960s on the same issue.

That black people can be found who disagree on affirmative action vs. self-help is surprising only to those, black and white, who think that blacks are incapable of thinking and speaking for themselves. What may make this particular disagreement unique is the fact that Clarence Thomas is not only disagreeing with some black leaders in America, but that he is so readily embraced by some in white America whose contempt for blacks is well known (Jesse Helms and Strom Thurmond).

Further troubling to many, is that he was elevated to this judicial pinnacle by two presidents whose administrations have presided over a steady reversal of civil-rights progress (Reagan and Bush).

As to the nomination of Clarence Thomas itself, let me list the areas of concern. Already widely discussed is his performance as head of the Equal Employment Opportunity Commission. That is readily the only public record available on this man. What his performance there promises to blacks, women, the elderly and others is no cause for enthusiasm. He savaged that agency. After only 16 months as an appeals court judge, there is little to suggest his views or his ability as a judge.

The real irony of this nomination is what it says about the shape and state of the U.S. Supreme Court for the next generation. George Bush has named to the court two men of incredibly low profile and even lower production of legal opinions and scholarly production. We know their ideology but we know nothing about their legal or judicial views.

Given the way in which all nominees since Bork (Kennedy-Scalia-Souter) have been coached for their confirmation hearings, we will not likely learn any more about Thomas until he is seated on the Court and begins to produce opinions. Given the issues that will confront the Court in the years to come (capital punishment, free speech, limiting police power, *Roe vs. Wade*, environmental policies and equal protection under the law). I wonder if the nation is well served by Supreme Court justices, seven of whom share the same conservative political ideology, and about whom so little is known.

We demand to know a lot about a nominee for a four-year term as president. For a lifetime term on the Supreme Court we seem content to accept legal and judicial unknowns, and are then asked to believe that the nomination carries no political overtones.

Finally, the NAACP regrets George Bush's lack of honesty in answering whether Thomas was named because he is black. Bush said that Thomas was the best man for the job. That is untrue by every measurement. The truth is Thomas was George Bush's choice to replace Thurgood Marshall. No one imagines that Clarence Thomas is the premier black federal judge in the United States. He is not yet in the same league as A. Leon Higgenbotham of the 3rd Circuit Court in Pennsylvania or Harry Edwards, who sat with Thomas on the 2nd Circuit Court in Washington D.C. Both of these men are primed for the high court, but they are not conservative ideologues.

I am hard-pressed to believe that Thomas would have been "the best man for the job on the merits" if Bush had to replace Harry Blackmun, who is also 82 years old and about to retire. This was a political decision by an increasingly conservative president. The shame is that Bush is unwilling to tell us that obvious truth.

The Congressional Record. July 22, 1991: E 2631.

WELFARE REFORM (APRIL 1992)

There are two general approaches to welfare policy, or programs that supply cash and food assistance to poor citizens, in the United States. In one approach, generally advocated by conservatives, needy people should be supported only in ways that either encourage them to seek further employment or provide a bare minimum of services for people who otherwise cannot work. Conservatives support this policy because they believe that this is the only way to ensure that welfare will not be abused. They also believe that this policy promotes work as a valuable part of human life.

By contrast, the other approach to welfare policy, generally supported by liberals, starts from the premise that people are affected by a great many social and political forces beyond their control. Government provides tax incentives and other supportive benefits to businesses; thus, they argue that it is appropriate to provide a range of support to citizens who cannot otherwise pay for health care, housing, and other basic needs.

President Bush supported welfare reform along the lines of the first approach. He argued that work was dignified, while welfare encouraged economic dependency and personal irresponsibility. He rejected the argument that welfare recipients could not acquire the necessary goods and services. Instead, he insisted that people should be encouraged to find work to live complete lives. Moreover, simply paying people to live meant transferring money from working people to the poor, which, Bush felt, was wrong.

Supporters of traditional welfare policies, including Senator Paul Simon (D-IL) and David Riemer, generally agreed with the idea that work was a benefit to everyone. They asked, however, whether it was realistic to suppose that everyone who wanted a job could get one, especially in a period of economic downturn or in areas where few businesses existed. Thus, if the United States made work a requirement for welfare, but jobs were not available, it would be condemning many people to great suffering for reasons they could not control.

During his administration, the Democratic-controlled Congress passed additional welfare reform based on the traditional, government-support model. Bush vetoed this legislation. His veto was sustained. Bush then supported allowing states to experiment with new kinds of welfare programs. No fundamental welfare reform occurred in his time in office, however.

Welfare reform was achieved during the Clinton presidency. Based on some of the experiments in welfare reform adopted by several states during Bush's presidency, welfare as a lifelong subsidy was eliminated during Clinton's term in office. By 2000 welfare rolls had declined substantially, and many states are not able to find enough beneficiaries to account for all the money they have allocated to these programs. Of course, it remains to be seen how successful these reforms will be if the economy sours. A fundamental premise of modern welfare is that everyone ought to work, but when the economy moves into recession, people lose their jobs, and there are not enough jobs to go around regardless of two-year time limits for welfare benefits. This is, at this time, a hypothetical problem—it has not yet happened.

BUSH'S RADIO ADDRESS TO THE NATION ON WELFARE REFORM

April 11, 1992

Today I want to focus on reforming our welfare system, especially on our Government's role in that reform process.

After years of trying to help those who are in need, we have found that too often our assistance does not help people out of poverty; it traps them there. It's not that people stopped caring; it's that the system stopped working. We want a welfare system that breaks the cycle of dependency before dignity is destroyed and before poverty becomes a family legacy. But today we must face this fact: Our system has failed.

I have repeatedly called for the forging of Federal-State partnerships that would make welfare reform a powerful, effective reality. Yesterday, at my direction, the Federal Government waived outdated rules to allow Wisconsin to try a new kind of welfare reform. The Wisconsin plan replaces some of the old assumptions of the welfare state and recognizes the importance of personal responsibility, self-respect, independence, and self-sufficiency.

In my State of the Union Address, I made a commitment to make it quicker and easier for States with welfare reform ideas to get the Federal waivers they need. By approving Wisconsin's waivers 24 days after we received their request, that commitment now has the force of action. . . .

We must balance America's generous heart with our responsibility to the taxpayers who underwrite governmental assistance. Our assistance should in no way encourage dependency or undermine our Nation's economic competitiveness. We pay twice for those who make welfare a way of life: once for the initial benefits, but even more because the Nation loses their contribution to the Nation's economic well-being.

Those who receive Government assistance have certain responsibilities: the responsibility to seek work or get education and training that will help them get a job, and the responsibility to get their lives in order. That means establishing lifestyles that will enable them to fulfill their potential, not destroy it.

We have responsibilities, too. We must structure our welfare programs so that they reverse policies which lock in a lifestyle of dependency and subtly destroy self-esteem. We must encourage family formation and family stability. Too often our welfare programs have encouraged exactly the opposite.

We must incorporate incentives for recipients to stay in school. For instance, in Wisconsin, teen parents are required by the Learnfare program to stay in school to obtain full benefits. They recognize that in many respects opportunity is equated with education. . . .

My approach to welfare reform should not only open the doors of opportunity for our citizens who are on public assistance but also prepare them to walk proudly and competently through those doors. Our goal is to build a system of welfare that will encourage self-respect, build strength of character, and develop to the fullest each individual's potential for a productive, meaningful life.

Public Papers of the President: George Bush. April 11, 1992: 592–593.

BUT ARE THERE ENOUGH JOBS FOR THE POOR?

February 21, 1991

Mr. Paul Simon (D-IL). Mr. President, I do not think, in all my years in Congress, I've ever asked that a letter to the editor be inserted into the *Congressional Record.* The other day I read a letter to the editor of the *New York Times* written by David R. Riemer, director of administration for the city of Milwaukee, that made so much sense, I believe it deserves larger circulation.

It talks about the need for a jobs program in this Nation.

It is one of the things that we seem to avoid facing.

We are either going to pay people for being productive or nonproductive, and I favor paying them for being productive.

I will be speaking more about the need for a jobs program on the floor of the Senate during the coming months, but I urge my colleagues to read this letter to the editor, which I ask to insert in the Record at this point.

The letter follows:

But Are There Enough Jobs for the Poor?

To the Editor:

Your series on poverty in America ("The Missing Agenda: Poverty and Policy," Jan. 27, 28, 29), while hitting most of the issues, missed the biggest one: Are there enough jobs for the poor?

If the number of low-income welfare recipients, unemployed and "discouraged workers" is less than the supply of available jobs, then either the conventional conservative solution (increase motivation by cutting benefits) or the conventional liberal solution (remove barriers to entry such as racial discrimination and lack of job training) may be sound public policy.

If, on the other hand, the number of those whom we expect to work substantially exceeds the supply of available jobs, then neither motivation nor the removal of barriers will do much good. Most of the poor will remain poor—because there will literally be too few jobs for them to fill.

We don't have a lot of data as to how the number of persons expected to work compares to the supply of unfilled jobs, but such data as do exist all point to the same conclusion: The supply of officially unemployed workers alone exceeds the supply of unfilled jobs.

National studies by Katherine Abraham and Harry Holzer show that—depending on the official unemployment rate—the number of officially unemployed consistently exceeds the number of unfilled jobs by ratios ranging from 10:1 to 3:1. When welfare recipients and "discouraged workers" are thrown into the mix, the ratios get worse. In Milwaukee, a forthcoming study by the Social Development Commission will show that, since 1987, the sum of welfare recipients plus unemployed plus discouraged workers has exceeded the estimated supply of unfilled jobs by ratios ranging from 10:1 to 6:1. And this when the official jobless rate was generally below both state and national averages.

. . .

To eliminate poverty, therefore, it is necessary to correct for . . . basic labor market deficiencies. Empowering the poor—as that concept is defined by Housing Secretary Jack Kemp, i.e., letting the poor choose to enroll in any school, buy public housing units, etc.; however meritorious, will not work, because empowerment neither creates millions of new extra jobs nor augments the earnings provided by the low-wage jobs at the bottom of the wage structure. More or better social services won't work either, for the same reasons: No new jobs are created and wages are not augmented.

Welfare reform generally won't work either, and again for largely the same reasons. Reform usually does not expand the supply of jobs, and it usually does not function to supplement low wages. To the extent that some welfare reform initiatives do achieve these goals, they suffer from two fundamental flaws. First, welfare reform's efforts to create jobs (by "workfare" or other means) or bolster wages (by letting benefits remain in place after recipients get employment) terminate at some fixed point in time. Second, and worse, welfare reform's attempts to create jobs or bolster wages help only the relatively small percentage of poor who get welfare in the first place. Welfare reform by its very nature does not help the vast majority of poor—who aren't on welfare—to get jobs or augment earnings.

The poor will benefit, of course, from any general expansion of employment in the economy—the last solution mentioned in your series. It is universally acknowledged, however, that the poor benefit in only a limited way when employment expands across the board. Too many of the new jobs are taken by non-poor competitors (such as teenagers, college students, second-earners, and the elderly), who always enter and advance quickly in the queue for "untargeted" new jobs when more jobs are created on a general scale. One can hardly begrudge these competitors: while not officially poor, many are far from well-off. They need the money too.

In the final analysis, there are only two practical methods of ending poverty in the United States. Give the poor money—so much money that they get out of poverty. Or get the poor into jobs—and then make sure the jobs they then take or already hold (for most poor adults work in the first place) yield an "earnings-related income," consisting of wages and earnings supplements, higher than the poverty line. Only these two approaches correct for the basic problem: the economy's shortage of jobs and its plethora of low-wage jobs.

The Congressional Record. February 21, 1991: S 2232.

BALANCED BUDGET AMENDMENT (JUNE 1992)

Given the context of massive budget deficits, a constitutional amendment requiring the budget of the United States to be balanced at all times except during emergencies like war seemed like a "magic bullet" that would force spending to be controlled, taxes to be raised, or some combination of the two to be enacted. The idea underlying the balanced budget amendment was that a constitutional amendment would force Congress, the president, and other political leaders to balance the budget.

President Bush supported the balanced budget amendment because he believed that the long-term consequences of massive deficits would hurt future generations: money spent paying off the debt could not be used for needed projects in the future. Also, a budget deficit is a transfer of burden between the generations: people today enjoy the benefit of government spending, but people tomorrow have to repay the debt. Finally, he argued that the political pressures preventing a balanced budget were too severe to be broken by ordinary politics. Therefore, only a constitutional amendment could break the impasse.

Opponents of the balanced budget amendment, including Congressman Romano Mazzoli (D-KY), rejected most of Bush's points. They admitted that budget deficits were a transfer of burden between generations and opposed continuing to run up massive deficits. However, they argued that a constitutional amendment was like trying to do brain surgery with a club: it was too crude a tool for the job. Ordinary political practice could, they insisted, create budgets that were balanced. They also pointed out that the amendment process is slow and uncertain; in the interim, large deficits might be maintained. Other critics also feared that budget reductions would largely come in the areas of domestic policy, cutting aid and support for programs aimed at the poor and at education.

The proposed balanced budget amendment never made it out of Congress. Despite calls for a convention of states to force an amendment—another means by which the Constitution can be amended—no action along these lines was taken, either. Instead, budget deficits continued to mount throughout the Bush administration.

However, due to a combination of tax increases and economic growth that began in the Bush administration and continued through Clinton's two terms, the federal budget began to run a surplus starting in 1998. In fact, projected surpluses surpass $1.6 trillion from 2000 to 2010. (These surpluses are only projections, however, and should the economy weaken thereby reducing tax revenues, should taxes be cut, or should government spending be increased, the projected surpluses will disappear.) As of 2000, then, the balanced budget amendment is a dead issue in contemporary politics.

BUSH'S RADIO ADDRESS TO THE NATION ON THE BALANCED BUDGET AMENDMENT

June 6, 1992

I want to talk to you today about a big idea, a big change in the way your Government works. For the past 12 years, President Reagan and I have tried to get Congress to act responsibly and restrain Federal spending. We've tried compromise. We've tried confrontation. And we've tried quiet diplomacy with the leaders of Congress. None of this has been enough. And so, my friends, the time has come to take some common-sense action. We must pass a constitutional amendment mandating a balanced budget.

For most of our Nation's history, there was an unwritten rule against deficit financing, against saddling future generations with a mountain of debt. But in recent times, we've moved away from that. Now, we're borrowing from the future to pay for indulgences of the present. Our future is at stake. To ensure long-term economic growth, we must get Federal spending under control.

I've called for big changes in many areas, reforms in how this Nation's gridlocked capital does business. Right now, we're coming out of tough times. The American people know that budget deficits threaten the long-term economic health of our country. Over the years, we've accumulated Federal debt totaling $65,000 for every family of four. This doesn't create more wealth. It merely helps pay for our current consumption. And that's like taking out a car loan and never buying a car.

To make our economic future strong, the balanced budget is where we must start. Beginning well before I became your President, I have fought for a balanced budget amendment. As a matter of fact, on February 9th, 1989, the very first legislative proposal that I made as President was for Congress to adopt a balanced budget constitutional amendment. In each of the three budgets I've submitted since, I've repeated that plea.

Why am I so fiercely dedicated to this issue? Look at your own family. You know what happens when you spend more than you make. The devil's going to come demanding his due. Well, that's what our American family faces right now.

When you hear about a deficit measured in hundreds of billions of dollars, remember that's not "Monopoly" money. Some day, that debt must be paid with your money, as sure as your own personal debts will have to be paid with your money. It's unacceptable when this spending riptide has us drowning in debt, dragging us further out to sea.

This amendment will bring us back to shore. Forty-four States already have some type of constitutional balanced budget requirement. Eighty percent of the American people want this amendment and the tougher scrutiny of Government spending which it will require.

We're fed up. We know it's time for partisan posturing to yield to responsibility to govern. It's time to stop treating our Federal Treasury like the corner cash machine.

Thomas Jefferson's words still ring true: "I place public debt as the greatest of the dangers to be feared." Today, we have within our grasp the power to conquer that fear. The key to this is twofold: We must control reckless Government spending, and we must encourage economic growth.

. . .

We have a moral imperative to act on behalf of future generations. They are not yet here to represent themselves. It's time to protect our children and our children's children. And we're determined to enact this solemn bond between generations.

Public Papers of the President: George Bush. June 6, 1992: 903–904.

WE DO NOT NEED TO LEGISLATE IN ORDER TO BALANCE THE BUDGET

June 9, 1992

Mr. Romano Mazzoli (D-KY). Mr. Speaker, we have reached the long awaited and much heralded balanced budget week. If there has ever been a week that has been oversold and hyped beyond belief, this is that week.

Let me try to go back to the start to frame the issue. We do not need, and let me say it again: We do not need to adopt any balanced budget legislation, whether it is a statute or an amendment, in order to balance the budget. We can balance the budget by having an enforcement package with teeth to cut spending and raise revenues, and we have to have, of course, the intestinal fortitude, or, as we say in Kentucky, the guts, to adopt this enforcement package.

But once again, Mr. Speaker, we do not need to pass any new legislation.

The enforcement package would be prickly, politically very potent and highly controversial, painful—all those things definitely. But that is the way to balance a budget.

Let me go back also for one other basic lesson. If a balanced budget amendment were adopted this week, that would not automatically balance the budget. Of course an amendment would have to go to the States for ratification, and that would take months, maybe years. Maybe it would never be ratified. But one way or the other, if a balanced budget amendment is adopted this week, we do not necessarily and automatically balance the budget.

I see that we have three options. One is the conventional option facing us this week. As we do so often when faced with a tough issue, we simply try to dodge it or finesse it, avoid it, and hope that somehow the confluence of time and events will cause that to sort of go away.

Now, we consider the balanced budget amendment first in the committee, where you only need a majority vote. But then the action of the committee has to be ratified by the House, where you need two-thirds. There is a possibility that we could wrangle for hours and go on for this entire week, pass a balanced budget amendment in the committee, but not adopt it in the House, come up empty handed, wring our hands, say how cruel fate is, and then maybe go back to business as usual.

That, I think, would be cynical. I think it would be hypocritical, and I think it would be deemed such by the people. I think it would deepen the cynicism and the concern people have, disaffection for the way business is being done in Washington. I hope we avoid that fate and outcome.

The second option I think we have, Mr. Speaker, is somewhat less conventional than option No. 1, and that is pass the Stenholm balanced budget amendment, with all the uncertainties that we have about it as to whether it will work or whether it might work too well, whether it will be ratified by the States, whether it will hurt the people we like to help and help the people we would like not to help. But one way or the other, we could do that.

That would be very unconventional, because we seldom pass balanced budget amendments, or any amendment, to the Constitution.

We could then—while it goes to the States for the 1 year or 2 years or whatever it takes to ratify it—go back to business as usual and not have any awareness of where we are in the budget cycle.

I would hope that if it were to be passed we would consider that framework, but it is possible we would not.

The third option, Mr. Speaker, is totally unconventional, revolutionary, but I just humbly offer it. I think what we should really do is to take 1 week or 2 weeks or 3 weeks off, clear the deck, and, under the openness of the most open rule put on this floor, the entire Internal Revenue Tax Code and all spending in all of the three categories of Government, domestic, international, and defense, and let this House and every Member in it have a go at developing a deficit reduction package. See what we could come up with.

All of the steps are vexatious, difficult, and painful for our friends and painful for all of the special interests, but I think that this procedure would give every Member of Congress a real feeling that he or she was involved in this, and, by extension, all the people of this country would be very much involved in what we did.

We would really be trying to get to the heart of the issue. Not to pass a balanced budget amendment or a balanced budget statute, but to really balance the budget.

So I would say, Mr. Speaker, as I have used my time, to go back to the basics. You do not need a balanced budget amendment to balance the budget. You do need the intestinal fortitude and a package.

I hope at the end of the day, whenever that day is, that Congress will measure up to that task.

The Congressional Record. June 9, 1992: H 4430.

NORTH AMERICAN FREE TRADE AGREEMENT
(DECEMBER 1992)

Free trade is one of the central components of the U.S. economy. By promoting the trading of goods and services across international borders easily and quickly, free trade makes it possible to hold costs to a minimum: goods and services can be produced in lower-cost nations and then brought to the United States, where the cost savings can be passed on to consumers in the form of lower prices. However, as a consequence of this cross-border trade, Americans who once produced the goods or service now being created elsewhere often lose their jobs. Thus free trade has real, painful consequences for some even as it benefits many others. This is a prescription for a controversial political issue.

George Bush promoted free trade, believing that on balance the benefits derived from open trade relations outweighed the costs. The greatest example of this philosophy negotiated by the United States in recent years was the North American Free Trade Agreement (NAFTA), which established free trade relations among the United States, Canada, and Mexico. Bush argued that such agreements would do more than just create an economic benefit for the United States; open relations would promote democracy, build trust, and assist in strengthening international police efforts to control drugs, illegal immigration, and other hemispheric problems.

Critics of NAFTA and other free trade agreements made a number of points. Congressman Peter Barca (D-WI) and others feared that the substantially lower cost of labor in Mexico and other relatively poor countries would cause American companies to move south and cost many Americans their jobs. (Businessman and former presidential candidate Ross Perot famously said that NAFTA would create a "giant sucking sound" of American jobs being pulled south of the border.) They also pointed out that even if benefits accrued to the United States, these benefits would not come for a long time. In the interim, many people would suffer. Finally, they were concerned that the lack of strong environmental, labor, and workplace safety rules in many countries outside the United States would mean that, morally, Americans were benefiting from the exploitation of international workers.

While it was negotiated and signed by President Bush, NAFTA was actually ratified by the U.S. Senate during Bill Clinton's presidency. While many Americans did lose their jobs as a consequence, the number lost never created the "giant, sucking sound" of Ross Perot's nightmares. The 1990s was, instead, a period of economic boom in the United States, although it is impossible to attribute such growth to NAFTA as a sole cause. The United States has continued to negotiate free trade agreements as part of its underlying economic philosophy, most recently with China.

BUSH'S REMARKS ON SIGNING THE NORTH AMERICAN FREE TRADE AGREEMENT

December 17, 1992

Let me just now get on with some comments about this agreement and about the common business that brings us all together, the affairs of this hemisphere. Throughout history, the destiny of nations has often been shaped by change and by chance and by the things—when I say chance, I'm talking about things that happen to them. And then there are those unique nations who shape their destinies by choice, by the things that they make happen.

Three such nations come together today, Mexico, Canada, and the United States. And by signing the North American free trade agreement, we've committed ourselves to a better future for our children and for generations yet unborn. This agreement will remove barriers to trade and investment across the two largest undefended borders of the globe and link the United States in a permanent partnership of growth with our first and third largest trading partners.

The peace and friendship that we've long enjoyed as neighbors will now be strengthened by the explosion of growth and trade let loose by the combined energies of our 360 million citizens trading freely across our borders.

. . .

It's especially fitting that an American President sign this agreement in this great Hall of the Americas, the home of the Organization of American States. You see, the NAFTA represents the first giant step towards fulfillment of a dream that has long inspired us all, the dream of a hemisphere united by economic cooperation and free competition. Because of what we have begun here today, I believe the time will soon come when trade is free from Alaska to Argentina; when every citizen of the Americas has the opportunity to share in new growth and expanding prosperity.

I hope and trust that the North American free trade area can be extended to Chile, other worthy partners in South America and Central America and the Caribbean. Free trade throughout the Americas is an idea whose time has come. A new generation of democratic leaders has staked its future on that promise. And under their leadership, a tide of economic reform and trade liberalization is transforming the hemisphere.

Today, as a result, the hemisphere is growing again. For the first time in years, more capital is flowing into the Americas for new investment than is flowing out. Every major debtor nation, from Mexico to Argentina, has negotiated a successful agreement to reduce and restructure its commercial bank debt under the Brady plan.

. . .

To fulfill its promise, democratic government must guarantee not only the right to regular elections but human rights and property rights, swift and impartial justice, and the rule of law. Democratic governments must deliver basic services. Their institutions must be strengthened and must be modernized. To defend democracy successfully, the OAS must strengthen the tools at its disposal, and I commend the new steps that you took this week to suspend nondemocratic regimes. Together we must also create new means to end historic border disputes and to control the competition in conventional weaponry.

In all of this, I believe my country, the United States of America, bears a special responsibility. We face a moment of maximum opportunity but also, let's face it, continued risk. And we must remain engaged, for more than ever before our future, our future, is bound up with the future of the Americas.

. . .

. . . And today with the signing of the North American Free Trade Agreement, we take another giant step towards making the dream a reality.

Public Papers of the President: George Bush. December 17, 1992: 2200–2203.

CRITICISM OF THE NORTH AMERICAN FREE TRADE AGREEMENT

November 16, 1993

Mr. Peter Barca (D-WI). Mr. Speaker, the goal of any trade agreement, including this NAFTA, must be to expand economic growth, enhance the export opportunities of American businesses, and promote a higher standard of living so that businesses can create more family-supporting jobs for American workers. Generally, providing free and fair trade throughout the world has helped to accomplish these goals. However, this NAFTA does not provide meaningful assurances that these goals can be accomplished. Therefore, I will oppose this NAFTA and work toward developing a better approach to meeting these goals.

It is imperative that we do not pass a flawed NAFTA because once Congress goes down this path, we set the standard for future free-trade agreements which will certainly be forthcoming. Most importantly, this NAFTA would lock the United States into a long-term agreement that would affect generations of Americans. The stakes are very high due to the fact that this agreement threatens American businesses' ability to provide family-supporting jobs for Americans. It has been a strong domestic economy which has propelled this Nation to be the leader of world economic growth since World War II.

. . .

There are three fundamental problems with this NAFTA which were not adequately addressed through the side agreements, problems that lead me to believe that this NAFTA is not in the best interest of our country.

First, the NAFTA was not negotiated on the most favorable terms to the United States. One of the problems is that current policies governing trade between Mexico and the United States are so badly slanted against this country. Mexican tariffs on United States goods are in many cases two or three times—and is some cases eight times—higher than United States tariffs on Mexican goods. NAFTA does not eliminate this imbalance in a timely manner.

. . .

The second fundamental problem with this NAFTA is that most of the benefits for our country will not accrue for a number of years, and then only if there is a growing standard of living for Mexican workers in order to provide them with more purchasing power to buy American goods.

. . .

The third fundamental problem with NAFTA is that the side agreements lack real enforcement mechanisms to ensure the enforcement of national environmental and labor laws, which is the stated goal of the side agreements.

. . .

In addition to these three fundamental problems with this NAFTA text itself, I have further concerns about how the agreement could affect our country.

NAFTA will serve as a dangerous pattern for negotiating trade agreements with other Latin American nations. Chile and the Caribbean nations are already waiting in line to gain the benefits of NAFTA. I am concerned that unless we negotiate the best possible terms under this NAFTA, we will end up creating a precedent that will be repeated again and again.

Also, and equally important, is attempting to finance the costs of implementing NAFTA, especially when the priority at the Federal level has been reducing the budget deficit. The administration must find a minimum of $2.5 billion in revenues or spending cuts up front to pay for the lower tariff revenues as a result of NAFTA and a bare bones worker retraining program. The total costs of NAFTA could exceed $30 billion, with funds earmarked for border cleanup and development and dislocated worker retraining. Regrettably, the proposal to raise more than $1 billion through increasing international airline passenger fees by 20 percent is not even directly related to NAFTA. There are not too many other revenue sources to finance NAFTA without hindering deficit reduction efforts.

Furthermore, this NAFTA comes at a time when our economy is still fragile. It would contribute to the loss of several hundred thousand American jobs based on credible estimates, with millions of related jobs made vulnerable. Our manufacturing jobs support a large number of related jobs in the community. That's why we can ill afford to further erode our job-supporting manufacturing base.

. . .

A vote against this NAFTA should not be interpreted as a vote to reject increased trade with Mexico and Canada. We already have a free-trade agreement with Canada which I publicly supported as a member of the State legislature. I strongly support free and fair trade, especially among industrialized countries and with the further goal of increasing trade throughout the Americas.

. . .

. . . The first step is to set aside this NAFTA. So I will be voting "no" when this NAFTA is presented to Congress and calling for an agreement that adequately addresses the concerns of the people of Wisconsin and accomplishes the goals of free and fair trade.

The Congressional Record. November 16, 1993: E 2909.

MILITARY AND FOREIGN POLICY

INVASION OF PANAMA (DECEMBER 1989)

Among recent U.S. presidents, Bush has been among the most willing to commit U.S. forces to combat. One example of this was the 1989 intervention in Panama to oust its leader, General Manuel Noriega. The United States has long had a special relationship with Panama: until 1999, the United States controlled the middle ten miles of Panama on either side of the Panama Canal; and the United States played a central role in the creation of Panama itself by supporting its independence from Colombia at the turn of the twentieth century. In 1989 a crisis developed in U.S.–Panamanian relations when General Manuel Noriega, once a close ally of the United States, seized power and rejected the election of a new government. Noriega was also accused of drug trafficking.

In December 1989, Bush ordered U.S. forces to occupy Panama, capture Noriega, and put the elected government back in power. He defended this policy on the grounds that Noriega was an accused drug dealer, had usurped power, and had threatened the lives of American citizens. His actions, Bush claimed, were intended to protect and restore democracy both in Panama and in the rest of the region.

Critics including Senator Ted Kennedy (D-MA) pointed out that the United States had long supported Noriega's rise to power, that Panama could hardly threaten the United States, and that by sending in troops the United States once again acted as it had so often in Central America: as the bully who imposed its will whenever it wanted. They also insisted that the U.S. action was illegal under international law. This point was backed up by the Organization of American States, an international organization that attempts to address issues of common concern in the Western Hemisphere.

The invasion of Panama was relatively easy, with the exception of a period of lawlessness in which U.S. troops stood by as local citizens looted and attacked targets in Panama City. Noriega was captured after hiding out in an embassy for several days. He has since been convicted of drug trafficking and is now in prison in the United States. Further, the invasion helped Bush's popularity: presidents often benefit from the "rally 'round the flag" phenomenon when international crises emerge and the American people support their leaders' actions. The support Bush received was short lived, however, and he lost the 1992 presidential election despite his success in Panama.

The elected government of Panama has remained democratic. In 2000, as required by a previously negotiated treaty, the United States turned control of the Panama Canal over to Panama itself. This transfer went smoothly, and the canal remains open to shipping from around the world. Panama remains a transit point for drug shipments from South America to the United States, however, and the 1989 intervention once again made relations between the United States and its southern neighbors difficult. At each intervention, the United States appears to its neighbors to be a bully that uses its powers to force others to follow rules that the United States itself often violates—such as not intervening in other nations' affairs. Mostly the U.S.–Panama relationship remains one of benign neglect: so long as nothing Panama does threatens or bothers the United States, the Americans leave Panama to handle its own affairs.

BUSH'S ADDRESS TO THE NATION ANNOUNCING UNITED STATES MILITARY ACTION IN PANAMA

December 20, 1989

My fellow citizens, last night I ordered U.S. military forces to Panama. No President takes such action lightly. This morning I want to tell you what I did and why I did it.

For nearly 2 years, the United States, nations of Latin America and the Caribbean have worked together to resolve the crisis in Panama. The goals of the United States have been to safeguard the lives of Americans, to defend democracy in Panama, to combat drug trafficking, and to protect the integrity of the Panama Canal treaty. Many attempts have been made to resolve this crisis through diplomacy and negotiations. All were rejected by the dictator of Panama, General Manuel Noriega, an indicted drug trafficker.

Last Friday, Noriega declared his military dictatorship to be in a state of war with the United States and publicly threatened the lives of Americans in Panama. The very next day, forces under his command shot and killed an unarmed American serviceman; wounded another; arrested and brutally beat a third American serviceman; and then brutally interrogated his wife, threatening her with sexual abuse. That was enough.

General Noriega's reckless threats and attacks upon Americans in Panama created an imminent danger to the 35,000 American citizens in Panama. As President, I have no higher obligation than to safeguard the lives of American citizens. And that is why I directed our Armed Forces to protect the lives of American citizens in Panama and to bring General Noriega to justice in the United States. I contacted the bipartisan leadership of Congress last night and informed them of this decision, and after taking this action, I also talked with leaders in Latin America, the Caribbean, and those of other U.S. allies.

. . .

The brave Panamanians elected by the people of Panama in the elections last May, President Guillermo Endara and Vice Presidents Calderon and Ford, have assumed the rightful leadership of their country. You remember those horrible pictures of newly elected Vice President Ford, covered head to toe with blood, beaten mercilessly by so-called "dignity battalions." Well, the United States today recognizes the democratically elected government of President Endara. I will send our Ambassador back to Panama immediately.

Key military objectives have been achieved. Most organized resistance has been eliminated, but the operation is not over yet: General Noriega is in hiding. And nevertheless, yesterday a dictator ruled Panama, and today constitutionally elected leaders govern.

I have today directed the Secretary of the Treasury and the Secretary of State to lift the economic sanctions with respect to the democratically elected government of Panama and, in cooperation with that government, to take steps to effect an orderly unblocking of Panamanian Government assets in the United States. I'm fully committed to implement the Panama Canal treaties and turn over the Canal to Panama in the year 2000. The actions we have taken and the cooperation of a new, democratic government in Panama will permit us to honor these commitments. As soon as the new government recommends a qualified candidate—Panamanian—to be Administrator of the Canal, as called for in the treaties, I will submit this nominee to the Senate for expedited consideration.

I am committed to strengthening our relationship with the democratic nations in this hemisphere. I will continue to seek solutions to the problems of this region through dialog and multilateral diplomacy. I took this action only after reaching the conclusion that every other avenue was closed and the lives of American citizens were in grave danger. I hope that the people of Panama will put this dark chapter of dictatorship behind them and move forward together as citizens of a democratic Panama with this government that they themselves have elected.

The United States is eager to work with the Panamanian people in partnership and friendship to rebuild their economy. The Panamanian people want democracy, peace, and the chance for a better life in dignity and freedom. The people of the United States seek only to support them in pursuit of these noble goals.

Public Papers of the President: George Bush. December 20, 1989: 1722–1724.

CRITICISM OF THE PANAMA INVASION

January 23, 1990

Mr. Ted Kennedy (D-MA). Mr. President, now that United States troops
are coming home from Panama, it is time for Congress to begin to reflect
on the implications of the United States invasion of that country.

No one questions the bravery of the American service men and women
who carried out this mission. They responded with skill and courage to
the call of the President, and all of us mourn those who were lost.

But I have serious reservations about the justification for the invasion
itself. The administration has offered four rationales for its action. It
claims that the invasion was necessary to:

Save American lives;

Protect the Panama Canal;

Restore democracy to Panama; and

Bring General Noriega to justice.

Nothing on the public record makes any of these justifications persuasive. Certainly, the United States does not have the right under international law or any other law that I know of to roam the hemisphere,
bringing dictators to justice or installing new governments by force on
other nations. Surely, it is a contradiction in terms and a violation of
America's best ideals to impose democracy by the barrel of a gun on
Panama or any other nation.

There was no imminent threat to the Panama Canal. In fact, for the
first time in its history, the canal was shut down—because of the U.S.
invasion.

Was the invasion necessary to save American lives? We will never
know the true answer to that question, because we will never know what
would have happened had there been no invasion. But we do know
certain facts.

In October, President Bush had been embarrassed and criticized for
failing to do enough to ensure the success of a coup against General
Noriega. The coup failed, perhaps because of U.S. blunders.

On the Friday before the invasion, the Noriega-created Panama Assembly passed a resolution saying that a "State of War Exists" in Panama, and listing a series of what it considered acts of aggression by the
United States against Panama, including United States economic sanctions. It is difficult to call this resolution a declaration of war by Panama
against the United States.

. . .

Contrary to the administration's threadbare and legalistic claims, the invasion violated our fundamental commitments under the United Nations Charter and the Charter of the Organization of American States. The administration's claim that the invasion was somehow justified as an act of self defense is not credible. It is no surprise that the United States was overwhelmingly rebuked for the invasion—by a vote of 20 to 1 in the Organization of American States, and by a vote of 75 to 20 in the United Nations General Assembly.

In the Declaration of Independence, the Founders of our Nation proclaimed their liberty and spoke of "a decent respect to the opinions of mankind." Two centuries later, we have still not learned to pay that respect.

The Congressional Record. January 23, 1990: S 12.

THE PERSIAN GULF WAR (JANUARY 1991)

When Iraq invaded and occupied Kuwait in August 1990, it took possession of a small, dusty country that happened to sit upon a significant percentage of the world's oil reserves. Iraq launched its invasion for a number of reasons, few of which were publicly discussed in the United States at the time: Kuwait and its ally, Saudi Arabia, were demanding repayment of loans given Iraq while Iraq was engaged in a long war with their mutual enemy, Iran; and there were territorial disputes between Iraq and Kuwait. Just days before the invasion, Iraq checked with the U.S. ambassador to Iraq to determine whether the United States was concerned about its dispute with Kuwait. The ambassador declared that the United States had "no opinion" about the conflict and considered it an internal Arab affair.

After Iraq occupied Kuwait, however, the United States developed an opinion. President Bush argued that it was necessary for the United States to drive Iraq out of Kuwait for a number of reasons. He was direct about the economic threat posed by a potentially hostile country controlling significant amounts of the world's petroleum reserves. He also noted that the Persian Gulf region needed to be stable if the American economy was to remain stable. Most important, he insisted that under American leadership a "new world order" could be created in which one nation's aggression against another would be met by the combined actions of the world's powers. This would lead to a new era of peace since no nation could reasonably expect to attack another and reap any benefit from its operation.

Opponents such as Congressman Charles Rangel (D-NY) made a number of counterarguments to Bush's statement. They pointed out that force seemed to be Bush's first option rather than his last. In addition, they noted that no real effort had been made to discover the sources of the original conflict; thus, while a military victory might be gained, no real solution to the problem could be generated. They also questioned whether a "new world order" meant anything other than the United States killing enemies in the name of peace. Finally, many critics doubted whether the operation fully complied with the War Powers Act, the 1973 law which requires the president to get the approval of Congress if U.S. forces will be in harm's way for more than sixty days.

The military operations against Iraq's forces were very successful when they were launched in January 1991. Iraq's forces were destroyed in seven weeks, although their leader, Saddam Hussein, was not driven from power, and Kuwait's government was restored. President Bush's popularity skyrocketed in the aftermath of the war. In spring 1991 his job approval ratings polled at 91 percent—a number no president had seen before or since. Yet, in the context of a weak domestic economy, his approval ratings did not translate to long-term popular support. Bush lost the 1992 presidential election despite his Persian Gulf triumph.

In the years following the Persian Gulf War, Iraq has remained a thorn in the side of U.S. policy makers. No-fly zones were established in northern and southern Iraq to prevent the Iraqi air force from engaging in operations against dissidents in those regions. These zones remain in effect, and U.S. forces continue to patrol and enforce the no-fly rules, regularly attacking targets in these areas. Also in the aftermath, an embargo and inspection program was established to force Iraq to end its biological, chemical, and nuclear weapons programs in return for the right to buy food and medical supplies on the world market. The sanctions remain in effect, and Iraq has suspended the inspections program. Finally, Saddam Hussein remains in power. However, in partial reward for U.S. support during the war, both Kuwait and Saudi Arabia flooded the world with oil in the 1990s, helping to keep its price low and the U.S. economy growing. Only in 2000 did this surplus of oil decline, leading to increased fuel costs and threatening U.S. economic growth.

BUSH'S ADDRESS TO THE NATION ANNOUNCING ALLIED MILITARY ACTION IN THE PERSIAN GULF

January 16, 1991

Just 2 hours ago, allied air forces began an attack on military targets in Iraq and Kuwait. These attacks continue as I speak. Ground forces are not engaged.

This conflict started August 2d when the dictator of Iraq invaded a small and helpless neighbor. Kuwait—a member of the Arab League and a member of the United Nations—was crushed; its people, brutalized. Five months ago, Saddam Hussein started this cruel war against Kuwait. Tonight, the battle has been joined.

This military action, taken in accord with United Nations resolutions and with the consent of the United States Congress, follows months of constant and virtually endless diplomatic activity on the part of the United Nations, the United States, and many, many other countries. Arab leaders sought what became known as an Arab solution, only to conclude that Saddam Hussein was unwilling to leave Kuwait. Others traveled to Baghdad in a variety of efforts to restore peace and justice. Our Secretary of State, James Baker, held an historic meeting in Geneva, only to be totally rebuffed. This past weekend, in a last-ditch effort, the Secretary-General of the United Nations went to the Middle East with peace in his heart—his second such mission. And he came back from Baghdad with no progress at all in getting Saddam Hussein to withdraw from Kuwait.

Now the 28 countries with forces in the Gulf area have exhausted all reasonable efforts to reach a peaceful resolution—have no choice but to drive Saddam from Kuwait by force. We will not fail.

. . .

Our objectives are clear: Saddam Hussein's forces will leave Kuwait. The legitimate government of Kuwait will be restored to its rightful place, and Kuwait will once again be free. Iraq will eventually comply with all relevant United Nations resolutions, and then, when peace is restored, it is our hope that Iraq will live as a peaceful and cooperative member of the family of nations, thus enhancing the security and stability of the Gulf.

Some may ask: Why act now? Why not wait? The answer is clear: The world could wait no longer. Sanctions, though having some effect, showed no signs of accomplishing their objective. Sanctions were tried for well over 5 months, and we and our allies concluded that sanctions alone would not force Saddam from Kuwait.

While the world waited, Saddam Hussein systematically raped, pillaged, and plundered a tiny nation, no threat to his own. He subjected the people of Kuwait to unspeakable atrocities—and among those maimed and murdered, innocent children.

While the world waited, Saddam sought to add to the chemical weapons arsenal he now possesses, an infinitely more dangerous weapon of mass destruction—a nuclear weapon. And while the world waited, while the world talked peace and withdrawal, Saddam Hussein dug in and moved massive forces into Kuwait.

While the world waited, while Saddam stalled, more damage was being done to the fragile economies of the Third World, emerging democracies of Eastern Europe, to the entire world, including to our own economy.

The United States, together with the United Nations, exhausted every means at our disposal to bring this crisis to a peaceful end. However, Saddam clearly felt that by stalling and threatening and defying the United Nations, he could weaken the forces arrayed against him.

While the world waited, Saddam Hussein met every overture of peace with open contempt. While the world prayed for peace, Saddam prepared for war.

I had hoped that when the United States Congress, in historic debate, took its resolute action, Saddam would realize he could not prevail and would move out of Kuwait in accord with the United Nation resolutions. He did not do that. Instead, he remained intransigent, certain that time was on his side.

Saddam was warned over and over again to comply with the will of the United Nations: Leave Kuwait, or be driven out. Saddam has arrogantly rejected all warnings. Instead, he tried to make this a dispute between Iraq and the United States of America.

Well, he failed. Tonight, 28 nations—countries from 5 continents, Europe and Asia, Africa, and the Arab League—have forces in the Gulf area standing shoulder to shoulder against Saddam Hussein. These countries had hoped the use of force could be avoided. Regrettably, we now believe that only force will make him leave.

Public Papers of the President: George Bush. January 16, 1991: 42–45.

HOW MUCH ABUSE CAN THE CONSTITUTION TAKE?

October 18, 1990

Mr. Charles Rangel (D-NY). Mr. Speaker, President Bush's decision to face down Iraqi aggression against Kuwait has won the wholehearted support of the United Nations. The United States Congress and the American people, too, have rightfully supported the President's decision to say no to the Iraqi dictator Saddam Hussein. I expected no less. The American people traditionally rally behind the flag and the President when it comes to defending our interest overseas.

But how much better would it have been—and how much more secure would the American people and Congress be in our decision to support the President—if he had come to us with a full explanation of his actions? And would we all not feel a lot more comfortable if the President had taken the trouble to get the Congress' approval before shipping off more than 200,000 of our young people to wait on the sands of Saudi Arabia for a war that hardly anyone wants?

In my view, and that of a growing number of Americans, the use of force must be avoided. A diplomatic solution must be found.

Now that our troops are there, I understand the President is trying to forestall the firestorm of protests from Congress that would probably be unleashed if he chose to take unilateral military action in the gulf. According to reports in the press, the President has been briefing selected Members of Congress on the possible use of force after the Congress adjourns for elections.

The President is correct in his anticipation of a congressional outcry; I for one would protest loudly if the Chief Executive opted to initiate another military adventure while no one was minding the store. That is why I have joined with other Members of Congress in asking speaker Thomas Foley to immediately reconvene the House in the event of the outbreak of conflict during the election recess. With thousands of young lives at stake, responsible Government demands Congress' constitutional checks and balances.

The President has twice spirited American military men and women thousands of miles from our shores; each time without the benefit of official prior notification of Congress. Last December during the Christmas holidays, we invaded Panama; and the last August, during the summer vacation, our troops were dispatched to the Persian Gulf. Neither time did the President officially inform the Congress of his full intentions or sought its approval, as required under the War Powers Act.

The War Powers Act of 1974 requires a president who commits U.S. forces to imminent hostility to inform Congress of his actions and get congressional approval within 60 days. In the case of the Persian Gulf, congressional notification would be required this month since our deployment of troops to the Persian Gulf began in August. But if the President repeats his performance in the Panama invasion, we in the Congress would not be made privy to impending war in the Persian Gulf—much less asked for approval. I had not the slightest inkling that 25,000 American troops had landed in Panama until I heard about it on CNN. The President has yet to consult or to inform the Congress officially under War Powers.

My concern about the War Powers Act is far from academic. Following the calamity of Vietnam, the law represents our only protection against unilateral, and potentially disastrous military adventures by the executive branch. The War Powers Act was put in place by the Congress to prevent another tragedy of the kind witnessed in Vietnam.

The law is meant, not to put unreasonable restraints on the President, but to ensure that the entire nation—through the Congress—is informed and consulted first in the event of dire action in the national interest. It was meant to prevent the ruinous political fracturing of the Nation such as occurred over Vietnam, by making sure the Congress—and thus the people—were fully behind the actions of the Commander in Chief.

Sadly, since its passage, the War Powers Act has been ignored by every president who could have used it to his advantage. Instead of abiding by the law to rally official congressional approval for controversial actions, they dodged; each time leaving our foreign policy open to charges of domestic as well as international lawlessness. So far, President Bush seems to be continuing in that tradition.

· · ·

What good does it do us as a nation to break our own laws while claiming to defend the sovereignty of Kuwait? How do we support American standards of justice and morality if, in defending the rest of the world, we offend the very Constitution that protects us at home?

After all, how much abuse can the Constitution take?

The Congressional Record. October 18, 1990: E 3348.

STRATEGIC ARMS REDUCTION TREATY (JULY 1991)

As the Soviet Union neared collapse, its leaders became more desperate to sign treaties with the United States to allow it to cut and control its extremely high costs for weapons, both nuclear and conventional. Thus, negotiations that had stalled for years began to be expedited in the early years of the Bush presidency. One example of this is the Strategic Arms Reduction Treaty (START). Aimed at reducing the number of nuclear weapons, not just controlling their proliferation as previous treaties had tried to do, START was an attempt to change the arms race into a process of arms reduction.

President Bush favored the treaty because he believed that the opportunity to reduce the size of the U.S. and Soviet nuclear arsenals was an important one. Further, he argued that since appropriate systems of verification had been put into effect by this treaty, cheating would be difficult and no side could gain an advantage. Finally, he insisted that building a positive relationship with the Soviet Union in the area of arms reduction would have long-term benefits for the United States.

Opponents of START, notably Senator Jesse Helms (R-NC), argued that with the collapse of the Soviet Union it was not clear whether any political authority in Russia could sign or administer the treaty. Moreover, they worried that Soviet/Russian cheating could put U.S. national security at risk.

START was ratified by the U.S. Senate in 1992. In the short term it had little effect: the deadline for beginning arms reductions was in the future, and most Americans did not have passionate feelings about the treaty. Accordingly, it did not help George Bush win the 1992 presidential election. In the longer term, however, the treaty set in motion a series of arms-control agreements among the United States, Russia, and several former Soviet territories which possessed nuclear weapons. The absolute number of nuclear weapons has been dramatically reduced in the 1990s, and no new weapons systems have been designed or deployed. The prospects of major-power nuclear war have been reduced to almost zero.

BUSH'S REMARKS AT THE SIGNING CEREMONY FOR THE STRATEGIC ARMS REDUCTION TALKS TREATY IN MOSCOW

July 31, 1991

The treaty that we sign today is a most complicated one—the most complicated of contracts governing the most serious of concerns. Its 700 pages stand as a monument to several generations of U.S. and Soviet negotiators, to their tireless efforts to carve out common ground from a thicket of contentious issues—and it represents a major step forward for our mutual security and the cause of world peace.

. . .

The START treaty vindicates an approach to arms control that guided us for almost a decade: the belief that we could do more than merely halt the growth of our nuclear arsenals. We could seek more than limits on the number of arms. In our talks we sought stabilizing reductions in our strategic arsenals.

START makes that a reality. In a historic first for arms control, we will actually reduce U.S. and Soviet strategic nuclear arsenals. But reductions alone are not enough. So, START requires even deeper cuts of the most dangerous and destabilizing weapons. The agreement itself is exceedingly complex, but the central idea at the heart of this treaty can be put simply: Stabilizing reductions in our strategic nuclear forces reduces the risk of war.

But these promises to reduce arms levels cannot automatically guarantee success. Just as important are the treaty's monitoring mechanisms so we know that the commitments made are being translated into real security. In this area, START builds on the experience of earlier agreements—but goes far beyond them in provisions to ensure that we can verify this treaty effectively.

. . . this treaty stands as both cause and consequence. Many times during the START talks, reaching agreement seemed all but impossible. In the end, the progress that we made in the past year's time—progress in easing tensions and ending the cold war—changed the atmosphere at the negotiating table, and paved the way for START's success. Neither side won unilateral advantage over the other. Both sides committed themselves instead to achieving a strong, effective treaty—and securing the mutual stability that a good agreement would provide.

. . . by reducing arms, we reverse a half-century of steadily growing strategic arsenals. But more than that, we take a significant step forward in dispelling a half-century of mistrust. By building trust, we pave a path to peace.

We sign the START treaty as testament to the new relationship emerging between our two countries—in the promise of further progress toward lasting peace.

Public Papers of the President: George Bush. July 31, 1991: 986–987.

THE START TREATY MUST BE POSTPONED

October 25, 1991

Mr. Jesse Helms (R-NC). Mr. President, on Tuesday, President Bush and President [Mikhail] Gorbachev will meet in Madrid. They will take time out from the Middle East peace discussions to talk about President Bush's recent announcement of unilateral reductions of nuclear weapons and President Gorbachev's announcement of Soviet unilateral cuts.

Of course, the word "Soviet" is obsolete, because no one has yet come up with a convenient word or phrase descriptive of the central government of the former Soviet Union. But that very dilemma points to something far more profound when we hear that the two Presidents will be discussing arms control matters.

The reason there is no simple description of the former Soviet Union is because Russia and its neighboring republics are in flux, both in their relationships to each other and their relationships to whatever central entity results from the breakup. We know that President Gorbachev is President, but we do not know what being President of that entity means anymore. We do not know what powers the central authority will have, or even if it will have the kind of strong authority necessary to carry out successful arms control and arms control verification.

Thus it is very disturbing that President Bush and President Gorbachev will be discussing arms control measures—a sort of minisummit for bilateral arms control in the midst of the Middle East negotiations. Even if clarifications in the separate proposals of the two Presidents are achieved, the result will be a kind of de facto START II, without a treaty to assure verification.

Mr. President, the irony of all of this is that START I—the treaty signed by President Bush and President Gorbachev on July 31—does not yet have a completed text. That text is still under negotiation, and is not scheduled to be sent to the Senate until January.

This is a highly unusual situation. Indeed, Mr. President, it is a totally unprecedented situation. The text of a treaty is always required to be completed before signing, and it is made available to the public immediately. But almost 3 months have gone by, and Congress still does not know what was agreed to in all specifics. This is more than a mere quibble. It is a profound defiance of the advice and consent process.

Because of the difficulty—indeed, I believe the impossibility—of adequate verification, the treaty definitions and formulas are intricate and long. Slight changes in those formulas can have profound impact on the implementation and impact of the treaty.

Experts who have seen the drafts report that major changes in key issues resulted from the postsigning negotiations, and that the text is presently in total disarray, filled with inconsistencies and undefined terms. The still-expanding draft is reported to be more than 750 pages long. Furthermore, there is the problem of the submitted Soviet data, which is reported to contain a serious flaw.

Moreover, while the July 31 treaty was still in the process of change, the Soviet Union itself began to disintegrate. Nineteen days after the signing, the coup of hardliners representing the Soviet KGB military-industrial complex overthrew the President who signed it. The restoration of Gorbachev by Boris Yeltsin, the President of the Russian Republic, did not mean the restoration of his authority. Rather, it meant the restoration of a mere transition figure, a mere placeholder without authority and without a constituency.

At the same time, the independence movements of the former constituent republics has thrown into doubt the practical workability of the START Treaty. If there were indeed a true successor regime to the old Gorbachev regime, the new regime could simply agree to accept the START Treaty as it stands.

But there is no simple successor regime to take up the duties of the old regime under international law. The breakup of the territory leaves installations limited and prohibited by START distributed throughout the geographic region, with command and control procedures impossible to put into effect.

. . .

Mr. President, I urge President Bush to be extremely cautious in accepting any clarifications or unilateral declarations on arms control in Madrid, or even in the near future. President Gorbachev is not an appropriate partner for such discussions, because he does not have the commanding authority to make sure even that his own wishes are carried out.

In fact, Mr. President, I go further. I urge President Bush not to send the July 31 START Treaty to the Senate. The treaty must be completely renegotiated, if and when there is a competent authority with whom to negotiate.

. . .

If the situation in Russia and the other republics solidifies, and if a competent central authority emerges in the future, then it will be time to renegotiate START, beginning on equal terms and resulting in an equal treaty.

The Congressional Record. October 25, 1991: S 15247–15248.

ECONOMIC SUPPORT FOR THE FORMER SOVIET UNION (APRIL 1992)

When the Soviet Union collapsed in 1991, it posed an important set of dilemmas for the United States and its allies. Supporting Russia by helping it with economic aid meant risking that Russia would restore itself to a position of power from which it could once again threaten its Cold War enemies. Allowing it to collapse meant risking that rebellions might break out across its territory—rebellions that might lead to dissident groups or military units taking possession of pieces of the Soviet nuclear stockpile or invading neighboring countries. Either choice was difficult.

President Bush advocated providing support to the former Soviet Union on a number of grounds. First, he insisted that on simple humanitarian grounds such aid ought to be provided: people would starve without it. Second, he noted that providing aid would establish positive relations with the new Russian government. Good relations could be expected to lead to new arms-control and diplomatic agreements that would promote peaceful relations between former adversaries. And third, Bush insisted that helping Russia restore its economy would help

American businesses as they provided the goods and services the Russians required and then marketed American products to a restored Russian market.

Opponents of such support, including Congressman Charles Bennett (D-FL), argued that aid to the former Soviet Union would not return positive benefits. Instead, the Russians would rebuild their power and again threaten the United States—as, he argued, they had done before. Other opponents went so far as to argue that the apparent collapse of the Soviet Union was a ruse intended to stimulate foreign investment, which would then be used to undermine the United States and its allies.

Bush's program was supported by Congress and most of the United States' allies. A program of economic aid, targeted loans, and nuclear nonproliferation support became law in 1992. As was the case with most of Bush's foreign policy initiatives, this plan did little to influence his reelection chances, nor did it have significant effects on the Russian people in the short term.

Over time, it has become clear that the Russian economy and political system are so weak that any limited aid package run through the Russian government is virtually doomed to fail. Corrupt government officials siphoned off billions of dollars of aid for their personal use; the Russian mafia stole much of the rest; and the Russian people struggled to make the transition from a system in which most of the basic goods of life— food, housing, and education—were provided by the government to one in which individuals have to fend for themselves. As of 2000, Russia's economy remains in shambles. It is returning to power in military affairs, however, and has signed extensive arms-control agreements with the United States. Several former Soviet client states have joined the U.S.-led North American Treaty Organization (NATO) coalition, and talks have begun to bring Russia itself into the alliance. While the United States and Russia are not allies, the level and nature of their competition changed dramatically in the 1990s.

BUSH'S MESSAGE TO THE CONGRESS TRANSMITTING THE FREEDOM SUPPORT ACT PROPOSED LEGISLATION

April 3, 1992

I am pleased to transmit a legislative proposal entitled the "Freedom for Russia and Emerging Eurasian Democracies and Open Markets Support Act of 1992" (the FREEDOM Support Act of 1992). . . .

. . . With the collapse of the Soviet Union, we face [an] unprecedented historical opportunity to help freedom flourish in the new, independent states that have replaced the old Soviet Union. The success of democracy and open markets in these states is one of our highest foreign policy priorities. It can help ensure our security for years to come. And the growth of political and economic freedom in these states can also provide markets for our investors and businesses and great opportunities for friendship between our peoples.

. . .

Just as Democrats and Republicans united together for over 40 years to advance the cause of freedom during the Cold War, now we need to unite together to win the peace, a democratic peace built on the solid foundations of political and economic freedom in Russia and the other independent states.

. . .

This proposal has 10 key elements:

First, this proposal provides the necessary flexibility for the United States to extend emergency humanitarian assistance to Russia and the other new independent states.

. . .

Second, this proposal will make it easier for us to work with the Russians and others in dealing with issues of nuclear power safety and de- militarization. This proposal broadens the authority for Department of Defense monies appropriated last fall for weapons destruction and hu- manitarian transportation to make these funds, as well as foreign mili- tary financing funds, available for nonproliferation efforts, nuclear power safety, and demilitarization and defense conversion.

Third, technical assistance can help the Russians and others to help themselves as they build free markets. Seventy years of totalitarianism and command economics prevented the knowledge of free markets from taking a firm hold in the lands of Russia and Eurasia. By providing know-how, we can help the peoples and governments of the new inde- pendent states to build their own free market systems open to our trade and investment. It will also allow agencies authorized to conduct activ- ities in Eastern Europe under the "Support for East European Democracy (SEED) Act of 1989": to conduct comparable but separate activities in the independent states of the former Soviet Union. Through organizations such as a Eurasia Foundation, we will be able to support a wide range of technical assistance efforts.

Fourth, this proposal will allow us to significantly expand our technical assistance programs that facilitate democratization in the new states, including our expanding rule of law program. It will authorize support for programs such as "America Houses." It also provides support for expanded military-to-military programs with Russia and the other new independent states to cultivate a proper role for the military in a democratic society.

Fifth, this proposal provides a clear expression of bipartisan support to continue to extend Commodity Credit Corporation credit guarantees to Russia and the other new independent states in light of the progress they are making toward free markets. As they overcome their financial difficulties, we should take into account their commitment to economic freedom in providing credit guarantees that will help feed their peoples while helping American farmers.

Sixth, for American business, this proposal expands authority for credit and investment guarantee programs such as those conducted by the Overseas Private Investment Corporation (OPIC) and the Export-Import Bank. It will allow us to waive statutory ceilings on credit guarantee programs of the Export-Import Bank Act and other agencies that applied to the Soviet Union and the restrictions of the Johnson Debt Default Act on private lending. In this way, it will expand U.S. exports to and investment in Russia and the other new independent states.

Seventh, this bill will facilitate the development of the private sector in the former Soviet Union. This bill removes Cold War impediments while promoting outside investment and enhanced trade. It will also allow waiver of restrictions on imports from the independent states of the former Soviet Union beyond those applied to other friendly countries. It will support efforts to further ease Coordinating Committee (COCOM) restrictions on high technology. The bill will also allow the establishment of Enterprise Funds and a capital increase for the International Financial Corporation.

Eighth, this proposal will allow the United States to work multilaterally with other nations and the international financial institutions toward macroeconomic stabilization. At the end of World War II, the United States stood alone in helping the nations of Western Europe recover from the devastation of the war. Now, after the Cold War, we have the institutions in place—the International Monetary Fund (IMF) and the World Bank—that can play a leading role in supporting economic reform in Russia and Eurasia.

. . .

Ninth, this proposal endorses a significant U.S. contribution to a multilateral currency stabilization fund. Working with the international financial institutions and the other members of the G-7, we are putting together a stabilization fund that will support economic reform in Russia and the other independent states.

Tenth, this proposal provides for an expanded American presence in Russia and the other new independent states, facilitating both government-to-government relations and opportunities for American business. Through organizations such as the Peace Corps and the Citizens Democracy Corps, we will be able to put a large number of American advisors on the ground in the former Soviet Union.

. . .

I call upon the Congress to show the American people that in our democratic system, both parties can set aside their political differences to meet this historic challenge and to join together to do what is right.

On this occasion, there should be only one interest that drives us forward: America's national interest.

Public Papers of the President: George Bush. April 3, 1992: 542–544.

ECONOMIC AID TO RUSSIA MANY YEARS AGO POORLY REMEMBERED BY LATER RUSSIAN LEADERSHIP

September 11, 1991

Mr. Charles Bennett (D-FL). Mr. Speaker, it may be that the United States will be asked to help the Soviet Union in its projected movement toward greater democracy and a market economy; but, if history repeats itself, we are not likely to receive much thanks for our efforts according to Brig. Gen. James D. Hittle—retired, U.S. Marine Corps. In a July 15 article published in the *Navy Times,* General Hittle points out, and I agree, that the Soviets are still vigorously arming themselves. What inflames their fears of our intentions? Do we not need to see some material reductions in Soviet arms productions? I think so! General Hittle wrote in part as follows:

Should the U.S. and other economically powerful nations rescue the Soviet Union from economic disaster? That could be one of the biggest strategic questions facing the United States today.

The dangers inherent in Russian economic disintegration are serious and they are real. And, of course, when the economic basket case is, paradoxically, a super military power, as is Russia, the situation is potentially more explosive. It's all very well for armchair strategists to say that Soviet Russia can't foot the bill for an aggressive war, or that its armed forces are too demoralized and fragmented with dissension to fight.

A proposed solution, involving a switch to a free market, and a thorough overhaul of the Russian economic system, has been put together at Harvard's Kennedy School of Government by Russian economist Grigory Yavlinsky and western economists. This proposal is being hailed—in spite of its five-year $100 billion price tag—as a "grand bargain." If accepted by the United States and the other western nations footing the bill, and if supported and implemented wholeheartedly by the various factions in Russia, it just might, considering the alternatives, be a worthwhile investment in global stabilization.

But, before the United States gets carried away with enthusiasm and puts its blessing on such a massive and expensive project, we'd better pause and look back about 70 years. That's when Herbert Hoover, later to be president of the United States, headed the American Relief Administration and was embarking on a massive relief effort in communist Russia.

Passage of time alters details, but there are fundamental similarities between Russia then and now. Then Lenin had seized control of the central government, and communism was already creating havoc in Russian agriculture and the economy as a whole. This, coupled with a civil war and a drought in the Ukraine, resulted in a terrible famine. Maxim Gorki, close friend of Lenin and a famed novelist, issued an appeal for U.S. help.

Herbert Hoover, a humanitarian but a very practical-minded administrator, replied. He said the American Relief Administration was willing to help. He also did something that we should remember today as the "grand bargain" is getting its media build-up. He set some very specific conditions for aid to Russia: release of Americans held in Soviet prisons, freedom of movement for relief officials, his organization's full control of distribution of food and equal treatment of all Russians regardless of "class origins." In August, 1921, the agreement was signed by Maxim Litvanov for the U.S.S.R. and Walter L. Brown for the American Relief Association. Hoover, a firm anti-communist, in reply to criticism over giving aid to the Lenin-Trotsky regime, is reported to have angrily replied, "Twenty million people are starving. Whatever their politics, they shall be fed." And, true to his word, they were.

Close to $90 million (over $700 million in today's dollars) went into Russian aid in two years. Millions were saved from starvation.

Did it help Lenin's government? According to former American ambassador to Russia, George Kennan, the effort "importantly aided" the government not only economically "but in its political prestige and capacity for survival."

Did Russia appreciate the vital U.S. help? On July 10, 1923, Leo Kamenev, as acting president, and other commissars signed a citation scroll on behalf of the Soviet government stating official appreciation for the famine relief. The citation is indeed noteworthy as it stated, in part, that "all the people inhabiting the Union of Socialist Soviet Republics never will forget the aid rendered to them by the American people, through the agency of the American Relief Administration, holding it to be a pledge of the future friendship of the two Nations."

But, unfortunately, events had already demonstrated the hypocrisy of the Soviet pledge of friendship. In spite of Hoover's conditions, practically from the beginning of the relief project Hoover's agents complained of "lack of cooperation" by Soviet authorities and told of secret police interference. This sabotage of Hoover's efforts was a mere sample of what was yet to come.

. . .

So, now events have come full circle. Again the Russian economy is a basket case. Politically, the nation is facing ethnic separatism, and governmental central control is eroding. And, again, the hat is being passed for economic aid, this time to the tune of around $100 billion. The potential dangers of Russian economic and political disintegration are so great as to argue against a summary turndown of help. One cannot forecast, for instance, what could be the ultimate results of the Kremlin's loss of control over Russia's nuclear missile arsenal.

But, this time let's not forget that we have been down the path of Russian relief a short 70 years ago. Let's learn from that experience. If we do not learn and apply the lessons of the past, we will not run, check in hand, to Moscow.

Instead, we should put all economic aid on an installment plan, with aid payments clearly attached to specific policies and actions by the U.S.S.R. High among these actions that must be completed, or firmly set in motion are: adoption of a market economy; convertability of the ruble and, with some necessary exceptions, the abolition of price controls; privatization of property; and a distribution system that will not result in our wheat and food assistance rotting beside Russian agricultural produce.

Not the least of our requirements must be a drastic downsizing of the Soviet armed forces. It doesn't make sense for us to pour our treasures into the Soviet system while at the same time that same system, in turn, pours its dwindling resources into improving its nuclear missiles aimed at the United States.

America's heart is usually big and generous toward nations in need. We opened our pocketbooks for our former enemies after World War II. A result today is that a resurgent Germany casts its potentially dominating shadow over continental Europe, and a booming Japan is an economic and industrial titan squeezing the lifeblood out of basic U.S. industries. This time around, let's hope the United States is sufficiently hardheaded in conditioning its aid so that we are not again the victims of our own beneficence.

The Congressional Record. September 11, 1991: E 2972.

RECOMMENDED READINGS

Adams, Bob. "Foreign Policy . . . Bush Was Aggressive Player in World Affairs, But Critics Question His Effectiveness." *St. Louis Post-Dispatch,* September 13, 1992, B1.

Albright, Madeleine. "America and the League of Nations: Lessons for Today." *U.S. Department of State Dispatch* 5 (1994): 192–195.

Alexander, Bruce K. "Alternatives to the War on Drugs." *Journal of Drug Issues* 20 (1990): 1–27.

Allen, Leslie J. "Varied Reaction to Disabilities Act . . . Business Gauges the Cost of Changes." *St. Louis Post-Dispatch,* May 24, 1990, C5.

Anderson, Martin, Gary Bauer, Warren T. Brookes, Milton Friedman, David D. Hale, Daniel Mitchell, J. Daniel, Stephen Moore, Grover Norquist, Richard W. Rahn, Alan Reynolds, Phyllis Schalfly, Richard Vedder, and Murry Weidenbaum. "The Great American Tax Debate." *Policy Review* 56 (1991): 53.

"As Russia's Economy Deteriorates, Calls for Western Aid Are Increasing." *Congressional Quarterly Researcher* 3, no. 10 (1993): 227.

Barrileaux, Ryan, and Mary Stuckey, eds. *Leadership and the Bush Presidency.* Westport, Conn.: Praeger, 1992.

"Bush Foreign Policy Criticized . . . Clinton Claims Rival Has Backed Dictators." *St. Louis Post-Dispatch,* October 2, 1992, A17.

Bush, George. Inaugural Address. The Bush Presidential Library. January 20, 1989. http://bushlibrary.tamu.edu/papers/1989/89012000.html.

"Bush Under Fire for Half-Hearted Support for Rebels in Failed Anti-Noriega Coup." *Latin America Regional Reports: Mexico and Central America,* October 26, 1989, 1.

Check, Dan. "The Successes and Failures of George Bush's War on Drugs." Think for Yourself: A Drug Policy Reading Room on the Drug War. October 12, 2000. http://www.tfy.drugsense.org/bushwar.htm.

Cohen, David B. "From START to START II: Dynamism and Pragmatism in the Bush Administration's Nuclear Weapon Policies." *Presidential Studies Quarterly* 27, no. 3 (1997): 412.

Conniff, Ruth. "Perspectives on Welfare Reform; Punishment Is No Cure for

Poverty; 'Welfare Reform,' as Practiced in Several States and Proposed in California, Is a Proven Failure." *Los Angeles Times*, January 10, 1992, B7.

Conroy, Michael E., and Amy K. Glasmeier. "Unprecedented Disparities, Unparalleled Adjustments Needs: Winners and Losers on NAFTA 'Fast Track.' " *Journal of Interamerican Studies and World Affairs* 34 (1992–1993): 1–37.

"The Costs of Retaining vs. the Cost of Retraining: An Analysis of the Family and Medical Leave Act." *Hofstra Labor Law Journal* 10, no. 2 (1993): 753.

Dionne Jr., E.J. " 'Defense Intellectuals' in a New World Order; Rand Analysts Rethink the Study of Conflict." *Washington Post*, May 29, 1990, A10.

———. "Odd Alliance Questions Gulf Policy; Coalition of Left and Right Unseen Since the Eve of World War II." *Washington Post*, November 13, 1990, A1.

"Does the War Make Sense?" *Economist* 310 (1989): 25–27.

"The Education President?" *Courier-Journal* [Louisville, Ky.], December 16, 1990, D2.

Farrell, John Aloysius. "Welfare Battlefield; Bush Stakes Out Issue by Attacking 'Cycle of Dependency.' " *Boston Globe*, April 19, 1992, 1.

Fletcher, Martin. "Start Marks the End of Treaties for Superpowers." *Daily Telegraph*, July 31, 1991, 9.

Francis, David R. "Slip in US Productivity Raises Questions on Government's Role." *Christian Science Monitor*, November 14, 1990, 8.

Galbraith, John Kenneth. "The Price of Comfort; the Reagan-Bush Faith in Laissez Faire and in the Wisdom of the Market Has Cracked America's Economic Foundations." *Los Angeles Times*, January 6, 1991, M1.

Garland, Susan B., and Stephen H. Wildstrome. "The Civil Rights Champion Trying to Mend Bush's Fences." *Business Week*, December 31, 1991, 63.

Gergen, David. "The Brief on Clarence Thomas." *U.S. News & World Report*, July 15, 1991, 84.

Gleckman, Howard. "Reaganomics, Sunny-Side Up." *Business Week*, May 7, 1990, 12.

Goshko, John M. "Bush Warns Against 'Retreat' to Isolationism." *Washington Post*, December 16, 1992, A22.

Greene, John R. *The Presidency of George Bush*. Lawrence: University Press of Kansas, 2000.

"Happiness Is a Gimmick; Balanced-Budget Amendment Won't Balance Budget, or Fool Anyone." *Los Angeles Times*, May 28, 1992, B6.

Harbrecht, Douglas, and Howard Gleckman. "Bush Needs a Domestic Agenda, but He's Getting a Domestic Squabble." *Business Week*, March 1, 1990, 47.

Hayes, Margaret Daly. "The U.S. and Latin America: A Lost Decade?" *Foreign Affairs* (1989): 180.

Hoffman, David. "Major Powers Differ on How to Aid Ex-Soviet States." *Washington Post*, January 23, 1992, A1.

Holmes, Steven A. "House Backs Bush Veto of Family Leave Bill." *New York Times*, July 26, 1990, A16.

Hurst, Steven. *The Foreign Policy of the Bush Administration*. New York: Cassell, 1979.

Ingwerson, Marshall. "Bush Speech Calls for New World Order." *Christian Science Monitor*, September 13, 1990, 7.

"It's a 'New Era' for Boris and George." *St. Petersburg Times*, February 2, 1992, A1.

Jackman, Robert W. "The Politics of Economic Growth, Once Again." *Journal of Politics* 51 (1989): 646–61.

Keene, Karlyn H., Carl Everett, Jennifer Baggette, John Benson, and Karl Zinsmeister. "Blacks and Whites Hand Down Opinions." *Public Perspective* 2, no. 6 (1991): 82.

Klein, Joe, and Ann McDaniel. "What Went Wrong." *Newsweek*, August 24, 1992, 22.

Kolb, Charles. *White House Daze*. New York: Free Press, 1994.

Kuttner, Robert. "Don't Worry So Much About the Budget Deficit." *Business Week*, July 6, 1992, 18.

Lerblance, Penn. "Introducing the Americans with Disabilities Act: Promises and Challenges." *University of San Francisco Law Review* 27, no. 1 (1992): 149.

MacKenzie, Hilary. "Tainted Victory; Cleared for the Supreme Court, Clarence Thomas Leaves the U.S. People Divided over Harassment." *Maclean's*, October 28, 1991, 24.

Maechling, Charles. "Washington's Illegal Invasion." *Foreign Policy* 79 (1990): 113–31.

Maldonado, Kirk F, "Questions and Answers Regarding the Family and Medical Leave Act of 1993." *Benefits Law Journal* 7, no. 1 (1994): 73.

Marcus, Ruth. "Bush Vows to Press for Balanced-Budget Amendment." *Washington Post*, June 4, 1992, A4.

Martin, Anderson, Gary L. Bauer, Mark Blitz, Edward H. Crane, James C. Miller III, Amy Moritz, and Pine Burton. "Mid-Term Grades for the Bush Administration." *Policy Review* 55 (1991): 32.

Mervin, David. *George Bush and the Guardianship Presidency*. New York: St. Martin's 1996.

Moore, W. John. "Rethinking Drugs." *National Journal* 23, no. 5 (1991): 267.

Morganthau,Tom, Mark Miller, and Ann McDaniel. "Bennett's Drug War." *Newsweek*, August 21, 1989, 16.

Mouat, Lucia. "Lessons from a Failed Coup." *Christian Science Monitor*, October 10, 1989, 7.

"The New World Order Passes Its First Hurdle." *Independent* [London], August 12, 1990, 18.

Norpoth, Helmut, and Bruce Buchanan. "Wanted: The Education President; Issue Trespassing by Political Candidates." *Public Opinion Quarterly* 56 (1992): 87–99.

Ordovensky, Pat. "Schools Are Worth a Tax Hike." *USA Today*, September 6, 1990, D1.

Parmet, Herbert. *George Bush: The Life of a Lone Star Yankee*. New York: Scribner, 1997.

PBS Newshour Interview between Jim Lehrer and George Bush. The Public Broadcasting Station. October 5, 1998. http://www.pbs.org/newshour/bb/international/july-dec98/bush_10-5.html.

Rauch, Jonathan. "The Growth Game." *National Journal* 23, no. 4 (1991): 210.

Reding, Andrew. "The Parliament of North America?; Freer Trade Means—Ultimately—Greater Political Integration on this Continent. NAFTA Is Just a First Step." *Gazette* [Montreal], September 2, 1992, B3.

Renner, Michael. "Critical Juncture: The Future of Peacekeeping." *Worldwatch Paper* 114 (1993): 3–74.

Roberts, Paul Craig. "Bush Is Burning the Mantle He Inherited from Reagan." *Business Week*, October 22, 1990, 18.

Rohter, Larry. "Fighting in Panama, Noriega Seeks Asylum at Vatican Embassy; Future Uncertain; Panamanians Cheer." *New York Times*, December 25, 1989, 1.

Rover, Julie. "New Cries for Welfare Reform Target Able-Bodied Poor." *Congressional Quarterly Weekly Report* 50 (1992): 809–10.

Rubin, Barry M. "Reshaping the Middle East." *Foreign Affairs* 69 (1990): 131–46.

Saunders, Debra. "Reforming Welfare: Two Different Plans." *St. Louis Post-Dispatch*, October 28, 1992, C3.

Savage, David. "Combat in Panama; Legality of US Invasion Spurs Debate." *Los Angeles Times*, December 21, 1989, A10.

Scheer, Robert. "Sagging Economy Hurting Jobs-Based Welfare Reform; Poverty: Recipients Feel Squeezed by the Lack of Good-Paying Positions." *Los Angeles Times*, October 29, 1992, A1.

"Should American Taxpayers Be Asked to Prop Up the Former Soviet Republics in the Post-Cold War Era?" *Congressional Quarterly Researcher* 3, no. 10 (1993): 219.

Spies, Karen Bornemann. *George Bush: Power of the President*. New York: Dillon Press, 1991.

Stokes, Bruce. "Tallying the Expenses of Free Trading." *National Journal* 24, no. 31 (1992): 1787.

"The Supreme Court: Doubting Thomas." *Economist*, September 7, 1991, 26–27.

Szanton, Peter L. "The Remarkable 'Quango': Knowledge, Politics and Welfare Reform." *Journal of Policy Analysis and Management* 10 (1991): 590–602.

Tiefer, Charles. *The Semi-Sovereign Presidency*. Boulder: Westview, 1994.

Toch, Thomas, Kenneth T. Walsh, and Ted Slafsky. "The President's Worst Subject." *U.S. News & World Report*, August 6, 1990, 46.

Towell, Pat, and Carroll Doherty. "START Gets Historic Terms for Nuclear Arms Cuts." *Congressional Quarterly Weekly Report* 49 (1991): 1993.

"The Walsh Iran/Contra Report, Chapter 28." The Federation of American Scientists. August 29, 2000. http://www.fas.org/irp/offdocs/walsh/chap_28.htm.

Will, George. "A Balanced Budget in Congress' Future." *St. Louis Post-Dispatch*, May 1, 1992, C3.

Woollacott, Martin. "How the West Got Lost: A Crisis of Leadership Has Afflicted the Rich and Industrialized World at Precisely the Moment when Greatest Change Seemed the Most Possible." *Toronto Star*, October 31, 1992, D1.

Zunes Stephen. "START Treaty Is Unlikely to Make the World Safer." *Seattle Times*, August 1, 1991, A9.

WILLIAM (BILL) CLINTON

(1993–2001)

INTRODUCTION

Bill Clinton became president on the cusp of a new era of American politics. The American economy was in the early stages of a boom that would last for a decade, drive unemployment rates to unprecedented low levels, and enjoy very low interest rates. These economic good times were matched by the promise of a government that was unified under the control of one party for the first time in over a decade. To the degree that members of one party share a common vision of what ought to be done, they can pass policies and programs designed to achieve their goals. Finally, with the end of the Cold War, many of the old assumptions about what had to be done in foreign policy were swept away. Thus Clinton was in a virtually unique position to accomplish most, if not all, of his political agenda, and to do so using new ideas and fresh perspectives on the problems of the day.

By the end of his term, the promise of Clinton's first days in office had been transformed. While he achieved many of his goals, and the United States had experienced a period of economic growth and social stability that was once considered impossible, Clinton's presidency will likely be labeled the "however" presidency forever. For example, future historians can be expected to look back at his term in office and write that the United States saw substantial economic growth in the 1990s; however Clinton was only the second president (and the first *elected* president) ever impeached by the House of Representatives and tried by the Senate. Others may look back at the period of budget surpluses that began in Clinton's time of office and appreciate their importance; however his term was marred by a substantial series of scandals, allegations of scandal, and controversy. Other people may examine the Clinton presidency and comment that he started with a government unified under the control of his party; however, he lost this control just two years into office, when the Republican Party took control of both branches of Congress for the first time since the 1950s—a takeover that was, in substantial measure, the result of the actions Clinton took in his first two years as president.

The Clinton presidency can be divided into three parts: 1993 through the 1994 midterm congressional elections, 1995 through the impeachment hearings, and the post-impeachment period. From 1993 to 1995, Clinton pursued a relatively progressive political agenda. In contrast with both Presidents Reagan and Bush, Clinton believed that government had a positive role to play in protecting people's rights, running programs intended to improve people's lives, and providing services that no other element of society could provide. Two examples of this progressive philosophy dominated his early years in office: the rights of gays and lesbians to serve in the U.S. military and the creation of a national health insurance system to ensure that everyone had access to decent health care. Thus, in contrast with established policy, Clinton believed that one's sexual orientation should not interfere with military service, and that government policies that excluded gays and lesbians from military service were unconstitutional violations of civil rights. Accordingly, early in his administration, he established a "don't ask, don't tell, don't pursue" strategy regarding sexual orientation and military service: so long as individuals did not make their sexual preference openly known, the military would be prevented from pursuing rumors of homosexuality and discharging gays and lesbians from the service. Government, then, would protect the rights of gays and lesbians to serve.

In the area of health care, Clinton noted that at least 37 million Americans lacked health insurance. When these citizens became ill they either suffered in silence or, in cases of last resort, went to hospital emergency rooms for care. In the emergency room, they often received very expensive treatment for the consequences of problems that might have been easily (and inexpensively) treated had they gone to a doctor earlier. Thus, Clinton argued, a program of national health insurance would actually save money and would make the lives of millions of Americans much better. Government, then, had a positive role to play in this area as well.

Finally, Clinton pushed for a tax increase in his early years in office. Faced by ever-growing budget deficits, and desiring to use the government to make people's lives better, Clinton advocated increasing the government's income by raising taxes. In combination with budget cuts and economic growth, Clinton believed that increasing taxes would substantially ameliorate America's budget crisis.

To suggest that these were controversial positions is to understate the case. Raising taxes is always painful. Moreover, many people are opposed to gays and lesbians as such; the idea that they should be allowed to serve in the military is disturbing to many people. Similarly, the cost and scope of a national health care system was overwhelming to both conservatives and to the businesses that would have to pay for much of the program. Such proposals, in combination with policies like the Brady Bill limiting on-the-spot handgun sales, stimulated intense opposition even as Clinton was laying out his new agenda.

Other controversial issues emerged in the first years of Clinton's administration. During the 1992 presidential campaign, Clinton was accused of two illegal acts: the sexual harassment of an Arkansas civil servant when he was governor of that state, and profiting from a real estate investment called Whitewater through illegal insider information. While these allegations did not prevent his election, they did set in motion a series of investigations that harmed his reputation and ultimately led to his impeachment and trial. They stimulated a profound level of anger in many opponents who then organized against him in Congress and in the electorate.

In addition, Clinton suffered a major political disaster in foreign affairs during his first year in office. Clinton inherited a policy in which U.S. troops were sent to Somalia to perform peacekeeping duties to try to end that country's vicious civil war. These troops ultimately took sides in the civil war and attempted to capture a local leader who was believed to be prolonging the conflict. Supporters of this Somali leader attacked U.S. forces, killed several servicemen, and dragged their bodies through the streets. As commander in chief, Clinton took a great deal of criticism for this disaster. This event, in combination with other alleged Clinton misdeeds, led many Americans to oppose his presidency fervently.

The Somalia intervention served as a preface to many similar issues that occurred during the Clinton administration. In the aftermath of the Cold War, many long-standing conflicts, which had been repressed in the name of international stability, began to reemerge. Yugoslavia, Rwanda, and Sierra Leone experienced remarkable levels of violence and destruction throughout the 1990s. U.S. troops were deployed to many areas as peacekeeping forces; however, the deployments were highly controversial during Clinton's eight years in office.

Ironically, these foreign policy and personal problems led many to overlook the accomplishments of the early Clinton administration. Due to his efforts, substantial progress was made in establishing peace among Catholics and Protestants in Northern Ireland. Peace between Palestinians and Israelis was also advanced, although it was challenged in an outbreak of violence near the end of his second term.

The 1994 midterm congressional elections served as a turning point in

Clinton's presidency. In response to the various tensions that shaped his early years in office, the Republican Party turned a long-standing pattern of American politics upside down: Democrats had controlled the House of Representatives in every year since 1953; suddenly, the Republicans took control of both houses of Congress. Many analysts suggested that the Republican victory spelled the end of Clinton's presidency. They predicted that he would be unable to pass any policies through the new Congress, and would lose the 1996 presidential election.

These predictions turned out to be partially true, and partially not. For example, in order to gain favor with the new Republican majority and so to pass any legislation at all, Clinton gave up most of his progressive agenda and turned to policies that were generally supported by most Republicans. Clinton supported such programs as welfare reform, crime control, and drug control, all of which are Republican favorites. In 1995 he engaged in a major confrontation with Republicans over the budget, vetoing several proposals that contained provisions he did not like. These vetoes caused the federal government to run out of money, forcing it to shut down. Americans blamed Republicans for the inconveniences resulting from the shutdown. Public opinion forced Republicans to accommodate Clinton's preferences in the budget. Thus, through skillful reinvention of his agenda and the artful use of public opinion, Clinton was able to develop political and public support for his presidency and was reelected in 1996.

Clinton's victory was short lived. The Republicans who came to Congress in 1994 were, for the most, conservative followers of Ronald Reagan's political ideology. They opposed Clinton's early, progressive agenda and were deeply offended by Clinton's alleged crimes in the areas of sexual harassment and Whitewater. They also believed that Clinton and his vice president, Al Gore, had engaged in illegal fund-raising activities during the 1996 presidential campaign. They insisted either that these activities be investigated by special prosecutors—attorneys who were given virtually unlimited power to explore allegations of wrongdoing by senior government officials—or that ongoing special prosecutor investigations be broadened to cover new areas of inquiry. When Attorney General Janet Reno agreed with these demands and empowered Special Prosecutor Kenneth Starr to investigate fully allegations of wrongdoing by President Clinton, she set in motion the process that led to Clinton's impeachment and trial in 1998–1999.

It is worth noting that Clinton continued to support new policies throughout this period. With the exception of the area of foreign policy, however, he enjoyed very little success. Thus, while Clinton continued to promote peace in Northern Ireland and between Israel and the Palestinians, and continued to enforce the post–Persian Gulf War embargo against Iraq and push for positive trade relations with China, Congress did not support much of Clinton's domestic policy agenda. Instead, Congress' attention was focused on the special prosecutor investigations and on the Republican agenda.

In late summer 1998, Special Prosecutor Kenneth Starr released the bulk of his findings. He alleged that President Clinton had committed several impeachable acts when he attempted to cover up a sexual affair he had carried on with a White House intern. Specifically, Starr alleged that Clinton had lied under oath when asked if he had engaged in sexual conduct with White House intern Monica Lewinsky. Starr also insisted that Clinton obstructed justice by lying about his conduct in public and to aides who later testified on the matter. This report persuaded the House of Representatives to vote to impeach Clinton, indicating that the majority of its members believed he had committed crimes that warranted his removal from office. By a simple majority vote, the House preferred impeachment charges against Clinton for lying under oath and obstruction of justice. Then, as prescribed by the U.S. Constitution, Clinton was put on trial by the U.S. Senate. It requires a two-thirds vote—67 of 100 senators—to convict the president and remove him from office. The Senate voted on two indictments but failed to reach the necessary two-thirds vote on either. It voted 55 to 45 in favor of conviction on the charge of lying under oath, and 50 to 50 on the charge of obstruction of justice. Thus, Clinton remained in office throughout his term.

In the last years of his term, Clinton focused on foreign policy issues. He traveled widely, pushed for permanent most-favored-nation status for China (MFN provides for relatively free trade relations between countries), and continued to support the peace processes in Northern Ireland and the Middle East.

As might be expected, given the intense emotions Clinton's presidency inspired, assessing his term is very difficult. Since so many people have such varying opinions of his leadership, it is necessary to specify exactly which dimension of his time in office is under consideration. In economic affairs, for example, the Clinton presidency was remarkable. Unemployment was low, as was inflation; the economy grew at unprecedented rates for the longest peacetime period in the modern era; and the stock market exploded in value, turning millions of ordinary citizens into substantial investors. Similarly, budget politics were transformed from an era of massive deficits to surpluses projected at $1.6 trillion through 2010. This surplus might be used for tax cuts, the elimination of the accumulated debt of the United States, or new programs such as health care and prescription drug coverage. In any case, the politics of surpluses are much easier to manage than the politics of deficits, and this transition came in Clinton's presidency. Finally, many of Clinton's peacemaking efforts abroad have paid off in new agreements among peoples who have warred for decades and centuries.

On the other hand, there is the "however" problem. He was impeached, his extramarital affair became public knowledge, and no solution for ending the internal conflicts ripping apart many of the world's societies has emerged. He promised to lead the most ethical administration in modern history, but Clinton and his appointees have been the subject of innumerable investigations. Liberal critics add to this list of failures the betrayal of his progressive agenda: for them, his decision to accommodate the Republicans when they came to power in Congress in 1995 is a sign of political weakness. Like it or hate it, the Clinton presidency was always an interesting one.

DOMESTIC AND ECONOMIC POLICY

NATIONAL SERVICE (MAY 1993)

As part of his progressive political agenda, Bill Clinton believed that government should support individuals who wished to work in their communities to improve neighborhoods, build trust, and promote participation. While Americans had traditionally volunteered to serve their communities without practical reward, Clinton supported the establishment of a National Service program, later called Americorps. Modeled after the Peace Corps, a program in which Americans volunteer to serve in poor and underdeveloped nations for three years to help communities improve health, social, and economic conditions, Americorps would pay people to serve in the United States itself. It would also provide support for continuing the individual's education. Such service, Clinton argued, would improve both the communities in which these individuals served and the lives of the individuals themselves.

Like other critics of the Americorps program, Congressman Gary Franks (R-CT) argued that it was silly to pay people to "volunteer": volunteering meant giving of one's own time without material reward. Otherwise, he argued, the program would encourage people to volunteer only when they were being paid. In addition, he argued that the program would be very expensive and would bust the budget in a crisis period. Thus, even if the program were a good idea, it would not be practical.

The National Service Trust Act was signed into law in 1993. Volunteers began to serve in 1994. Like so many programs he sponsored, the short-term effects of this program must be evaluated in terms of how a person views Clinton as president: liberals supported Clinton for Americorps on the grounds that it was helping poor communities around the United States; conservatives felt that it was an example of government intrusion into policy areas that ought to be managed by state and local governments. This dispute, around the question of the government's proper role in political life, was central to the 1994 congressional elections in which conservative Republicans, advocating less federal government in local affairs, took over Congress.

After the Republican takeover of Congress in 1994, funding for the program was substantially reduced. Thus the program never reached its target of 150,000 volunteers per year, although a smaller number of people do serve under its rules annually. After the 1994 midterm elections, Clinton gave up advocacy of programs like Americorps in favor of proposals to increase the numbers of teachers and police officers in the

United States. Neither major party candidate in the 2000 election proposed to fund Americorps at its original target. Thus, while the program survives, it is only a shadow of its intended self.

CLINTON'S MESSAGE TO THE CONGRESS TRANSMITTING PROPOSED LEGISLATION ON NATIONAL AND STUDENT LOAN REFORM

May 5, 1993

I am pleased to transmit today for your immediate consideration and enactment the "National Service Trust Act of 1993." . . . [It] represents innovative public policy grounded on traditional American values: offering educational opportunity, rewarding personal responsibility, and building the American community. In affirming these values, the Act(s) reject wasteful bureaucracy—instead reinventing government to unleash the ideas and initiative of the American people. Also transmitted is a section-by-section analysis.

. . .

The . . . Act is designed to meet these basic American needs. The National Service Trust Act of 1993 establishes a domestic Peace Corps, offering hundreds of thousands of young people the opportunity to pay for school by doing work our country needs. . . .

The National Service Trust Act of 1993 establishes a definition of national service that is clear but broad. National service is work that addresses unmet educational, environmental, human, or public safety needs. It enriches the lives of those who serve, instilling the ethic of civic responsibility that is essential to our democracy. And national service does not displace or duplicate the functions of existing workers.

Building on the National and Community Service Act of 1990 and the flourishing community service programs of nonprofit organizations and States, the initiative rejects bureaucracy in favor of locally driven programs. In the spirit of reinventing government, the Act will empower those with the greatest expertise and incentives to make national service work.

The Act enables citizens of all backgrounds to serve and use their educational awards where they see fit. While many participants will be recent college graduates, Americans will be eligible to enter the program at any time in their adult lives. Both full-time and part-time service will be encouraged. And whatever their education level, those who complete a term of service will receive an award of $5,000. The award will be payable toward past, present, or future educational expenses in 4- and 2-year colleges, training programs, and graduate and professional schools.

. . .

The National Service Trust Act of 1993 encourages Americans to join together and serve our country—at all ages and in all forms. The Act enhances the Serve-America program for school-age youth; extends and improves the VISTA and Older Americans Volunteer Programs authorized under the Domestic Volunteer Service Act; supports the Civilian Community Corps and Points of Light Foundation; and pulls these efforts under the new Corporation. The Act will help instill an ethic of service in elementary and secondary school students, encourage them to serve in their college years, and give them further opportunities later in their lives.

. . .

Opportunity, responsibility, and community go beyond politics. They are basic American ideals. Enactment . . . will express the Nation's commitment to these ideals and to our shared future.

Public Papers of the President: William J. Clinton. May 5, 1993: 574–576.

CRITICISM OF THE NATIONAL SERVICE TRUST ACT OF 1993

August 3, 1993

Mr. Gary Franks (R-CT). Mr. Chairman, the Clinton administration and some of my colleagues here in the House are arguing that this national service plan has many outstanding goals. I agree that we in Congress can play an important role in providing educational opportunity to Americans and in fostering community service. However, I do not believe that creating an expensive, bureaucracy-laden Government program is a good way to achieve these goals. In fact, passage of this plan will send a disturbing signal to the millions of volunteers in this country that community service needs a Government imprimatur to be legitimate. This act would also undermine the American idea of community service by paying people to help others. Finally, this bill, expensive as it is, can only play a very limited role to open educational opportunities to our Nation's college students. This bill is just another make-work summer jobs program, except this program is intended to make work for social activists on our Nation's campuses.

First, I want to make clear that I believe that volunteer community service has been and is an intrinsic quality of the American people. In 1991, 94.3 million adult Americans volunteered in some way to our communities and averaged more than 4.2 hours of service a week. No country can be a utopia, and therefore even our great Nation is indebted to people who are willing to make our communities better and help those who through no fault of their own are in need. However, I believe that many of our Nation's problems can be solved through the local level within the community. In contrast, President Clinton is subverting community service with his idea of national service: creating a federally directed volunteer organization designed to fulfill a national political agenda.

. . .

This national service plan has other philosophical flaws. If a person gets genuine compensation for doing work, that person is doing a job. The first definition of job in the Merriam-Webster Dictionary is "a piece of work; especially a small miscellaneous piece of work undertaken on order at a stated rate." Mr. Chairman, this bill undermines the entire idea of helping others without compensation out of empathy for fellow members of the community. Participants in national service will receive an hourly minimum wage, a $5,000 stipend, and federally subsidized health care. College students who have children can receive federally subsidized child care. I haven't received monetary compensation and benefits for my service—I thought my service transcended materialism. This plan will truly destroy the spirit of service.

Let me discuss the cost of this program and the percentage of students it will actually benefit. National service will cost $7.4 billion over the next 4 years. The Peace Corps has received less than half of that sum in its 31 years of existence. While this sum provides between $15,000 and $20,000 in taxpayer money to each participant, remember that much of the money will go toward a massive new Federal bureaucracy and clone bureaucracies in each State. By 1997, when the bureaucracy begins to mature, national service will cost over $22,600 per participant. Who knows how high the Federal deficit will be in 1997? To at least limit the costs of this program, I will support Congresswoman Molinari's amendment to eliminate the minimum wage stipend, the federally subsidized health care, and the federally subsidized child care for students.

Few of my constituents will benefit from this national service plan. Even after $7.4 billion is spent creating jobs for students, only 150,000 will be involved in 1997. This year more than 16 million students were enrolled in some form of higher education. Who will be the special people that get this Government ride for their education? This program is going to be highly susceptible to cronyism, discrimination, and abuse. I will support Congressman Goodling's amendment to make educational awards under this program need-based.

This program is also subject to abuse from labor unions and interest groups with pointed political agendas. This bill will allow labor unions to be involved in the approval process for an applicant's grant. While this seems fair on the surface to prevent participants from taking jobs, it has a different meaning when one finds out that, under this bill, unions can apply for the same grants themselves. I will vote for Congressman Ballenger's amendment to prevent this conflict-of-interest from occurring. Nevertheless, I am still concerned that this national service plan could create a pool of potential secretaries for political lobbyists.

Some Members on my side of the aisle support this national service plan because it allows students to pay for their education by working. I say to these Members: If President Clinton was concerned about giving students an opportunity to finance their education, why didn't he propose to use the existing college work study program as an administrative framework for providing paid community work? Why the creation of a new Corporation for National Service? The educational benefits of the National Service Trust Act are a cover for bigger Government and the creation of a phalanx of taxpayer-funded political activists. I will vote against this bill.

The Congressional Record. April 9, 1993: E 1960.

MOST-FAVORED-NATION TRADE STATUS FOR CHINA
(MAY 1993)

Relations with China are a common point of contention in American politics. China, the world's most populous nation, is a potentially vast market for American products. Moreover, many U.S. companies produce their goods in China, where labor is cheap. This allows them to sell their products in the United States as inexpensively as possible. However, China, the world's largest Communist power, is repressive of human rights, is a competitor against U.S. interests around the world, and has the potential to become a superpower on the international stage. Accordingly, China trade policy provides a flash point among those who promote economic value as the highest good, those who think that the United States should advocate human rights as its primary foreign policy goal, and those who think trade and rights can reinforce one another.

Like Presidents Reagan and Bush, President Clinton favored giving

China most-favored-nation (MFN) trade status. Under this rule, nations put very few restrictions on the goods and services brought in from their trading partners. This promotes the relatively free exchange of goods and services, which in turn is expected to promote economic growth. Clinton, of course, supported economic growth; however, he also insisted that as Chinese people were exposed to capitalism and to the freedoms of the West, they would push for democracy in their own country. Thus, trade promoted freedom and linked the ideals of advocates of both growth and human rights.

Congressman Frank Wolf (R-VA), like most opponents of MFN for China, focused on that regime's oppressive treatment of its citizens in objecting to the policy. As critics saw it, open trade relations would stimulate economic growth in China. This growth would provide the government with the resources it needed to continue to repress human rights. Thus, rather than promoting freedom, trade would stimulate oppression.

MFN for China remained a controversial issue for the whole of Clinton's term of office, as did other questions related to trade. In the short term, Clinton won. However, conservatives criticized him for failing to control Communist aggression, while liberals attacked him for deemphasizing human rights in U.S. trade policy. Eventually, in a manifestation of these critiques, Congress failed to renew the president's authority to negotiate trade through fast-track agreements that expedited congressional approval of trade pacts. As with most domestic policies Clinton advocated in his first years in office, the policy of most-favored-nation status for China served as a foundation for the anti-Clinton backlash of 1994.

In 2000 permanent MFN status for China was approved when China was admitted to the World Trade Organization (WTO), an international body that promotes free trade worldwide. As of this writing it is unclear whether such open trade relations have had any effect on human rights and freedoms in China, or anywhere else for that matter. Many critics remain opposed to supporting China because of its human rights violations. Although others remain critical because of the threat to U.S. interests a powerful China may eventually oppose, MFN for China is a reality.

CLINTON'S STATEMENT ON MOST-FAVORED-NATION TRADE STATUS FOR CHINA

May 28, 1993

Yesterday the American people won a tremendous victory as a majority of the House of Representatives joined me in adopting our plan to revitalize America's economic future.

Today, members of Congress have joined me to announce a new chapter in United States policy toward China.

China occupies an important place in our nation's foreign policy. It is the world's most populous state, it's fastest growing major economy, and a permanent member of the United Nations Security Council. Its future will do much to shape the future of Asia, our security and trade relations in the Pacific, and a host of global issues, from the environment to weapons proliferation. In short: our relationship with China is of very great importance.

Unfortunately, over the past four years our nation spoke with a divided voice when it came to China. Americans were outraged by the killing of pro-democracy demonstrators at Tiananmen Square in June of 1989. Congress was determined to have our nation's stance toward China reflect our outrage. Yet twice after Congress voted to place conditions on our favorable trade rules toward China—so-called Most Favored Nation status—those conditions were vetoed. The annual battles between Congress and the Executive divided our foreign policy and weakened our approach over China.

It is time that a unified American policy recognize both the value of China and the values of America. Starting today, the United States will speak with one voice on China policy. We no longer have an Executive Branch policy and a congressional policy. We have an American policy.

. . .

We are here today because the American people continue to harbor profound concerns about a range of practices by China's communist leaders. We are concerned that many activists and pro-democracy leaders, including some from Tiananmen Square, continue to languish behind prison bars in China for no crime other than exercising their consciences. We are concerned about international access to their prisons. And we are concerned by the Dalai Lama's reports of Chinese abuses against the people and culture of Tibet.

We must also address China's role in the proliferation of dangerous weapons. The Gulf War proved the danger of irresponsible sales of technologies related to weapons of mass destruction. While the world is newly determined to address the danger of such missiles, we have reason to worry that China continues to sell them.

Finally, we have concerns about our terms of trade with China. China runs an $18 billion trade surplus with the U.S.—second only to Japan. In the face of this deficit, China continues practices that block American goods.

. . .

We take some encouragement from the economic reforms in China—reforms that by some measures place China's economy as the third largest in the world, after the United States and Japan. China's coastal provinces are an engine for reform throughout the country. The residents of Shanghai and Guangzhou are far more motivated by markets than by Marx or Mao.

We are hopeful that China's process of development and economic reform will be accompanied by greater political freedom. In some ways, this process has begun. An emerging Chinese middle class points the antennae of new televisions towards Hong Kong to pick up broadcasts of CNN. Cellular phones and fax machines carry implicit notions of freer communications. Hong Kong itself is a catalyst of democratic values—and we strongly support Governor Patten's efforts to broaden democratic rights.

. . .

We are prepared to build a more cooperative relationship with China, and wish to work with China as an active member of the international community. Through some of its actions, China has demonstrated that it wants to be a member of that community. Membership has its privileges, but also its obligations. We expect China to meet basic international standards in its treatment of its people, its sales of dangerous arms, and its foreign trade.

With one voice, the United States Government today has outlined these expectations.

Public Papers of the President: William J. Clinton. May 28, 1993: 770–771.

URGING REJECTION OF RENEWAL OF MOST-FAVORED-NATION STATUS FOR CHINA

May 23, 1994

Mr. Frank Wolf (R-VA). Mr. Speaker, the time of decision about whether or not to renew most-favored-nation [MFN] status for China is upon us. Although the Secretary of State has until June 3 to make his recommendation to President Clinton, all bets are that he will make the call in the next week just after Members leave town and just before his D-day trip to Europe.

I stand before this body and the Nation today to urge President Clinton to stand behind his Executive order and revoke MFN in light of the new crackdown in China against religious and political dissent. No one disputes that the President's Executive order was clear, and no one disputes that there has been overall, significant regression instead of progress in human rights in China.

Let us look at recent evidence.

Only a week ago correspondent Lena Sun of the [Washington] *Post* reported that—

China amended its public order law to broaden the already extensive powers of the police to detain and restrict the activities of democracy and labor activists as well as religious and national minority groups— new regulations essentially give authorities the right to detain anyone they regard as a threat to the socialist system.

New regulations include:

First, carrying out activities under the name of a social organization without registration;

Second, organizing activities of superstitious sects and secret societies to disrupt public order;

Third, disturbing public order and damaging people's health through religious activities;

Fourth, stirring up conflicts between nationalities, hurting their unity and inciting separation of nationalities;

Fifth, fabricating or distorting facts, spreading rumors or otherwise disrupting public order, or doing harm to the public interest through other means.

About the same time these regulations came out, some Tibetan nuns received longer prison stays for singing patriotic songs while in detention.

Then last Thursday, Human Rights Watch/Asia released a new report citing almost 500 previously unknown prisoners of conscience jailed for their involvement in the Tiananmen Square demonstration. Further, this seminal report details the "charade" ICRC prison inspection that was later canceled by Beijing. Inmates were allowed their first showers in a year, sick prisoners with "unattractive appearances" were moved, and window glass was partially installed in windows normally covered in paper.

Yes, we are grateful for the release of some prominent Tiananmen leaders like Wang Juntao and Chun Ziming, but they are a drop in the bucket as China continues to arrest many more activists.

On the categories in which the President stated we must see "overall, significant" progress, we are clearly seeing "overall, significant" regression—leaving the administration claiming new Chinese promises to "talks" on Red Cross visits and "talks" about not jamming Voice of America broadcasts as purported progress in the categories that follow the two "must do" conditions.

The two "must do" conditions for MFN renewal are: First, progress on resolving outstanding emigration cases; and, second, progress on tightening the 1991 Memorandum of Understanding [MOU] on prohibition of forced labor exports from China.

The Chinese have helped resolve limited emigration cases.

In spite of the much-lauded progress on the MOU, the Chinese have only agreed to make a toothless agreement a bit less weak—leaving themselves plenty of turnaround time to sanitize prison labor camps before allowing visits by United States officials. I know some guys in Pyongyang and Baghdad who would love to sign up for that kind of inspection regime.

Harry Wu just returned from a covert trip to China in which he visited 26 prisons, bringing back fresh evidence that the Chinese knowingly violate both the letter and the spirit of their agreement not to export forced labor products into China. He even implicated two U.S. companies which the prison factory officials admitted to be importers of their slave labor products.

Purported progress on the MOU is clearly a sham.

. . .

Let us face it, trade is the only leverage that carries any true weight with the Chinese regime which is bolstered by our dollars—which make up almost 40 percent of their export market. And, in answer to the reply that MFN pressure has not achieved our desired result, I say that we have to date not revoked MFN. The lack of progress is probably due to mixed signals and idle threats the Chinese do not believe we'll carry out.

I believe the real question is whether or not we'll honestly call Beijing's bluff and do the morally right thing: revoke MFN in light of continued Chinese repression. If we do not, I believe we will not only let many in China down who are hoping we will stand firm for democracy, but only lose our credibility with the dictators of Beijing and the entire region. The message is: make our commitments seem too painful to carry out, and we will cave.

The Congressional Record. May 23, 1994: H 3793–3794.

HOMOSEXUALS IN THE MILITARY (JULY 1993)

Military forces inevitably reflect the biases of the societies they serve. Thus, for most of American history, African Americans either were banned from military service or were allowed to serve only in segregated units led by white officers. Similarly, gays and lesbians have been banned from military service in the United States, and anyone who is discovered to be homosexual while in service is given a dishonorable discharge.

During his candidacy, Bill Clinton pledged to overturn the military's ban on gays. When he became president and faced a near-rebellion of senior military leaders, however, he amended his position to create a policy of "don't ask, don't tell, don't pursue." Under this policy, the military is banned from asking about a service person's sexual preference, and as long as the individual does not disclose his or her orientation, military officials are banned from pursuing rumors of a person's sexuality. Service people can still be dismissed from the military if their sexual preference is revealed, however. For Clinton, this policy was important because he believed that discrimination based on sexual preference was a violation of people's civil rights. Additionally, he noted that many gays and lesbians had served with distinction; removing them from the service would harm America's defense.

Congressman Duncan Hunter (R-CA) and other opponents of Clinton's policy argued that many servicemen and servicewomen did not want to serve with gays and lesbians. It would be difficult to recruit new servicemen and women, and in those units in which gays were known to serve, unit cohesion would decline. (Interestingly, identical arguments were made against desegregating military units in the 1950s.) Other opponents feared that the combat effectiveness of the military would erode. Gay and lesbian opponents of Clinton's plan noted that it was not as far-reaching as his campaign promise. They wanted all-out acceptance of their service in the military.

Clinton's policy was highly controversial, and at least in the short term it stimulated much opposition. It provided some of the impetus behind the conservative backlash against Clinton that led to the Republican takeover of Congress in 1994. Thus, while his plan was adopted and remains the military's policy regarding sexuality and military service, it hurt him politically.

Over time, however, the policy has declined in controversy: the U.S. Supreme Court has ruled that the policy is constitutional, and both major party candidates for the presidency in 2000 supported "don't ask, don't tell." As conservatives feared, recruitment for military service has been low; however, this is an artifact of the good economy—fewer people want to serve in the military when high-paying civilian jobs are readily available. Indeed, military leaders desperate for recruits have been increasingly open to the idea of gays in the military—although gays are still dishonorably discharged if their sexuality is discovered. Similarly, declines in military readiness are clearly the result of budget cuts, not a policy of gays in the military. As of 2000, the "don't ask, don't tell" policy is relatively noncontroversial for most Americans.

CLINTON'S REMARKS ANNOUNCING A NEW POLICY ON HOMOSEXUALS IN THE MILITARY

July 19, 1993

I have come here today to discuss . . . our nation's policy toward homosexuals in the military.

The policy I am announcing today is, in my judgment, the right thing to do and the best way to do it. It is right because it provides greater protection to those who happen to be homosexual and want to serve their country honorably in uniform, obeying all the military's rules against sexual misconduct. It is the best way to proceed because it provides a sensible balance between the rights of the individual and the needs of our military to remain the world's number one fighting force. As President of all the American people, I am pledged to protect and to promote individual rights. As Commander in Chief, I am pledged to protect and advance our security. In this policy, I believe we have come close to meeting both objectives.

. . .

Let me review the events which bring us here today. Before I ran for President, this issue was already upon us. Some of the members of the military returning from the Gulf War announced their homosexuality in order to protest the ban. The military's policy has been questioned in college ROTC programs. Legal challenges have been filed in court, including one that has since succeeded. In 1991, the Secretary of Defense Dick Cheney was asked about reports that the Defense Department spent an alleged $500 million to separate and replace about 17,000 homosexuals from the military service during the 1980s, in spite of the findings of a government report saying there was no reason to believe that they could not serve effectively and with distinction. Shortly thereafter, while giving a speech at the Kennedy School of Government at Harvard, I was asked by one of the students what I thought of this report and what I thought of lifting the ban. This question had never before been presented to me, and I had never had the opportunity to discuss it with anyone. I stated then what I still believe: that I thought there ought to be a presumption that people who wish to do so should be able to serve their country if they are willing to conform to the high standards of the military, and that the emphasis should be always on people's conduct, not their status.

For me, and this is very important, this issue has never been one of group rights, but rather of individual ones—of the individual opportunity to serve and the individual responsibility to conform to the highest standards of military conduct. For people who are willing to play by the rules, able to serve, and make a contribution, I believe then and I believe now we should give them the chance to do so.

The central facts of this issue are not much in dispute. First, notwithstanding the ban, there have been and are homosexuals in the military service who serve with distinction. . . .

Second, there is no study showing them to be less capable or more prone to misconduct than heterosexual soldiers. Indeed, all the information we have indicates that they are not less capable or more prone to misbehavior.

Third, misconduct is already covered by the laws and rules which also cover activities that are improper by heterosexual members of the military.

Fourth, the ban has been lifted in other nations and in police and fire departments in our country with no discernible negative impact on unit cohesion or capacity to do the job, though there is, admittedly, no absolute analogy to the situation we face and no study bearing on this specific issue.

Fifth, even if the ban were lifted entirely, the experience of other nations and police and fire departments in the United States indicates that most homosexuals would probably not declare their sexual orientation openly, thereby, making an already hard life even more difficult in some circumstances.

. . .

Clearly, the American people are deeply divided on this issue, with most military people opposed to lifting the ban because of the feared impact on unit cohesion, rooted in disapproval of homosexual lifestyles, and the fear of invasion of privacy of heterosexual soldiers who must live and work in close quarters with homosexual military people. However, those who have studied this issue extensively have discovered an interesting fact. People in this country who are aware of having known homosexuals are far more likely to support lifting the ban. In other words, they are likely to see this issue in terms of individual conduct and individual capacity instead of the claims of a group with which they do not agree; and also to be able to imagine how this ban could be lifted without a destructive impact on group cohesion and morale.

. . .

These past few days I have been in contact with the Secretary of Defense as he has worked through the final stages of this policy with the

Joint Chiefs. We now have a policy that is a substantial advance over the one in place when I took office. I have ordered Secretary Aspin to issue a directive consisting of these essential elements: One, servicemen and women will be judged based on their conduct, not their sexual orientation. Two, therefore, the practice, now six months old, of not asking about sexual orientation in the enlistment procedure will continue. Three, an open statement by a service member that he or she is a homosexual will create a rebuttable presumption that he or she intends to engage in prohibited conduct, but the service member will be given an opportunity to refute that presumption; in other words, to demonstrate that he or she intends to live by the rules of conduct that apply in the military service. And four, all provisions of the Uniform Military Justice will be enforced in an even-handed manner as regards both heterosexuals and homosexuals. And, thanks to the policy provisions agreed to by the Joint Chiefs, there will be a decent regard to the legitimate privacy and associational rights of all service members.

. . .

Thus, on grounds of both principle and practicality, this is a major step forward. It is, in my judgment, consistent with my responsibilities as President and Commander in Chief to meet the need to change current policy. It is an honorable compromise that advances the cause of people who are called to serve our country by their patriotism, the cause of our national security and our national interest in resolving an issue that has divided our military and our nation and diverted our attention from other matters for too long.

The time has come for us to move forward. As your Commander in Chief, I charge all of you to carry out this policy with fairness, with balance and with due regard for the privacy of individuals. We must and will protect unit cohesion and troop morale. We must and will continue to have the best fighting force in the world. But this is an end to witch hunts that spend millions of taxpayer dollars to ferret out individuals who have served their country well.

Public Papers of the President: William J. Clinton. July 19, 1993: 1109–1112.

OPPOSITION TO CLINTON'S POLICY ON HOMOSEXUALS IN THE MILITARY

June 22, 1993

Mr. Duncan Hunter (R-CA). Mr. Speaker, it has become fairly clear today, through news reports, that the President, the Secretary of Defense and the Department of Defense are on the verge of putting forth a policy with respect to allowing homosexuals to serve in the Armed Forces of the United States.

. . .

I rise, Mr. Speaker, to talk a little bit about the hearings that have been held on the Republican side of the aisle and the testimony that has come forth in the full hearings that we have held on the House Committee on Armed Services and the importance of this decision and the potential damage of this decision by President Clinton to the men and women who serve in the Armed Forces of the United States.

Now, the small unit commanders who testified and the retired NCO's who testified, to both the Republican Research Committee task forces and the full Committee on Armed Services on the homosexuals in the military issue, basically laid out the problems that this country is going to acquire with respect to the readiness of our Armed Forces, if this happens.

One thing that they went to was unit cohesion. The point is that American military men and women go forth in battle and in certain times die in battle because they feel that they have common cause with the United States of America and that their own set of values, Judeo-Christian values that have evolved over the years, are in concert with the values of this country.

When those values come into conflict there is a great damage to morale. We have said that, of course, when we have had massacres in the past and units have been involved in those things. We have seen the morale go straight downhill in those units that were involved.

The facts are, as has been illustrated by all of the polls that have been taken since this issue arose, the American fighting forces, the men and women who make up the fighting forces, overwhelmingly do not want to see the present ban on homosexuals in the military lifted. . . .

If we change this ban in any way, if we erode it, if we allow it to be compromised, we are going to see young men and women who serve in the Armed Forces because they feel it is consistent with their values finding that it is not consistent with their values, and we are going to see a degradation of morale and a degradation of unit cohesion. That, I think, has been the great weight of the testimony that has come forth.

Second, in the area of recruitment, we understand now that the decision to go into the military is a family decision in many cases. America's families send their young people to serve in the Armed Forces because they believe that the Armed Forces are a wholesome environment for their young people. If they come to the conclusion that the Armed Forces is not a wholesome environment for their young people, and all the information we have is, if we lift the ban on homosexuals in the military,

America's families that traditionally send their young people to the Armed Forces will come to that conclusion, will feel that the environment is no longer wholesome, is no longer good for their young person, then we are going to see a downward spiral in the volunteering for America's military that has made our modern military forces the best in the world. That is going to greatly damage our capability to project power around the world, to protect our own freedom, and to protect the freedom of our allies.

I want to simply say, duty, honor, and country are the three pillars on which our military is based. Our military leaders, whose assent must be taken, must concur before the American people will agree to any change in this policy, I would pray that they would look long and hard at any decision to in any way compromise the ban that is in place now that serves all of the fighting personnel in our Armed Forces.

The Congressional Record. June 22, 1993: H 3913.

THE FIRST CLINTON ECONOMIC PLAN (JULY 1993)

When President Clinton took office in 1993, the annual budget deficit of the United States was over $300 billion per year. During twelve years of Republican administrations, many domestic programs Clinton favored had undergone major budget cuts. Finally, the economy was in a slow period; few people could get better jobs, and many could not get jobs at all.

Clinton's response to this situation was a reversal of the Reagan-Bush economic plans. He advocated increasing taxes, particularly for more affluent people, and increasing spending on many social programs. He did promote some budget cuts; however, unlike Presidents Reagan and Bush, he pushed for cuts in the military's budget. Such a combination, Clinton insisted, could promote economic growth, establish fiscal responsibility, and ensure that the United States was fulfilling its commitments to the needy.

Opponents of the Clinton plan, including Senator Slade Gorton (R-WA), argued in favor of the Reagan-Bush approach. They preferred a policy that promoted continuing tax cuts and spending controls. Such a policy, they believed, would guarantee that the government did not become involved in projects it should not undertake, and would keep the financial pressure on government to control its budget. This combination would promote economic growth.

Clinton's economic plan was passed by Congress in 1993. The taxing and spending priorities reflected his progressive, liberal ideology that the federal government had an important role to play in improving the lives of its citizens. As such, it added fuel to the fire of controversy about what the proper role of the federal government actually is; conservatives used this debate to promote their plans and agendas. The Clinton tax plan was a key variable in the conservative political backlash that led to the Republican takeover of Congress in 1994.

In the ensuing years, the United States entered into its longest period of economic growth during peacetime in its history. It has also entered a period of budget surpluses—cumulatively, these are the biggest surpluses in history. Conservatives insist that the growth and surplus have resulted despite the Clinton tax increase; liberals argue that the tax increase promoted growth and the surplus. Whichever is right—or even if neither is right—the United States has entered a new era of the politics of budget surpluses which can be expected to dominate well into the twenty-first century.

CLINTON'S RADIO ADDRESS TO THE NATION

July 31, 1993

Five months ago in my state of the union address to Congress, I pledged to the American people that I would do my best to fulfill the campaign commitment of 1992 to change the way Washington works. That means reviving our economy by reducing our deficit; cutting spending; reversing trickle-down economics by asking the wealthiest Americans to pay their fair share of taxes; increasing incentives to business to create new jobs; helping the working poor; and renewing the skills and productivity of our workers, our students, and our children.

Now the members of both Houses of Congress are preparing to decide on a final version of my economic growth plan that meets the objectives I discussed when I presented it five months ago. This plan will contain the largest reduction in our deficit in the nation's history. With nearly one quarter of a trillion dollars in real enforceable spending cuts, every new dollar of taxes will be matched by a dollar of spending cuts, and 80 percent of the new taxes now will be raised from individuals earning over $200,000 a year. No working family earning less than $180,000 will pay more in income taxes. That will be a real change from the trickle-down economics of the past dozen years. The average family will pay only one tax—less than a dime a day in an energy tax devoted entirely to deficit reduction. That's about $33 a year for a family of four with an income of $40,000 or $50,000 a year. I think that's a modest and fair price to pay for the change we seek and the progress we're making. We pledged to have the lightest possible burden on the middle class, and I think that we have done.

Because we need the private sector to grow, the plan provides investments in job creating capacities of American business and in the education and skills of our people. For example, the plan supports small business by dramatically increasing the tax incentive they get to invest in their own operations. Under this plan, more than 90 percent of the small businesses in America will actually be eligible for a reduction in their taxes. The plan also gives other incentives to business for new plant and equipment, to invest in research and development for high tech firms, to invest in new fast growing firms that create so many of our jobs. And perhaps most important to many middle class families, this plan opens the doors of college for millions of families by reforming the student loan program and making college affordable again to all Americans.

We do all this without imposing harmful cuts on programs that benefit older Americans and building a better future for our children without asking unreasonable sacrifice from their grandparents. It's time for Congress to pass this plan. It's time for Washington to show the courage to change, just as people all across America are showing that kind of courage.

. . .

This is a new economic direction for our country. If you want it, if you want the jobs it will provide and the growth for our economy, you must make your voices heard. Tell your Senators and Representatives that this plan, with its deficit reduction, with its lower interest rates, with its investment in private sector jobs, means more jobs and a better future for America, and it is time to pass it.

Public Papers of the President: William J. Clinton. July 31, 1993: 1253–1254.

IT'S NOT THE MESSENGER WE NEED TO CHANGE—IT'S THE MESSAGE

May 20, 1993

Mr. Slade Gorton (R-WA). Mr. President, it is no secret to any Member of this Chamber that the President's economic program is in deep trouble. Deep trouble not just with Republicans in the House and the Senate, but with a large number of members of his own party in both Houses of Congress and, more significantly, across the United States as a whole.

This new President is a gracious, a hardworking, likable individual. He still has a great reservoir of popularity in the country. All Americans wish him well because, if he does well, the country itself will be well. The President and many of his advisers are concerned that his message is losing its punch because of the lack of focus. They are now attempting to focus the President more sharply on his economic program and on the economy of the country.

That concern I believe, Mr. President, is entirely misplaced. It is not the messenger with whom the people of the United States are concerned, it is the message. The economic program is in trouble not because it is misunderstood by the people of the United States. It is in trouble because it is becoming to be understood far too well across this country.

Yesterday, the distinguished senior Senator from Texas utilized this chart to show how far the message of the President has varied from that which won him election in November. During the campaign, the President promised $3 in spending cuts for every $1 in tax increases. At the time of the confirmation of his Office of Management and Budget Director, it was $2 in spending cuts for $1 in tax increases. In the State of the Union Address, it was dollar for dollar. In the budget submitted to us, it turned out to be $3 in tax increases for $1 in spending cuts. And now, with the reconciliation bill before the House of Representatives, it is $5 to $1.

The day before yesterday, a courageous citizen in San Diego, Lauren Fleming, a self-employed businessman, asked the President at one of his town meetings point blank:

Can you tell me of any time in history when higher taxes and greater Government spending led to prosperity?

The President, somewhat discomfited by the question, nevertheless answered it honestly by saying that he knew of no such example. He went on to say that this was not, however, his program.

The problem, Mr. President, is that it is his program. The program before us is very heavy on tax increases; it is very light on spending cuts. The American people have told us to cut spending first.

What is needed in this administration is not more focus on the part of the President. It is not trips out of Washington, D.C., to sell a flawed program, it is a revised program which lives up to the promises which he made during the course of his campaign.

If the President will trust the people to spend their own money, if he will trust the people to build the economy, if he will not rely so greatly on huge additions in Government spending, there will be no question about his focus. There will be renewed popularity not only of the President but of the President's program. There will then be bipartisan support for the President's plan and economic success for this country.

It is not the messenger we need to change, Mr. President, it is the message.

The Congressional Record. May 20, 1993: S 6167.

HEALTH CARE REFORM (SEPTEMBER 1993)

The ability of the modern American health care system to cure desperate illnesses, promote health, and otherwise care for people is astonishing. It is also extremely complex and expensive. Unfortunately, at least 37 million Americans lack health insurance because they do not work, or they work at jobs that do not provide insurance, or they are the children of people who lack insurance. Accordingly, they have to pay all the costs of their health care. The costs of such care often cause such people to avoid doctors, or to wait until their illnesses require treatment in public hospital emergency rooms. Care at the latter stages of disease is usually vastly more expensive than it is in the early days of illness—delaying treatment causes greater expenditures.

To address such problems, President Clinton advocated creating a national health care system for the United States. Under Clinton's plan, similar to those of Canada, England, and France, everyone would be entitled to a basic insurance plan organized by the federal government and paid for by taxes exacted from working people. Thus, workers would provide sufficient money to pay for insurance for the poor, and since the poor would no longer delay receiving treatment, the overall costs of health care in the United States would be reduced. Such a plan would reduce costs, provide insurance to all, and treat health care as a right for all people.

A massive campaign was mounted in opposition to Clinton's plan. Congressman Christopher Cox (R-CA) and others objected to the cost of the plan: at over $42 billion per year, it would potentially bust the budget and lead to substantial increases in taxes. Additionally, many feared that the federal government would run the program inefficiently, causing it to be more expensive than it needed to be. Finally, other critics feared that patients would lose the power to choose their medical care providers inasmuch as many doctors might choose not to accept the insurance or might drop out of medicine in protest.

Clinton's health care plan was declared "dead on arrival" when it was sent to Congress; no national health care plan emerged. Opponents focused on its costs, the way in which it was created (Clinton's wife, Hillary, had acted as director of the program's development, and many meetings had been held in secret), and the underlying premise that working people ought to subsidize heath care for the poor. Backlash against the Clinton plan was partially responsible for the return of the Republican Party to power in Congress in 1994.

However, by 1999, discussion of a scaled-down national health care plan began again since more and more people work in jobs that lack health insurance. Scaled-down versions of national health care (prescription drug coverage for senior citizens and increased funding for programs to deliver health care to children) became centerpieces of the 2000 presidential election for both the Democratic candidate, Al Gore, and the Republican candidate, George W. Bush. Thus, while it is unlikely that any plan as ambitious as Clinton's will emerge in the near future, expanded health care coverage does seem inevitable despite Clinton's 1993 loss.

CLINTON'S ADDRESS TO A JOINT SESSION OF THE CONGRESS ON HEALTH CARE REFORM

September 22, 1993

My fellow Americans, tonight we come together to write a new chapter in the American story. Our forebears enshrined the American Dream—life, liberty, the pursuit of happiness. Every generation of Americans has worked to strengthen that legacy, to make our country a place of freedom and opportunity, a place where people who work hard can rise to their full potential, a place where their children can have a better future.

. . .

Millions of Americans are just a pink slip away from losing their health insurance, and one serious illness away from losing all their savings. Millions more are locked into the jobs they have now just because they or someone in their family has once been sick and they have what is called the preexisting condition. And on any given day, over 37 million Americans—most of them working people and their little children—have no health insurance at all.

. . .

Now, if I might, I would like to review the six principles . . . mentioned earlier and describe how we think we can best fulfill those principles.

First and most important, security. This principle speaks to the human misery, to the costs, to the anxiety we hear about every day—all of us—when people talk about their problems with the present system. Security means that those who do not now have health care coverage will have it; and for those who have it, it will never be taken away. We must achieve that security as soon as possible.

. . .

The second principle is simplicity. Our health care system must be simpler for the patients and simpler for those who actually deliver health care—our doctors, our nurses, our other medical professionals. Today we have more than 1,500 insurers, with hundreds and hundreds of different forms. No other nation has a system like this. . . .

. . .

The third principle is savings. Reform must produce savings in this health care system. It has to. We're spending over 14 percent of our income on health care—Canada's at 10; nobody else is over nine. We're competing with all these people for the future. And the other major countries, they cover everybody and they cover them with services as generous as the best company policies here in this country.

. . .

So how will we achieve these savings? Rather than looking at price control, or looking away as the price spiral continues; rather than using the heavy hand of government to try to control what's happening, or continuing to ignore what's happening, we believe there is a third way to achieve these savings. First, to give groups of consumers and small businesses the same market bargaining power that large corporations and large groups of public employees now have. We want to let market forces enable plans to compete. We want to force these plans to compete on the basis of price and quality, not simply to allow them to continue making money by turning people away who are sick or old or performing mountains of unnecessary procedures. But we also believe we should back this system up with limits on how much plans can raise their premiums year in and year out, forcing people, again, to continue to pay more for the same health care, without regard to inflation or the rising population needs.

. . .

People may disagree over the best way to fix this system. We may all disagree about how quickly we can do what—the thing that we have to do. But we cannot disagree that we can find tens of billions of dollars in savings in what is clearly the most costly and the most bureaucratic system in the entire world. And we have to do something about that, and we have to do it now. The fourth principle is choice. Americans believe they ought to be able to choose their own health care plan and keep their own doctors. And I think all of us agree. Under any plan we pass, they ought to have that right. But today, under our broken health care system, in spite of the rhetoric of choice, the fact is that that power is slipping away for more and more Americans.

. . .

The sixth and final principle is responsibility. We need to restore a sense that we're all in this together and that we all have a responsibility to be a part of the solution. Responsibility has to start with those who profit from the current system. Responsibility means insurance companies should no longer be allowed to cast people aside when they get sick. It should apply to laboratories that submit fraudulent bills, to lawyers who abuse malpractice claims, to doctors who order unnecessary procedures. It means drug companies should no longer charge three times more for prescription drugs made in America here in the United States than they charge for the same drugs overseas.

. . .

Forty years from now, our grandchildren will also find it unthinkable that there was a time in this country when hardworking families lost their homes, their savings, their businesses, lost everything simply because their children got sick or because they had to change jobs. Our grandchildren will find such things unthinkable tomorrow if we have the courage to change today. This is our chance. This is our journey. And when our work is done, we will know that we have answered the call of history and met the challenge of our time.

Public Papers of the President: William J. Clinton. September 22, 1993: 1556–1565.

REMARKABLE EROSION OF SUPPORT FOR HEALTH CARE REFORM AMONG MIDDLE-INCOME AMERICANS

August 17, 1994

Mr. Christopher Cox (R-CA). Mr. Speaker, there has been a remarkable erosion of support among middle Americans, that is to say Americans of middle-income, for the Clinton health care bill and for the Clinton health care bill in its legislative form in the other body, where it is the Clinton-Mitchell bill, and in the House, where it is the Clinton-Gephardt bill. The same phenomenon occurred last year during consideration of the Clinton tax bill. During the 1992 campaign as a candidate he talked about a middle-class tax cut, but in fact we know how quickly that evaporated once we got down to brass tacks. Instead this Congress pushed through the biggest tax increase in American history, one that directly impacted the middle class, for example, seniors receiving Social Security making $14,000 got a 70-percent effective rate increase on their Social Security benefits. That is how much their income taxes went up on Social Security benefits.

That record-breaking tax increase passed by the Congress will pale in comparison to the Clinton-Gephardt bill that we are likely to take on here in the House, although it is difficult for us to talk about it as Members of Congress because while we have looked at the press releases and press statements about the bill, we are still waiting, we are still waiting for a bill even though we are just days away from adjournment. And the Congress hopes to act on health care before we adjourn. But we do not have a bill. The Congressional Budget Office has not been able to give us an estimate of how much precisely in the way of new taxes the bill contains and precisely how much in the way of new spending the bill contains. We simply have not read it. This is more than a trivial point. Health care comprises one-seventh of our Nation's economy. It is also on a more personal level a matter of life and death for every American. One would think that a new health care plan prescribed by the Federal Government for the whole country would therefore be the most carefully studied document since the Constitution.

But instead when, as, and if this Congress and House get around to seeing and voting on a bill, we are going to find that Members have not had a chance to read it, that in fact when we vote, Members will know more about O.J. Simpson's blood type than they will about the content of our own health care legislation. But we operate necessarily in an environment of uncertainty. We do not have a bill, but we must debate what it is we anticipate because after all the vote will be upon us and that will be it and we will have an election. We must adjourn at some point, and that point is arriving rather quickly.

Why are people skeptical of what they have been seeing? The Heritage Foundation did an analysis of the Clinton-Gephardt bill as it was released. What they found is that the new taxes, and there are many of them in the Clinton-Gephardt bill, would amount to $42.6 billion in the first full effective year of the plan in 1999, on top of the current costs on the system. People who are saying these new taxes are only going to displace existing health care costs or somehow limit the growth of health care costs must face this fact; $42.6 billion in new taxes will be imposed by the Clinton-Gephardt health care bill on top of our current estimates for how much the existing system is going to cost.

Now, the average additional tax burden per individual as a result of the Clinton-Gephardt bill, according to the Heritage Foundation is $430 per individual on average. The Clinton-Gephardt bill unquestionably is going to offer Americans less choice. It does not quite do justice to the fact to say less, almost none compared to what presently an insured American has available.

Congress and the Federal Government are going to prescribe a standard health care plan. And that is going to be the norm for the country, like it or not. If your existing plan is different than the standard plan, if you continue to get those benefits, you will pay a tax, not only will you pay a tax but your employer will pay a tax. The new taxes imposed by the Clinton-Gephardt bill are going to be split 80 percent by the employer and 20 percent by the individual. So 20 percent of these new taxes will come directly out of the paycheck of the American worker. There will be far more bureaucracy in this plan because for a substantial part it is going to rely upon something called Medicare Part C. Medicare Part C is, in effect, a Government-run insurance plan that will extend, together with the existing Medicare program to over half the entire population or to about half the entire population, according to our best estimates. Half of the American people at that point will be getting their health care from a Government plan, as compared to the current system.

The Congressional Record. August 17, 1994: H 8574.

NORTH AMERICAN FREE TRADE AGREEMENT
(NOVEMBER 1993)

Free trade is one of the central components of the U.S. economy. By promoting the trading of goods and services across international borders easily and quickly, free trade makes it possible to hold costs to a minimum: goods and services can be produced in nations with lower costs and then brought to the United States, where the cost savings can be passed on to consumers in the form of lower prices. However, as a consequence of this cross-border trade, Americans who once produced the goods or service now being created elsewhere often lose their jobs. Thus free trade has real, painful consequences for some even as it benefits many others. This is a prescription for a controversial political issue.

President Clinton promoted free trade, believing that on balance the benefits derived from open trade relations outweighed the costs. The greatest example of this philosophy negotiated by the United States in recent years was the North American Free Trade Agreement (NAFTA), originally promoted by President George H.W. Bush, which established free trade relations among the United States, Canada, and Mexico. Clinton argued that such agreements would do more than just create an economic benefit for the United States; open relations would promote democracy, build trust, and assist in strengthening international police efforts to control drugs, illegal immigration, and other hemispheric problems.

Critics of NAFTA and other free trade agreements made a number of points. Like Congressman Sander Levin (D-MI), and others feared that the substantially lower cost of labor in Mexico and other relatively poor countries would cause American companies to move south and cost many Americans their jobs. They also pointed out that even if benefits accrued to the United States, these benefits would not come for a long time. In the interim, many people would suffer. Finally, they were concerned that the lack of strong environmental, labor, and workplace safety rules in many countries outside the United States would mean that, morally, Americans were benefiting from the exploitation of international workers.

NAFTA was ratified in 1993. While many Americans did lose their jobs as a consequence, the 1990s was a period of economic boom in the United States. The United States has continued to negotiate free trade agreements as part of its underlying economic philosophy.

CLINTON'S LETTER TO CONGRESSIONAL LEADERS ON NAFTA

November 15, 1993

As we approach the end of an intense debate over the North American Free Trade Agreement (NAFTA), I want to share with you my reasons for believing Congressional approval on NAFTA is essential to our national interest.

We share a commitment to ensuring that our country has the world's strongest and most competitive economy, to maintaining and creating jobs for our workers, and to making sure that opportunities are there for our children as they join the workforce of the future. That is why I am fighting for the approval of NAFTA. I am convinced that it will help strengthen our economy—in the near term and in the long run.

Our nation's prosperity depends on our ability to compete and win in the global economy. It is an illusion to believe that we can prosper by retreating behind protectionist walls. We will succeed only by ensuring that we have the world's most competitive companies, productive workers, and open markets in which to sell our manufactured goods, services, and agricultural products.

I understand that NAFTA is, for many, a reminder of the economic hardships and insecurities that have grown over the past 20 years. Obviously, NAFTA did not cause those problems. In fact, it is part of the solution. We are world-class producers of everything from computers and automobiles to financial services and soybeans. We can compete anywhere, but we need to ensure that markets around the world are open to our products.

. . .

NAFTA provides us preferential access to the Mexican market: 90 million people, in one of the most dramatic growing economies in the world, who look to us for consumer goods, agricultural products and the infrastructure needed to build a modern economy. It is the gateway to the fast growing markets of Latin America, which are also opening, where we have a natural advantage over Japan and the European Community. Turning away from this opportunity would be a serious self-inflicted wound to our economy. It would cost us jobs—in the short and long term.

Many opponents of NAFTA say that they don't oppose a trade agreement with Mexico. They say they just oppose this NAFTA, and suggest that it be renegotiated. We should be under no illusions. This is a far-reaching and fair agreement. It was negotiated painstakingly over three years with input from a broad array of groups, and it is in the best interest of the United States, Mexico and Canada. It represents an unprecedented effort to include in a trade agreement provisions to enhance environmental protection and worker's rights. It was negotiated by a Republican President, and endorsed and strengthened by a Democratic President. If it were defeated, no government of Mexico could return, or would return, to the negotiating table for years to come. Mexico would turn to others, like Japan and the European Community, for help in building a modern state—and American workers, farmers, and businesses would be the losers.

Of course, NAFTA is not a magic bullet for all our economic problems. But there is no question that NAFTA will benefit every region of our country. It is no accident that NAFTA has the support of more than two-thirds of the nation's governors and Members of Congress from every part of the nation. They understand the benefits that will flow to their states, regardless of region.

My main reason for supporting NAFTA is that it will be good for the competitive U.S. economy that we are trying to build. But there is another critical issue that I ask you to consider. After World War I, the United States chose the path of isolation and protectionism. That path led directly to the Depression, and helped set the world on the path to World War II. After World War II, we chose to engage with the world, through collective security and expanded trade. We helped our allies rebuild, ushered in a period of unprecedented global economic growth, and prevailed over communism.

. . .

Rejecting NAFTA would, quite simply, put us on the wrong side of history. That is not our destiny. I ask the House of Representatives to join me in choosing the path of expanded trade, to make the decision to compete in the world, rather than to retreat behind our borders. We are a great country, and we cannot shrink from this test.

Public Papers of the President: William J. Clinton. November 15, 1993: 1991–1995.

NAFTA MATH: IT DOESN'T ADD UP

October 20, 1993

Mr. Sander Levin (D-MI). Mr. President, today I am releasing a booklet I prepared to explain how the administration is using distorted math to claim job gains from NAFTA. It's called *NAFTA MATH: It Doesn't Add Up.*

This booklet challenges the administration's often stated claim that we will gain 200,000 jobs from NAFTA.

Obviously, people will make their own decision about whether or not to support NAFTA, but they should do so based on a full picture of the facts, not just on what they get from listening to the supporters of NAFTA.

Let me explain. The underlying premise supporting NAFTA is that United States exports to Mexico will increase and all exports create jobs.

The Commerce Department hands out a book—this book, which I have here—showing State-by-State exports to Mexico and the Commerce Department translates every billion dollars in exports into roughly 20,000 additional American jobs.

President Clinton himself has said: "Every time we sell $1 billion of American products and services overseas, we create about 20,000 jobs."

The administration has estimated that exports to Mexico will rise by "$10 billion over the next 3 years with NAFTA." And, according to the administration's math, or NAFTA math, since each $1 billion in exports creates about 20,000 jobs, $10 billion in additional exports would create about 200,000 jobs.

The Secretary of the Treasury, Lloyd Bentsen, says: "We calculate we'll pick up 200,000 more jobs" from NAFTA.

But that claim of 200,000 more jobs and NAFTA's very foundation is based on highly distorted export figures.

First, those calculations are based on export figures alone. The projection of 200,000 additional jobs from NAFTA conveniently ignores the job loss which results from imports from Mexico to the United States, which will be increased under NAFTA. It is a major distortion to only look at half the picture and claim job gains based on exports alone. It is like looking at half a ledger sheet—the revenue half—and ignoring the expense half of the ledger.

The administration has even acknowledged, after being pressed in a *Washington Post* article, that it does not deduct job losses from the added imports which will result from Mexico in its overall job gains claim.

An October 13 article by Howard Kurtz says a "USTR official confirmed that the 200,000 estimate is not a net figure." In other words, it only looks at the alleged gains from exports and does not deduct the jobs which will be lost as a result of increased imports. The Commerce Department does not give us figures on job losses from increased imports; it does not give us net job figures. All it gives us is the 200,000 additional jobs claim and totally ignores the job losses from imports.

Second, Mr. President, even if you only look at exports, one-third of American exports to Mexico go across the border for a few days or weeks for assembly and then come right back to America for consumption.

But, believe it or not, the Department of Commerce classifies as exports those American parts that are temporarily sent to Mexico for assembly and then shipped right back to the United States for consumption here. In reality, one-third of American exports represent little more than trading with ourselves. It is a little like an actor mailing himself fan mail and then citing that as evidence of his box office appeal.

What is more, Mr. President, that same one-third of American exports that the Commerce Department shows going to Mexico not only does not represent jobs gained, they often actually represent lost jobs to Americans.

Let me just give you an example. Take an assembly plant in the United States with a thousand workers that closes and moves to Mexico—1,000 jobs are lost. But some United States parts suppliers continue to supply the new Mexican assembly plant.

Mr. President, according to NAFTA math, if every American assembly plant closed and moved to Mexico, we would have a big jump in job creation in America. Because as long as some of the parts and components previously assembled here go to Mexico for assembly, they count as exports. And since exports are translated into job creation, the closing of every assembly plant in America would be a big job increaser, according to the Commerce Department, just so long as some of the parts and components are shipped to those assembly plants after they move to Mexico.

. . .

It is time for the administration to abandon attempts to sell this agreement with distortions and NAFTA math.

The Congressional Record. October 20, 1993: S 13981.

GUN CONTROL (THE BRADY BILL) (NOVEMBER 1993)

For many Americans, the phrase "gun control" constitutes fighting words. On one side of the debate, advocates of limiting Americans' access to guns, particularly handguns, is a first step in making society safer. The image of millions of angry citizens carrying guns is nightmarish for these people. By contrast, defenders of the right to carry guns believe that this constitutional right is a force for stability and crime control. On both sides, passions run high.

President Clinton supported a version of gun control known as the Brady Bill, named for James Brady, a close aide of former President Reagan who was seriously wounded and suffered permanent brain damage during the 1981 assassination attempt on President Reagan. The Brady Bill put limits on the numbers of handguns individuals can purchase, mandates background checks on weapons purchasers to prevent anyone from acquiring a gun who is not legally entitled to do so, and imposes a waiting period on handgun sales so that an angry person could not go to a store, buy a gun, and use it in a moment of passion. It also places limits and even bans on military-style assault weapons which are deemed to be intended to hunt people, not animals. Combined, Clinton argued that these limitations would help prevent guns from falling into the wrong hands and protect the broader community.

Clinton was passionately opposed by millions of Americans. Like Congressman Ronald Coleman (D-TX), opponents of the Brady Bill argued that all the Brady Bill would do was limit the rights of law-abiding citizens to own guns. Criminals, they insisted, are likely to acquire guns through illegal means. Similarly, the crimes most people are worried about—children bringing guns to school, the use of guns in violent crime, and so on—were not addressed by the Brady Bill. Accordingly, they argued that the Brady Bill would not improve safety in the United States even as it limited the rights of law-abiding citizens.

The Brady Bill passed Congress and was signed into law in 1993; it has been extensively amended in subsequent years. Hundreds of thousands of people who wished to purchase firearms but could not pass the background check for various reasons have been denied the opportunity to buy a gun. However, criminals still obtain guns illegally, and sales of military-style weapons continue as manufacturers make cosmetic changes to avoid Brady Bill restrictions. Moreover, backlash against these restrictions informed the anger that caused the Republican takeover of Congress in 1995.

Guns are still pervasive in U.S. society, but as the crime rate has declined in the 1990s so have incidences of gun violence. There is no clear evidence that Brady Bill restrictions have made a meaningful difference in controlling gun violence or the access of criminals to illegally attained weapons. Criminals who obtain guns illegally and are then arrested, however, are subject to additional penalties for the violation. Gun control remains a highly controversial issue in American society.

CLINTON'S REMARKS ON SIGNING HANDGUN CONTROL LEGISLATION

November 30, 1993

Everything that has been—that should be said about this has already been said by people whose lives are more profoundly imbued with this issue than mine. But there are some things I think we need to think about that we learned from this endeavor as we look ahead to what still needs to be done.

Since Jim and Sarah [Brady] began this crusade, more than 150,000 Americans—men, women, teenagers, children, even infants—have been killed with handguns. And many more have been wounded. One hundred and fifty thousand people from all walks of life who should have been here to share Christmas with us. This couple saw through a fight that really never should have had to occur; because still, when people are confronted with issues of clear common sense and overwhelming evidence, too often we are prevented from doing what we know we ought to do by our collective fears, whatever they may be.

The Brady Bill has finally become law, in a fundamental sense not because of any of us, but because grass roots America changed its mind and demanded that this Congress not leave here without doing something about this. And all the rest of us, even Jim and Sarah, did was to somehow light that spark that swept across the people of this country and proved once again that democracy can work. America won this battle. Americans are finally fed up with violence that cuts down another citizen with gunfire every 20 minutes.

And we know that this bill will make a difference. As Sarah said, The

Washington Post pointed out that about 50,000 people have been denied the right to buy a handgun in just four states since 1989. Don't let anybody tell you that this won't work. I got a friend back home who sold a gun years ago to a guy who had escaped from a mental hospital that he hadn't seen in 10 years. And he pulled out that old form from the 1968 act, and said, have you ever been convicted of a crime? Have you ever been in a mental hospital? The guy said, no, no—and put the form back in the drawer. And 12 hours later six people were dead and my friend is not over it to this day. Don't tell me this bill will not make a difference. That is not true. It is not true.

But we all know there is more to be done. The crime bill not only has 100,000 new police officers who, properly trained and deployed, will lower the crime rate by preventing crime, not just by catching criminals. It also has a ban on several assault weapons, long overdue; a ban on handgun ownership and restrictions on possession of handguns by minors; the beginning of reform of our federal firearms licensing systems; and an effort to make our schools safer. This is a good beginning. And there will be more to be done after that.

. . .

So, I plead with all of you today, when you leave here to be reinvigorated by this; to be exhilarated by the triumph of Jim and Sarah Brady and all these other folks who didn't let their personal losses defeat them but instead used it to come out here and push us to do better.

And each of you in turn, take your opportunity not to let people ever again in this country use a legitimate part of our American heritage in ways that blinds us to our obligation to the present and the future. If we have broken that, then there is nothing we cannot do. And when I go and sign this bill in a minute, it will be step one in taking our streets back, taking our children back, reclaiming our families and our future.

Public Papers of the President: William J. Clinton. November 30, 1993: 2079–2081.

BRADY BILL OPPOSED

November 10, 1993

Ronald D. Coleman (D-TX) . . . I rise today in opposition to the Brady bill. I oppose this measure not because of what it does; but for what it fails to do. I agree with the proponents of this measure that we ought to have an automated system by which we can determine whether or not someone is legally barred from owning a gun. . . . However, I must oppose this legislation because it is not a crime control solution. The Brady bill will not reduce crime, nor will it prevent handgun violence. Indeed, it will not even prevent those who are legally barred from possessing a gun from doing so.

Let me say that this was not a decision I made lightly or quickly. I have weighed very carefully the arguments on both sides of this debate. Personally, I have found the increasing levels of gun violence, especially among our children, very distressing. Every day, approximately 135,000 children bring a gun to school. Every day, 14 children die in gun accidents, suicides and homicides. Every day, 30 American children are wounded by guns. There was a time, not that long ago, when accidents were the leading cause of death among our young people. This is no longer the case. Gun deaths are now the leading cause of death among young people, particularly in minority communities.

However, the Brady bill will do nothing to stem the violence which now confronts our Nation's youth. Handgun Control has stated that 1.2 million elementary aged, latch-key children have access to guns in their homes. I respectfully invite anyone in this body to explain to me exactly how enactment of the Brady bill will change this situation. The truth is no one can, because enactment of the Brady bill will do nothing to reduce a child's access to guns in his or her home. More importantly, this bill does nothing to address the fact that guns are being sold to children in the streets by criminals. Brady will do nothing to reduce, curb or prevent gang and other violence which now threatens our young people because it does not apply to them. Passing the Brady bill will not prevent acts of youth violence.

I also must question just how effective Brady will be in combating other types of violent crime. Just how many violent criminals do we honestly believe will submit to a background check and 5-day wait to purchase their weapons. I suggest that significantly less than 1 percent are likely to do so, the rest will simply continue to purchase their weapons as they are already doing illegally. This measure will not combat crime in the least. The people most impacted by enactment of the Brady bill are those who have a legal right to purchase a firearm and exercise that right through a licensed firearms dealer. If we are attempting to combat crime, then let us do that; to my colleagues I say that we should honestly admit that the Brady bill is not the proper vehicle for achieving that end.

To address the very real problem of violent crime, I respectfully urge my colleagues on the Judiciary Committee to act on measures which will ensure swift justice. If we are serious that we want to get tough on crime let us do that. We should appropriate additional funds for more courts, more prosecutors and more prisons. This vote today on the Brady bill is nothing more than a feel good vote which will do nothing to address the problem of violence in our society. I understand why this legislation is attractive to many; but it simply will not further our nation's efforts to combat crime. In casting my vote against this measure, I urge my colleagues to join me in focusing our attention on the root causes of crimes and our actions against those who perpetrate them.

The Congressional Record. November 17, 1993: E 2923.

DRUG CONTROL (APRIL 1996)

Drugs are a perennial issue in post-1960s America. The Reagan-Bush strategy was to punish drug users, imprison drug dealers, and use U.S. military and other forces in an attempt to interdict and cut off the supply of drugs coming into the United States. The effect of these policies was to increase the number and cost of prisons in the United States; however, drug use did not decline. Clinton articulated a new strategy that added drug treatment and economic development to the Reagan-Bush strategy.

Clinton's argument was that if Americans want people to remain drug free, the nation has to help them. In addition, he argued that increasing economic opportunities would make drugs less attractive. Thus, while interdiction and destroying drug networks were important, it was also important to give people hope for the future. A combined strategy of punishment and reward would go further to resolving America's drug crisis than discipline alone.

Opponents of the Clinton strategy, including Senator Alfonse D'Amato (R-NY), articulated the Reagan-Bush line. In their view, the cost of drug use and drug dealing had to be raised so high that no one would be willing to pay it. Accordingly, they advocated longer sentences for both dealers and users, increases in prison building and terms of imprisonment, and greater efforts at drug interdiction.

The basic outline of Clinton's drug-control strategy was largely rejected by Congress. Since Congress was controlled by Republicans, its members supported a drug-control strategy similar to that of Presidents Reagan and Bush: more prisons, more arrests, and greater penalties. Treatment, from this perspective, supports drug abuse; it does not prevent it. Accordingly, Clinton's plans were rejected.

Drugs remain a problem in U.S. society. While rates of drug use declined in the first years of Clinton's term, recent evidence suggests they are rising again, particularly among the young. New, "designer" drugs are now drawing increasing numbers of users. Budgetary support for both treatment and interdiction have declined. It is estimated that fully half of all U.S. prisoners are serving drug-related sentences. Interdiction and punishment obviously have not ended the drug problem. Whether treatment would work has not been tested. However, neither major party candidate in the 2000 presidential election advocated developing treatment policies; thus, such programs are unlikely in the near future.

CLINTON'S MESSAGE TO THE CONGRESS TRANSMITTING THE NATIONAL DRUG CONTROL STRATEGY

April 29, 1996

I am pleased to transmit to the Congress the 1996 National Drug Control Strategy. This Strategy carries forward the policies and principles of the 1994 and 1995 Strategies. It describes new directions and initiatives to confront the ever-changing challenges of drug abuse and trafficking.

This past March I convened the White House Leadership Conference on Youth, Drug Use, and Violence in order to focus the Nation's attention on two major health problems faced by young people today—drug use and violence....

... In the last few years our nation has made significant progress against drug use and related crime. The number of Americans who use cocaine has been reduced by 30 percent since 1992. The amount of money Americans spend on illicit drugs has declined from an estimated $64 billion five years ago to about $49 billion in 1993—a 23 percent drop. We are finally gaining ground against overall crime: drug-related murders are down 12 percent since 1989; robberies are down 10 percent since 1991.

At the same time, we have dealt serious blows to the international criminal networks that import drugs into America. Many powerful drug lords, including leaders of Colombia's notorious Cali cartel, have been arrested. A multinational air interdiction program has disrupted the principal air route for smugglers between Peru and Colombia. The close cooperation between the United States, Peru, and other governments in the region has disrupted the cocaine economy in several areas. Our efforts have decreased overall cocaine production and have made coca planting less attractive to the farmers who initiate the cocaine production process. And I have taken the serious step of cutting off all non-humanitarian aid to certain drug producing and trafficking nations that have not cooperated with the United States in narcotics control. Further, I have ordered that we vote against their requests for loans from the World Bank and other multi-lateral development banks. This clearly underscores the unwavering commitment of the United States to stand against drug production and trafficking.

Here at home, we have achieved major successes in arresting, prosecuting, and dismantling criminal drug networks. In Miami, the High Intensity Drug Trafficking Program, through its operational task forces, successfully concluded a major operation that resulted in the indictments of 252 individuals for drug trafficking and other drug-related crimes. Operations conducted by the Drug Enforcement Administration's Mobile Enforcement Teams program (MET), a highly successful federal tool for assisting local law enforcement, have resulted in more than 1,500 arrests of violent and predatory drug criminals in more than 50 communities across the nation.

But as the White House Leadership Conference on Youth, Drug Use, and Violence showed, now is the time to press forward. . . .

There are many reasons why young people do continue to use drugs. Chief among these are ignorance of the facts about addiction and the potency of drugs, and complacency about the danger of drugs. Unfortunately, all too often we see signs of complacency about the dangers of drug use: diminished attention to the drug problem by the national media; the glamorization and legitimization of drug use in the entertainment industry; the coddling of professional athletes who are habitual drug-users; avoidance of the issue by parents and other adults; calls for drug-legalization; and the marketing of products to young people that legitimize and elevate the use of alcohol, tobacco, and illicit drugs.

All Americans must accept responsibility to teach young people that drugs are illegal and they are deadly. They may land you in jail; they may cost you your life. We must renew our commitment to the drug prevention strategies that deter first-time drug use and stop the progression from alcohol and tobacco use to marijuana and harder drugs.

The National Drug Control Strategy is designed to prevent a new drug use epidemic through an aggressive and comprehensive full-court press that harnesses the energies of committed individuals from every sector of our society. As I said in the State of the Union, we must step up our attack against criminal youth gangs that deal in illicit drugs. We will improve the effectiveness of our cooperative efforts among U.S. defense and law enforcement agencies, as well as with other nations, to disrupt the flow of drugs coming into the country. We will seek to expand the availability and improve the quality of drug treatment. And we will continue to oppose resolutely calls for the legalization of illicit drugs. We will increase efforts to prevent drug use by all Americans, particularly young people.

Public Papers of the President: William J. Clinton. April 29, 1996: 660–661.

CRITICISM OF THE 1995 NATIONAL DRUG CONTROL STRATEGY

March 22, 1995

Mr. Alfonse D'Amato (R-NY) . . . The Office of National Drug Control Policy [ONDCP] has now released its annual National Drug Control Strategy, dated February 1995. I regret that this strategy continues in the direction established in the 1994 strategy, a direction I strongly criticized at the time. The administration has produced another deeply flawed document that will not advance the war against drugs.

In this document the administration outlines its priorities for dealing with illicit drugs. The document extols treatment and prevention as the primary tools in combating the drug problem. The strategy never addresses interdiction. It stresses policy changes to enhance the administration's demand side approach to dealing with the flood of foreign illegal drugs entering the United States, rather than enforcement efforts.

. . . The strategy frequently contradicts itself from one chapter to the next in its interpretation of its findings, whether the findings were based on surveys or medical reports. This strategy provides an overinflated justification for expanded treatment and prevention efforts, without ever dealing with the underlying problem of the ease with which illegal drugs can be obtained.

Furthermore, this document attempts to distinguish between the drug user and the drug dealer, claiming one is a public health problem while the other is a criminal. The truth of the matter is that both using and dealing are criminal violations and the dealer could not exist, much less profit, without the user. Drug dealers can only be arrested by working through drug users. Therefore, enforcement efforts against users should not be curtailed, but instead reinforced.

. . .

While demand reduction is the ultimate key to victory in the war on drugs, this approach completely disregards the immediate problems of the availability of illicit drugs, the monetary rewards for dealing illegal drugs, and the constant flow of illegal drugs into the United States. Furthermore, most drug dealers are also drug users. How are the courts to differentiate between the classes of criminals as described within this strategy?

Law enforcement efforts and the criminal penalties for illegal drug activities directly affect drug availability, financial incentives for drug trafficking, and the flow of these illegal drugs. Once the supply is reduced, then treatment can be effective to further reduce demand. The section of the strategy closes with 14 listed goals to be used as the measure of success for the strategy. The top eight goals are all treatment or prevention measures. Once again this strategy of targeting treatment without addressing illegal drug availability and drug law enforcement concerns is akin to the old problem of putting the cart before the horse.

. . .

In my remarks on the drug problem in prior years, I emphasized the importance of social delegitimization of illegal drug use. I believe that the crop of new users reported by ONDCP is, in important part, the product of a relegitimization of illegal drug use, flowing from messages of tolerance implicit in the administration's statements and actions on this subject, taken as a whole.

Mr. President, it is not premature to issue a serious assessment of this administration's performance in the war on drugs. It has been dismal, and will only get worse. The problem is that the full penalty for this administration's failures—in analyzing and understanding the problem, in crafting a policy and budgetary response to it, and in implementing its decisions—will be paid by future generations of Americans.

The Congressional Record. March 22, 1995: S 4394.

MEGAN'S LAW (MAY 1996)

Sex-related crimes are among the most vicious in our society. Victims of such crimes are often either killed or damaged for life. Accordingly, there is a strong backlash against those who perpetrate such crimes, and many citizens want to know whether sex offenders have moved in to their neighborhoods. This is particularly important since the recidivism, or repeat, rate for sex crimes is very high. However, under U.S. law, after a person has served his or her sentence for a crime, the person is not obliged to inform others of the conviction. People who have served their time are entitled to the same right to privacy as other Americans.

President Clinton favored a policy requiring that, on their release from prison, convicted sex offenders personally inform their neighbors of the nature of their crime and that they have moved into the area. This policy is named Megan's Law for a New Jersey girl who was killed by a recently released sex criminal who had moved into her neighborhood without the knowledge of the neighbors. Clinton argued that the safety of the community was more important than the right to privacy of convicted sex offenders. Moreover, he insisted that states had an obligation to inform communities of the whereabouts of sexual offenders in their areas. Armed with this information, then, parents and others can protect their children and themselves from potentially dangerous individuals.

Opponents of Megan's Law were in a difficult position: arguing that criminals had rights in the face of the horrible murder of a seven-year-old child was difficult. While a few critics made the argument that sex offenders deserved the same right to privacy as other people, the short terms of sex offenders were more commonly criticized by the Libertarian party: They were back too soon on the street potentially to cause more harm. (Ironically, the quick release of sex offenders is related to the war on drugs: as American prisons have filled with minor drug offenders, many other criminals convicted of non–drug related charges have to be released to make room for drug offenders serving mandatory sentences.)

Megan's Law passed easily. Both Republicans and Democrats wanted to be on the right side of this issue: in an election year, no one wanted to face an election opponent who would accuse them of being soft on sex offenders. Indeed, Clinton made Megan's Law a centerpiece of his campaign for reelection: it stood, he said, as an example of his status as a "New Democrat" not afraid to attack crime. While his reelection cannot be attributed to Megan's Law, Clinton's New Democrat philosophy did aid his easy victory in 1996.

Megan's Law has been upheld by the U.S. Supreme Court as an appropriate limitation of privacy in favor of community safety. Published incidences of convicted sex offenders committing similar crimes in their new areas of residence have lessened. However, there have been attacks against individual offenders by community members, highlighting the tension between the right to privacy and the right of a community to defend itself.

CLINTON'S REMARKS IN THE BILL SIGNING CEREMONY FOR MEGAN'S LAW

May 17, 1996

This has been a week in which our country is moving to combat crime and violence. A couple of days ago we awarded over 9,000 new police officers to some 2,500 communities. That brings us to 43,000 police officers in 20 months along the road to our goal of 100,000. We're ahead of schedule and under budget.

But today the valiant presence of five American parents reminds us that this fight against crime is so much more a fight for peace and for safety for our people, and especially for our children. Richard and Maureen Kanka, Patty Wetterling, Marc Klaas and John Walsh have suffered more than any parent should ever have to suffer. They have lived through the greatest pain a parent can know—a child brutally ripped from a parent's love. And somehow they found within themselves the strength to bear a further burden. They took up the parents' concerns for all children's safety and dedicated themselves to answering that concern.

Each of you deserves the fullest measure of your country's thanks. Because of you, steps have already been taken to help families protect their children. Study after study has shown us that sex offenders commit crime after crime. So two years ago, we gave every state the power to notify communities about child sex offenders and violent sex offenders who move into their neighborhoods. We're fighting now to uphold these laws in courts all across the country, and we will fight to uphold them all the way to the Supreme Court.

Today we are taking the next step. From now on, every state in the country will be required by law to tell a community when a dangerous sexual predator enters its midst. We respect people's rights, but today America proclaims there is no greater right than a parent's right to raise a child in safety and love. Today, America warns: If you dare to prey on our children, the law will follow you wherever you go, state to state, town to town. Today, America circles the wagon around our children. Megan's Law will protect tens of millions of families from the dread of what they do not know. It will give more peace of mind to our parents.

To understand what this law really means, never forget its name—the name of a seven-year-old girl taken wrongly in the beginning of her life. The law that bears a name of one child is now for every child, for every parent and every family. It is for Polly and Jacob and Adam, and, above all, for Megan.

Public Papers of the President: William J. Clinton. May 17, 1996: 763–764.

LIBERTARIANS ASK: WILL MEGAN'S LAW PROTECT POLITICIANS—OR OUR CHILDREN?

August 29, 1997

Megan's Law will be better at protecting the jobs of politicians than protecting the lives of children, the Libertarian Party charged today.

"When politicians talk about community notification, what they really mean is: 'We've just set more child rapists free in your neighborhood,' " said Steve Dasbach, the party's national chairman. "Megan's Law may make politicians feel better, but it won't make our children any safer."

The New Jersey law, which was upheld by a federal appeals court last week, allows states to notify communities when sex offenders are released. The law is named for Megan Kanka, the 7-year-old girl who was raped and murdered in 1994 by Jesse Timmendequas, who lived across the street.

"The fact is, Megan would be alive today if this predator, who had been convicted twice of sexual attacks on children, had been kept behind bars where he belonged," said Dasbach. "But instead of protecting her, politicians have virtually guaranteed that many more Megans will be brutalized."

The reason: Child molesters serve an average of just 37 months in prison, according to the U.S. Department of Justice—which is less than half the average sentence for such crimes.

"In other words, child molesters get to spend three to four extra years roaming your neighborhood—instead of serving out their full jail terms," said Dasbach. "Forget Megan's Law: Wouldn't Americans feel safer if these criminals were behind bars, instead of living next door?"

So why are dangerous child molesters—who have terrifyingly high recidivism rates—being sprung from jail so early? It's part of an ongoing national trend to imprison fewer violent criminals, noted Dasbach.

"In 1980, a full 48.2% of newly sentenced offenders had been convicted of violent crime. By 1992, that number had fallen to 28.5%," he said. "During the same time, the number of people in jail for drug crimes skyrocketed from 6.8% to 30.5%."

"Politicians had a choice: They could either keep child molesters behind bars, or imprison people for smoking marijuana. They chose to release psychopathic criminals who prey on children, and the murder of Megan Kanka is the price we've paid for that policy," he said.

In response to public outcry, politicians passed Megan's Law—to show that they care about protecting vulnerable Americans from violent crime, said Dasbach.

"But their actions speak louder than their laws. And politicians' actions say they expect panicked parents to play police officer and be on the lookout for the dangerous psychopaths who they've turned loose," he said.

In addition, Dasbach said, Megan's Law won't work anyway, is almost certainly unconstitutional, and guarantees that innocent people will be persecuted. Specifically . . .

- Megan's Law covers just one out of five child molesters.

- "According to a Justice Department study, half of all child molesters are friends or distant relatives of the victim, and a third are their parents—meaning that just 20% are strangers," Dasbach said. "Community notification may lull parents into a false sense of security, causing them to stop looking for signs of sexual abuse by people closer to home."

- Community notification punishes people twice for the same crime—in clear violation of the Constitution.
- "Politicians can't have it both ways," Dasbach said. "Either these people are dangerous criminals, who should be in prison, or they aren't—in which case they should be released with their full civil rights restored. Politicians shouldn't be allowed to use fear of crime as an excuse to molest the Constitution."

August 29, 1997. http://www.lp.org/rel/970829-Megan.html

INVESTIGATION AND IMPEACHMENT (JANUARY 1999)

William Jefferson Clinton has the distinction of being only the second president—and the only elected president—to be impeached by the House of Representatives and put on trial by the U.S. Senate. Impeachment came after years of investigations undertaken by various special prosecutors who examined Clinton's business dealings. In the aftermath of the Watergate (1972–1974) scandal, in which President Richard Nixon fired an investigator looking into Nixon's illegal activities, the U.S. Congress passed a law creating the position of "special prosecutor"—an individual with broad power to investigate senior government officials but who cannot be fired by the president. Several such investigators examined Clinton's record during his time in office; one, Kenneth Starr, released a report summarizing the results of his investigation and asking the U.S. House of Representatives to impeach the president.

Investigators examined whether Clinton and his wife had profited from illegal insider information in the Whitewater real estate development in Arkansas. They investigated whether Clinton had abused his powers by firing the Bush-era appointees who ran the White House travel office. They looked into whether Clinton and his wife had conspired to cover up any potentially illegal activities by hiding White House documents that subsequently appeared in First Lady Hillary Clinton's White House office. Investigators questioned whether the suicide of Clinton friend and advisor Vince Foster was really a murder intended to protect Clinton from prosecution. They also examined allegations of sexual harassment lodged against Clinton for actions taken while he was the governor of Arkansas. Clinton's administration was one of the most investigated in American history.

Despite the scope of these investigations, Clinton was impeached for only two alleged crimes: lying under oath that he did not have a sexual relationship with a White House intern, and obstructing justice by attempting to convince his friends and advisors that he did not have a relationship with the intern. Clinton did have an affair, but this is not illegal. The allegations were based on questions he was asked as part of a sexual harassment lawsuit filed by Paula Jones. Jones alleged that Clinton had sexually harassed her when he was governor of Arkansas and she was an Arkansas state employee. As part of that investigation, Clinton was asked about subsequent relationships he might have had. His evasive answers to those questions were the source of the alleged lying under oath and obstruction of justice.

Clinton's defense on the allegations moved forward on multiple fronts. First, he claimed that he did not, technically, lie under oath because the questions he was asked were vague. Accordingly, vague answers did not constitute lies. Second, he argued that even if senators believed that he had lied he should not be removed from office because lying about a sexual affair did not constitute the condition of "high crimes and misdemeanors" specified by the Constitution for removing a president from office. No president, he said, should be "unelected" in such circumstances.

Advocates for Clinton's removal, including Congressman James Talent (R-MO), argued that presidents, even more than ordinary citizens, have an obligation to follow the law even in embarrassing circumstances. The fact that Clinton did not want to admit to a private affair was irrelevant: he was asked a legal question in a legal proceeding and so had a legal obligation to answer fully and truthfully. In addition, anyone who would lie in such circumstances could not be trusted to serve as president. They also insisted that Clinton's actions to hide the affair constituted an abuse of his executive power and so easily met the standard of high crimes and misdemeanors for which presidents can be removed from office.

After the House of Representatives impeached Clinton on four counts by a simple majority vote on December 11–12, 1998, he was put on trial by the Senate as required by the Constitution. A two-thirds majority of the senators must vote to remove a president from office. On February 12, 1999, the Senate voted 55 to 45 to convict Clinton of lying under oath and 50 to 50 to convict him of obstruction of justice. Both votes failed to meet the two-thirds requirement, and Clinton remained in office. His power was diminished, yet, as president, his power to veto and to shape budgets remained intact. He remained a formidable force in American and world politics through the rest of his term.

Perhaps the most significant long-term effect of the impeachment trial was on the 2000 presidential election. The Republican candidate, Texas Governor George W. Bush, made ethics, honesty, and credibility a centerpiece of his campaign. His strategy emphasized the scandals of the Clinton administration and tried to exploit the nation's "Clinton fatigue":

its exhaustion at hearing about the scandals of Clinton's time in office. By contrast, the Democratic candidate, Vice President Al Gore, was forced to distance himself from Clinton to avoid the taint of scandal even as the general conditions of the nation—its economy; its peaceful status; its lowering of crime, abortion, and unemployment rates—would encourage him to wrap himself in Clinton's mantle. Thus, even though he was not convicted, Clinton clearly affected the 2000 presidential campaign adversely.

TRIAL MEMORANDUM OF PRESIDENT WILLIAM JEFFERSON CLINTON

(Excerpts from brief written by Clinton defense team and submitted to the U.S. Senate before the impeachment trial opened.)

January 13, 1999

The Senate, in receipt of Articles of Impeachment from the House of Representatives, is now gathered in trial to consider whether that decision should be set aside for the remaining two years of the President's term. It is a power contemplated and authorized by the Framers of the Constitution, but never before employed in our nation's history. The gravity of what is at stake—the democratic choice of the American people—and the solemnity of the proceedings dictate that a decision to remove the President from office should follow only from the most serious of circumstances and should be done in conformity with Constitutional standards and in the interest of the Nation and its people.

The Articles of Impeachment that have been exhibited to the Senate fall far short of what the Founding Fathers had in mind when they placed in the hands of the Congress the power to impeach and remove a President from office. They fall far short of what the American people demand be shown and proven before their democratic choice is reversed. And they even fall far short of what a prudent prosecutor would require before presenting a case to a judge or jury.

. . . and we see clearly that the House of Representatives asks the Senate to remove the President from office because he:

- used the phrase "certain occasions" to describe the frequency of his improper intimate contacts with Ms. Monica Lewinsky. There were, according to the House Managers, eleven such contacts over the course of approximately 500 days.

Should the will of the people be overruled and the President of the United States be removed from office because he used the phrase "certain occasions" to describe eleven events over some 500 days? That is what the House of Representatives asks the Senate to do.

- used the word "occasional" to describe the frequency of inappropriate telephone conversations between he and Monica Lewinsky. According to Ms. Lewinsky, the President and Ms. Lewinsky engaged in between ten and fifteen such conversations spanning a 23-month period.

Should the will of the people be overruled and the President of the United States be removed from office because he used the word "occasional" to describe up to 15 telephone calls over a 23-month period? That is what the House of Representatives asks the Senate to do.

- said the improper relationship with Ms. Lewinsky began in early 1996, while she recalls that it began in November 1995. And he said the contact did not include touching certain parts of her body, while she said it did.

Should the will of the people be overruled and the President of the United States be removed from office because two people have a different recollection of the details of a wrongful relationship—which the President has admitted? That is what the House of Representatives asks the Senate to do.

The Articles of Impeachment are not limited to the examples cited above, but the other allegations of wrongdoing are similarly unconvincing. There is the charge that the President unlawfully obstructed justice by allegedly trying to find a job for Monica Lewinsky in exchange for her silence about their relationship. This charge is made despite the fact that no one involved in the effort to find work for Ms. Lewinsky—including Ms. Lewinsky herself—testifies that there was any connection between the job search and the affidavit. Indeed, the basis for that allegation, Ms. Lewinsky's statements to Ms. Tripp, was expressly repudiated by Ms. Lewinsky under oath.

. . .

In the final analysis, the House is asking the Senate to remove the President because he had a wrongful relationship and sought to keep the existence of that relationship private.

Nothing said in this Trial Memorandum is intended to excuse the President's actions. By his own admission, he is guilty of personal failings.

As he has publicly stated, "I don't think there is a fancy way to say that I have sinned." He has misled his family, his friends, his staff, and the Nation about the nature of his relationship with Ms. Lewinsky. He hoped to avoid exposure of personal wrongdoing so as to protect his family and himself and to avoid public embarrassment. He has acknowledged that his actions were wrong.

By the same token, these actions must not be mischaracterized into a wholly groundless excuse for removing the President from the office to which he was twice elected by the American people. The allegations in the articles and the argument in the House Managers' Trial Memorandum do not begin to satisfy the stringent showing required by our Founding Fathers to remove a duly elected President from office, either as a matter of fact or law.

The Congressional Record. January 13, 1999: S 59–68.

IN SUPPORT OF THE ARTICLES OF IMPEACHMENT

January 6, 1999

Mr. James Talent (R-MO). Mr. Speaker, it is not my preference or custom to speak on matters relating to the misconduct of others who hold public office. I have never done so before during my time in Congress. I hope never to have to do so again.

But the Constitution confides in Members of this House the obligation to decide whether high officers have acted in a manner that requires their impeachment. Where an official has a legal or moral obligation to judge misconduct and when that obligation cannot honorably be avoided, it is necessary to stand without flinching for what is clearly right.

Those failing to do so become inevitably part of the wrong against which they failed to act. The issue before the House is not whether Bill Clinton has acted with integrity. We all know the answer to that question. The issue is whether we have the integrity to do our duty under the Constitution and laws.

Public men and women commit private wrongs, just like everyone else. And just like everyone else, they are usually called to account for those wrongs in the fullness of time. If they act honorably when called to account, and accept responsibility for what they have done, they can emerge with a measure of their integrity intact. If they act less than honorably and refuse to own up to their actions, they may, and often are judged by the voters.

Their fellow officers in government have no warrant to judge them formally if they at least conform to the minimum standards of law and morality in how they react. But the minimum standards are just that: the minimum that we have the right to expect and insist upon. No one can fall below those standards with impunity. No officer of government can actively subvert the law, abuse the powers of his office and flout the standards of decency without facing the consequences that any other person in a position of trust would have to face.

That is the gravamen of the charges against President Clinton. The genesis of this matter was the President's liaison with Monica Lewinsky. But that affair, however sordid, was a private wrong. The Articles of Impeachment deal exclusively with what the President did to avoid the consequences when that private wrong reached the eyes and ears of the public. When the President was called to account before the people, he lied to the people; when he was called to account before a civil deposition, he lied under oath; and then, to cover up those initial lies, he tampered with witnesses, abused the trust of other officers of government, perjured himself before a federal grand jury, and abused the powers of the Presidency to avert investigations into his wrong doing.

From the record before the House, it is impossible to conclude anything other than that the President is guilty of these wrongs. He is therefore, in my judgment unfit to hold any position of trust, much less the Presidency.

. . .

The term "high crimes or misdemeanors" means a deliberate pattern of misconduct so grave as to disqualify the person committing it from holding a position of trust and responsibility. The President's misconduct qualifies as such an offense according to the commonly accepted understandings of civic responsibility, never before questioned until this controversy arose. No one would have argued a year ago that a President could perjure himself, obstruct justice, and tamper with witnesses without facing impeachment, and no one would argue that a business, labor, educational, or civic leader should stay in a position of trust having committed such misconduct. Congress has impeached and removed high officers for less than the President has done. Are we to lower the standards of our society because the President cannot live up to them?

. . .

Mr. Speaker, this whole affair, distasteful as it is, presents an opportunity for the House to make a clear statement. There is such a thing as right and wrong. No society, and certainly not a constitutional republic like America, can endure without acknowledging that fact; and if we believe in right and wrong, we must give life to that belief by trusting that the right thing will be the best thing for our country. I urge each member of the House to do his duty today in the faith that only in that way can America emerge stronger.

The Congressional Record. January 6, 1999: E 12.

TAX CUTS AND BUDGET SURPLUS (SEPTEMBER 1999)

In 1998, when the United States began to enjoy budget surpluses for the first time since the 1960s, a debate broke out about what to do with the excess money the federal government was collecting. Three basic options emerged: tax cuts, or returning the extra revenues to citizens; debt reduction, or paying off the accumulated debt of the United States; and Social Security and Medicare reform, or saving the excess to pay for benefits for retired persons.

President Clinton favored using the surplus to reduce the debt and to "save" Social Security and Medicare. In his view, the debt was a burden accumulated during his lifetime, and unless it was paid off quickly it would be later generations who would be burdened by the task. This, he said, was not fair. In addition, he argued that unless extra money was saved for Social Security and Medicare, these important programs would not have enough money to pay for benefits for the large number of people who were going to start to retire after 2020. Accordingly, he opposed tax cuts in favor of using the money on these other programs.

Proponents of tax cuts, such as Congressman Jim Bunning (R-KY), made two, central arguments. First, they noted that taxes constitute citizens' income taken by the government; if government does not need so much money, it should return it to the people who earned it. Second, they claimed that Clinton and other Democrats wanted to increase government spending and would not use the excess to reduce the debt, save Social Security, and fund Medicare.

President Clinton vetoed the Republican tax cut bill. This veto was not overturned; accordingly, taxes were not lowered. This veto became a centerpiece of the 2000 presidential campaign since it serves as a symbol of the difference between Republicans and Democrats regarding tax policy: Republicans favor tax cuts; Democrats favor new government spending and debt reduction.

Since Clinton's veto, and in the context of the 2000 presidential campaign, the debate about what to do with the surplus has intensified as estimates of its projected size have continued to expand. By 2010, the ten-year accumulated surplus is estimated, conservatively, at $1.6 trillion. The politics of budget surpluses can be expected to be a central part of U.S. politics through 2010 at the least.

CLINTON'S RADIO ADDRESS TO THE NATION

September 25, 1999

For almost seven years now, Vice President Gore and I have pursued a new economic strategy that focused on fiscal discipline, expanding trade in American products and services and investing in our people and new technology.

The results are now clear. The past six and a half years have produced the longest peacetime expansion in history; more than 19 million new jobs; rising wages; the lowest unemployment, welfare and crime rates in a generation; the highest levels of homeownership ever; a balanced budget; and the largest surplus ever. It has given the American people more money in their paychecks, lower interest rates for homes and cars, more help through efforts like the HOPE Scholarship to open the doors of college to all. We're on a path of progress and prosperity. The American people want it to continue.

That's why two days ago, I vetoed the Republicans' risky, $792 billion tax plan. It was just too big, too bloated; it would place too big a burden on our economy and run the risk of higher interest rates and lower growth. Also, it didn't add a day to the Social Security trust fund or a dollar to Medicare. And it would have forced cuts of nearly 50 percent in everything from education to health care to the environment to veterans programs to national security—even in air traffic safety.

It would have created an untenable choice for the Congress: these irresponsible cuts on the one hand; or on the other, diverting ever more funds from the Social Security surplus and from debt reduction. We said, all of us did, just a few months ago, that we shouldn't spend the Social Security surplus anymore. Today, I say again to the congressional majority, we don't have to do that. I gave them a plan to expand the life of the Social Security trust fund 50 years, to extend Medicare over 25 years and add prescription drug coverage, to invest in education and other priorities, to provide an affordable tax cut and still to pay down the debt and make us debt-free as a nation for the first time since 1835.

But the congressional majority continues on a track that doesn't adequately fund America's real priorities, while already spending large amounts of the Social Security surplus, instead of preserving it for debt reduction. A month ago, their own Congressional Budget Office estimated they'd used $16 to $19 billion of the surplus for Social Security, and steps they've taken since then have only made it go higher. They have used what the *Wall Street Journal*, the *New York Times* and others have called "budget gimmicks" to give the impression that they have simply created $17 billion out of thin air.

At the same time, they're still not providing nearly enough for education and other vital priorities. In fact, the very same day I vetoed their budget-busting tax plan, they passed a bill out of committee that would seriously undermine our efforts to strengthen education. It would eliminate our effort to hire 100,000 quality teachers and reduce class size—something they themselves endorsed last year at election time. It would deny hundreds of thousands of young people access to after-school programs.

It would eliminate our mentoring program, which is designed to get poor children into college. It doesn't improve or expand Head Start. It cuts the successful America Reads program, which now involves students from a thousand colleges going to tens of thousands of our young children to make sure they can read. It cuts our efforts to connect all our classrooms and schools to the Internet by the year 2000. And, again, there's not any funding for our plan to build or modernize 6,000 schools. All this at a time when we need to be doing more, not less, to prepare for the 21st century—for what is now the largest group of schoolchildren in our history.

There's a better way. The Republicans should work with us to create a budget that pays for itself with straightforward proposals like our tobacco policy. They should work with us to create a real Social Security lockbox, that would devote the entire surplus to debt reduction from Social Security taxes and extend the life of Social Security until the middle of the next century—something their plan doesn't do.

. . .

I'm reaching out to the Republicans to engage with us on Medicare. I want to do the same on education, on Social Security, on paying down our debt. We owe it to the American people to give it our best efforts. The results could make the 21st century America's best days.

September 25, 1999. http://www.pub.whitehouse.gov/uri-res/I2R?urn:pdi://oma.eop.gov.us/1999/9/27/2.text.1

SUPPORT FOR THE TAXPAYERS REFUND AND RELIEF ACT OF 1999

August 5, 1999

Mr. Jim Bunning (R-KY). Mr. President, I rise in strong support on conference report on the Taxpayers Refund and Relief Act of 1999 and urge my colleagues to support it. I congratulate Senator Roth and his staff on getting such a great bill to the floor of the Senate. I urge the President of the United States to reconsider his threat to veto it.

It is a good bill. It is responsible in its timing. It is responsible in its provisions. And it is definitely responsible to let the American taxpayers keep a little more of their own money.

. . .

Federal tax rates are at an all-time, peace-time high, consuming more than 20.6 percent of the Nation's economic output. That is a higher tax rate than any year except 1944 at the height of World War II when Federal taxes consumed 20.9 percent of the gross domestic product.

At the same time, we are anticipating record budget surpluses. The economists tell us that over the next 10 years, the Federal Government will take in nearly $3 trillion more than it needs. Even if we set aside $1.9 trillion of that surplus to safeguard Social Security and pay down the public debt, the Federal Government will still have $1 trillion more than it needs over the next 10 years.

It is hard to imagine a more opportune or reasonable time to cut taxes. Tax rates are at record highs—budget surpluses are at record highs. What more do you need?

In a similar vein, it is difficult to dispute any of the major provisions in this bill on the basis of fairness. It does a lot of good things.

It reduces each of the personal income tax rates, which currently range from 15 percent to 39.6 percent by 1 percentage point so that low- and moderate-income taxpayers receive a larger real cut than those in higher income brackets.

It reduces the capital gains tax moderately and indexes capital gains to account for inflation. It encourages savings by increasing IRA contribution limits from $2,000 to $5,000.

It would eliminate the odious death tax which destroys family businesses and farms. Point by point, it is difficult to portray any of these provisions as radical or unfair.

It is also difficult to question the fairness of the bill's provisions which try to eliminate the marriage penalty that exists under current tax law and which forces 20 million married couples to pay about $1,400 a year more in taxes than unmarried couples.

In an effort to eliminate this inequity, the Taxpayer Refund Act increases the standard deduction and raises the upper limit of the 14-percent bracket for married couples.

The individual provisions in the tax cut bill are reasonable and fair.

Still, the President insists that a $792 billion tax cut is irresponsible and reckless. Even though our Republican plan sets aside $1.9 trillion to secure Social Security and pay down the public debt—even though it reserves another $277 billion to pay for Medicare reform or other essential services—even though the tax cuts are phased in slowly over 10 years, the President claims it is reckless and irresponsible.

It is easy to understand why. He wants to spend more. He says cutting taxes $792 billion is reckless but he didn't have any qualms about proposing 81 new spending programs that would cost $1.033 trillion in his budget proposal this year.

He clearly believes that the money belongs to the Federal Government—not the taxpayers. And he clearly plans to find ways to spend that surplus if given the chance. That is the big question that faces the Nation right now. Whose money is it and is it more responsible to give some of it back to the taxpayers than it is to spend it?

I have heard a lot about Federal Reserve Board Chairman Alan Greenspan's recent testimony before a Senate Committee on which I serve and, admittedly, he was not overly enthusiastic about cutting taxes right now.

He would prefer that we use all the budget surplus to pay down the debt. But, he also made it clear that the worst thing we could do is to spend the surplus on new programs. He made it clear that cutting taxes would be preferable to expanding Federal spending. Our tax bill already pays down the debt more than the President's plan and if we don't cut taxes now, make no mistake about it, the President will find plenty of ways to spend the rest of that surplus.

This bill simply says that when tax rates are at record highs and the Government has more money than it needs to protect Social Security and Medicare and to pay down the debt, the responsible thing to do is to give some of that money back to the people who pay the taxes.

There is nothing reckless about the Republican tax cut. It protects Social Security and Medicare. It reduces the debt more than the President's plan.

It reserves several hundred billion to pay for essential services or to pay the debt down even more. The timing is right. The provisions are fair. It simply allows the Nation's taxpayers to keep a little more of their own money.

The Congressional Record. August 5, 1999: S 10307.

MILITARY AND FOREIGN POLICY

PEACEKEEPING IN SOMALIA (OCTOBER 1993)

When he came to office, President Clinton inherited a policy established by President Bush whereby U.S. forces were stationed in Somalia as peacekeepers. Somalia had been engaged in a long civil war that occurred at the same time as a serious drought. Hundreds of thousands of Somalis were dying as a result of the drought and the war. U.S. forces were sent to ensure that relief supplies being sent to Somalia by the rest of the world were not being stolen by warring forces. Over time, and after President Clinton took office, the mission of these U.S. forces changed. Military and political leaders reasoned that, if the war could be stopped, the need for U.S. forces could be eliminated. Accordingly, they ordered U.S. troops to capture the leaders of the warring factions. In the course of one of these operations, however, U.S. forces were trapped by enemy fire. A U.S. helicopter was shot down and several troops were killed. To add fuel to the political fire, the bodies of these soldiers were desecrated and then dragged through the streets of Mogadishu, Somalia's capital.

President Clinton defended the policy that sent U.S. forces into these military operations on a number of grounds. First, he insisted that such operations were necessary to protect the relief efforts. Second, he noted that, in the absence of an end to the war, U.S. troops might be permanently stationed in Somalia. Third, he insisted that without U.S. troops on the ground the situation in Somalia would again become an international disaster.

At least three criticisms were aimed at Clinton's policy. Congressman Benjamin Gilman (R-NY) objected to Clinton's refusal to invoke the War Powers Act of 1973, which requires that presidents get approval from Congress if U.S. forces will be in danger for more than sixty days. Critics believed that the United States had, in effect, given complete control of all military forces to the president to use however he chose, in this case with disastrous consequences. Other critics doubted whether the United States had a compelling reason to send its forces to Somalia, and still others questioned the policy of involving U.S. forces in direct confrontations with warring factions.

U.S. forces remained in Somalia for a brief period after the events in Mogadishu; however, as soon as a peace agreement was worked out among the warring parties, the United States pulled out. Images of dead American servicemen being burned and dragged through the streets were used by Republicans during the 1994 midterm elections to support their claims that Clinton was incompetent and to urge the election of Republican candidates to office. The Somalia crisis was another factor in the Republican takeover of Congress in 1994.

Since 1993 Somalia has again degenerated into war and famine; however, as of 2000, no discussions are currently under way to send U.S. forces there again. Indeed, the negative consequences of U.S. operations in Somalia can be seen to shape U.S. reluctance to involve itself in international problems anywhere, even in Europe. Peacekeeping and addressing human rights may be important components of U.S. policy, but U.S. capacity is limited. Somalia was proof of that. Since Somalia, the United States has tended to send its forces into peacekeeping missions only when they are likely to face little immediate danger.

CLINTON'S ADDRESS TO THE NATION ON SOMALIA

October 7, 1993

Today I want to talk with you about our Nation's military involvement in Somalia. A year ago, we all watched with horror as Somali children and their families lay dying by the tens of thousands, dying the slow, agonizing death of starvation, a starvation brought on not only by drought, but also by the anarchy that then prevailed in that country.

This past weekend we all reacted with anger and horror as an armed Somali gang desecrated the bodies of our American soldiers and displayed a captured American pilot, all of them soldiers who were taking part in an international effort to end the starvation of the Somali people themselves. These tragic events raise hard questions about our effort in Somalia. Why are we still there? What are we trying to accomplish? How did a humanitarian mission turn violent? And when will our people come home?

These questions deserve straight answers. Let's start by remembering why our troops went into Somalia in the first place. We went because only the United States could help stop one of the great human tragedies of this time. A third of a million people had died of starvation and disease. Twice that many more were at risk of dying. Meanwhile, tons of relief supplies piled up in the capital of Mogadishu because a small number of Somalis stopped food from reaching their own countrymen.

Our consciences said, enough. In our Nation's best tradition, we took action with bipartisan support. President Bush sent in 28,000 American troops as part of a United Nations humanitarian mission. Our troops created a secure environment so that food and medicine could get through. We saved close to one million lives. And throughout most of Somalia, everywhere but in Mogadishu, life began returning to normal. Crops are growing. Markets are reopening. So are schools and hospitals. Nearly a million Somalis still depend completely on relief supplies, but at least the starvation is gone. And none of this would have happened without American leadership and America's troops.

. . .

We started this mission for the right reasons, and we're going to finish it in the right way. In a sense, we came to Somalia to rescue innocent people in a burning house. We've nearly put the fire out, but some smoldering embers remain. If we leave them now, those embers will reignite into flames, and people will die again. If we stay a short while longer and do the right things, we've got a reasonable chance of cooling off the embers and getting other firefighters to take our place.

We also have to recognize that we cannot leave now and still have all our troops present and accounted for. And I want you to know that I am determined to work for the security of those Americans missing or held captive. Anyone holding an American right now should understand, above all else, that we will hold them strictly responsible for our soldiers' well-being. We expected them to be well-treated, and we expect them to be released.

So now we face a choice. Do we leave when the job gets tough, or when the job is well done? Do we invite a return of mass suffering, or do we leave in a way that gives the Somalis a decent chance to survive?

. . .

. . . If we were to leave today, we know what would happen. Within months, Somali children again would be dying in the streets. Our own credibility with friends and allies would be severely damaged. Our leadership in world affairs would be undermined at the very time when people are looking to America to help promote peace and freedom in the post-cold-war world. And all around the world, aggressors, thugs, and terrorists will conclude that the best way to get us to change our policies is to kill our people. It would be open season on Americans.

That is why I am committed to getting this job done in Somalia, not only quickly but also effectively. To do that, I am taking steps to ensure troops from other nations are ready to take the place of our own soldiers. We've already withdrawn some 20,000 troops, and more than that number have replaced them from over two dozen other nations. Now we will intensify efforts to have other countries deploy more troops to Somalia to assure that security will remain when we're gone.

. . .

So let us finish the work we set out to do. Let us demonstrate to the world, as generations of Americans have done before us, that when Americans take on a challenge, they do the job right.

Public Papers of the President: William J. Clinton. October 7, 1993: 1703–1706.

DEATH OF THE WAR POWERS RESOLUTION IN SOMALIA

August 4, 1993

Mr. Benjamin Gilman (R-NY). Mr. Speaker, today, August 4, 1993, may very well be remembered as the day that the War Powers Resolution died. Its death was caused by the election of President Clinton and by the erosion of popular support for his policy in Somalia.

Sixty days ago, on June 5, combat involving United States Forces broke out in Somalia and has continued ever since. Under any reasonable reading of the War Powers Resolution, the President was required to withdraw United States Forces from Somalia by today. He has not, and Congress has decided to look the other way. In so doing, Congress has acquiesced in a legal rationale that will make the War Powers Resolution a dead letter.

The War Powers Resolution provides that whenever U.S. Armed Forces are deployed into a situation of hostilities, or imminent involvement in hostilities in a foreign country, they must be withdrawn in 60 days unless Congress declares war or passes a joint resolution authorizing continuation of the deployment. United States Forces were first sent to Somalia on December 8, 1992. President Bush informed Congress at that time that he did not intend for U.S. Forces there to become involved in hostilities, meaning that the 60-day clock would not apply. While one could debate whether hostilities were imminent after December 8, in fact there was little combat, and therefore it was tenable to contend that the War Powers Resolution did not apply. President Clinton adopted the same position after taking office.

. . .

On June 5, serious fighting broke out in Mogadishu. U.S. Forces have engaged in considerable combat since that time, and by all accounts, southern Mogadishu is a war zone. No Americans have yet been killed, but over a dozen have been wounded.

On June 15, I wrote to Secretary of State [Warren] Christopher to ask whether the United States was now [engaged] in hostilities in Somalia, such that the 60-day clock applies. The administration responded on July 21. In essence, the administration said that Somalia involves only "intermittent military engagements," each lasting less than 60 days, and therefore, does not involve "sustained hostilities" that might compel the withdrawal of United States Forces after 60 days.

The problem with that logic, of course, is that all wars consist of a series of discrete military engagements. Under this reasoning, it would not be too difficult to argue that a conflict on the scale of World War II falls outside that War Powers Resolution. After all, Pearl Harbor, the Battle of Midway, and the Battle of the Bulge each lasted less than 60 days.

. . .

By looking the other way while the administration eviscerates the War Powers Resolution, Congress has avoided an embarrassing disagreement with our new President. But the precedent set today will be available to all future Presidents.

History will inevitably show that the War Powers Resolution died in Somalia.

The Congressional Record. August 4, 1993: E 1984–1985.

PEACEKEEPING IN YUGOSLAVIA AND BOSNIA (FEBRUARY 1994)

For most of the period since the end of World War II, Yugoslavia was a stable, multiethnic state which, although Communist, was not closely allied with the Soviet Union. When the Communist leadership of the country was overthrown, however, decades of built-up ethnic tensions were exploited by local leaders to split the country into many pieces. War broke out among these new countries, and civil wars broke out among ethnic groups living in the same region. Because Yugoslavia is centrally located in Europe, neither the major European powers nor the United States was willing to let the post-Yugoslavia conflicts rage out of control. The question was, what to do and why?

One of the most brutal conflicts in the former Yugoslavia occurred in Bosnia. Bosnia, whose capital, Sarajevo, had hosted the winter Olympics in 1984, was destroyed while ethnic Serbs, Croats, and Bosnians warred over history, territory, and religion. (Serbs and Croats are mostly Orthodox Christians; Bosnians are generally Muslim.) In particular, forces from both Serbia and Croatia invaded Bosnia in 1993 with the intent of keeping it part of the remnants of Yugoslavia by whatever means necessary.

This brutal conflict led to the mass killings of civilians and other atrocities. Clinton advocated a policy of air strikes to force the Serbs and Croats to stop the war in Bosnia. He also supported sending peacekeeping troops (not Americans) to Bosnia to separate the warring ethnic groups. Finally, he advocated negotiating a peace agreement among the various groups to stabilize the situation. Such efforts, Clinton argued, would protect Europe, promote respect for human rights, and stabilize the volatile politics of the region.

Opponents, including Congressman Pete Geren (D-TX), pointed out that no one was a pure victim in the Bosnian conflict. All sides had committed atrocities in the name of ethnic purity—the idea that one's own ethnic group is better than everyone else's group; for "us" to be happy and safe, "we" must eradicate "them." More, the risk of U.S. intervention was high: Yugoslavia is a mountainous territory populated by people who were committed to their cause; accordingly, the simple presence of U.S. troops could not be expected to end the conflict and indeed might intensify it, leading to the death of many Americans. Finally, they wondered if U.S. involvement could address tensions that were hundreds of years old.

Eventually, U.S. forces were introduced into Bosnia as peacekeepers after a peace agreement was worked out among the warring powers. This agreement involved using outside troops as peacekeepers between warring groups; U.S. forces were placed in territories where fighting had been comparatively light. This policy was highly controversial—many Americans were opposed to sending U.S. forces into hostile areas.

Since this time, Bosnia has remained relatively stable. However, other conflicts in the former Yugoslavia have broken out, most notably in Kosovo. In 2000, the Serbian leader who had led the war in Kosovo, Slobodan Milosevic, was removed from office after losing an election and facing a popular uprising. U.S. and other European forces remain stationed in the former Yugoslavia.

CLINTON'S RADIO ADDRESS TO THE NATION

February 19, 1994

My fellow Americans, this morning I want to speak with you about the conflict in Bosnia. My administration has worked for over a year to help ease the suffering and end the conflict in that war-torn land. Now, a prolonged siege of the Bosnian capital of Sarajevo has brought us to an important moment.

In the coming days, American war planes may participate in NATO air strikes on military targets around Sarajevo. We do not yet know whether air strikes will be necessary. But I want to talk with you about what American interests are at stake and what the nature and goals of our military involvement will be if it occurs.

The fighting in Bosnia is part of the broader story of change in Europe. With the end of the Cold War, militant nationalism once again spread throughout many countries that lived behind the Iron Curtain, and especially in the former Yugoslavia. As nationalism caught fire among its Serbian population, other parts of the country began seeking independence. Several ethnic and religious groups began fighting fiercely. But the Serbs bear a primary responsibility for the aggression and the ethnic cleansing that has killed tens of thousands and displaced millions in Bosnia.

This century teaches us that America cannot afford to ignore conflicts in Europe. And in this crisis, our nation has distinct interests.

We have an interest in helping to prevent this from becoming a broader European conflict, especially one that could threaten our NATO allies or undermine the transition of former communist states to peaceful democracies. We have an interest in showing that NATO, the world's greatest military alliance, remains a credible force for peace in the post–Cold War era. We have an interest in helping to stem the destabilizing flows of refugees this struggle is generating throughout all of Europe. And we clearly have a humanitarian interest in helping to stop the strangulation of Sarajevo and the continuing slaughter of innocents in Bosnia.

I want to be clear. Europe must bear most of the responsibility for solving this problem, and, indeed, it has. The United Nations has forces on the ground in Bosnia to protect the humanitarian effort and to limit the carnage. And the vast majority of them are European, from all countries in Europe who have worked along with brave Canadians and soldiers from other countries. I have not sent American ground units into Bosnia. And I will not send American ground forces to impose a settlement that the parties to that conflict do not accept.

But America's interest and the responsibilities of America's leadership demand our active involvement in the search for a solution. That is why my administration has worked to help contain the fighting, relieve suffering and achieve a fair and workable negotiated end to that conflict.

Over a year ago, I appointed a special American envoy to the negotiations to help find a workable, enforceable solution acceptable to all. And I have said that if such a solution can be reached, our nation is prepared to participate in efforts to enforce the solution, including the use of our military personnel.

. . .

Our military goal will be straightforward—to exact a heavy price on those who refuse to comply with the ultimatum. Military force alone cannot guarantee that every heavy gun around Sarajevo will be removed or silenced, but military force can make it more likely that Bosnian Serbs will seek a solution through negotiation rather than through Sarajevo's strangulation, and that more innocent civilians will continue to live.

Public Papers of the President: William J. Clinton. February 19, 1994: 283–285.

AVOID UNITED STATES INVOLVEMENT IN FORMER YUGOSLAVIA

February 9, 1994

Mr. Pete Geren (D-TX). Mr. Speaker, the carnage of last weekend in the former Yugoslavia that was brought into all of our living rooms over the television set I fear has brought us to the brink of intervention in a bloody 1,000-year-old civil war in what was the former Yugoslavia.

Mr. Speaker, as we consider this as a Congress and as a nation, I think it is important that we consider it very soberly and consider the implications. You do not get a little bit into a war. You do not get a little bit into the middle of a conflict. We talk about just using airstrikes. But once you have made the commitment of putting American men and women into combat, you have stepped over a line from which there is no coming back.

The media accounts of the conflict in Yugoslavia have given us the impression that there are some good guys in that conflict and some bad guys in that conflict. The media has painted the Serbs as the aggressors. I would like to just share an anecdote from a hearing in front of the Committee on Armed Services when we were having hearings on the Bosnian situation.

We had a former NATO commander, a general from Canada, speak to us. He said first let me disabuse all of you of the notion that there are any good guys in this conflict. If we in NATO or if you Americans choose to engage yourselves in this conflict, you are choosing among degrees of serial killers. Perhaps 1 has killed 100, and the other has killed 75, and the other has only killed 50. If that provides you a basis to choose one or the other, well, so be it. But you need to know going in, there are no white hats over there. There is no natural ally for the United States of America in that conflict. And it is a conflict which, if you look at history, is a conflict without end.

. . .

As our country debates whether or not to get into this war, I would like to go back to a speech that then-Secretary of Defense Caspar Weinberger gave in 1984, as he tried to give us a blueprint to lead us into this post-cold-war era, a blueprint that has been used repeatedly over and over by our great military leaders since that time.

Let me quote from that speech:

I believe the postwar period has taught us several lessons, and from them I have developed six major tests to be applied when we are weighing the use of U.S. combat forces abroad. Let me now share them with you:

First, the United States should not commit forces to combat overseas unless the particular engagement or occasion is deemed vital to our national interest or that of our allies. That emphatically does not mean that we should declare beforehand, as we did with Korea in 1950, that a particular area is outside our strategic perimeter.

Second, if we decide it is necessary to put combat troops into a given situation, we should do so wholeheartedly, and with the clear intention of winning. If we are unwilling to commit the forces or resources necessary to achieve our objectives, we should not commit them at all. Of course if the particular situation requires only limited force to win our objectives, then we should not hesitate to commit forces sized accordingly. When [Adolf] Hitler broke treaties and remilitarized the Rhineland, small combat forces then could perhaps have prevented the Holocaust of World War II.

Third, if we do decide to commit forces to combat overseas, we should have clearly defined political and military objectives. And we should know precisely how our forces can accomplish those clearly defined objectives. And we should have and send the forces needed to do just that. As [Carl von] Clausewitz wrote, "No one starts a war—or rather, no one in his senses ought to do so—without first being clear in his mind what he intends to achieve by that war, and how he intends to conduct it."

. . .

Fourth, the relationship between our objectives and the forces we have committed—their size, composition and disposition—must be continually reassessed and adjusted if necessary. Conditions and objectives invariably change during the course of a conflict. When they do change, then so must our combat requirements. We must continuously keep as a beacon light before us the basic questions: "Is this conflict in our national interest?" "Does our national interest require us to fight, to use force of arms?" If the answers are "yes," then we must win. If the answers are "no," then we should not be in combat.

Fifth, before the U.S. commits combat forces abroad, there must be some reasonable assurance we will have the support of the American people and their elected representatives in Congress. This support cannot be achieved unless we are candid in making clear the threats we face; the support cannot be sustained without continuing and close consultation. We cannot fight a battle with the Congress at home while asking our troops to win a war overseas or, as in the case of Vietnam, in effect asking our troops not to win, but just to be there.

Finally, the commitment of U.S. forces to combat should be a last resort.

As we as a nation consider this weighty decision, I think that we must reflect back on these questions asked by Secretary Weinberger and also ask ourselves is this a fight we are willing to go to the finish. I do not think so, Mr. Speaker. I hope that the carnage of the last weekend, the tremendous emotional appeal and the desire of every honorable person in the world to do something about this does not cause us to act imprudently. I fear that the Bosnian crisis is a riddle without an American solution.

The Congressional Record. February 9, 1994: H 394.

INTERVENTION IN HAITI (SEPTEMBER 1994)

Since the pronouncement of the Monroe Doctrine in 1819, the United States has claimed a special right to influence the politics and economics of countries in the Western Hemisphere. The United States has, on innumerable occasions, sent its forces and agents into the countries of Central and South America to promote and impose policies preferred by the United States. While this makes sense from the U.S. point of view—the United States is the most powerful nation in the region and does not wish to face enemies near its borders—these repeated interventions have caused resentment and have complicated relations with the other nations of the Western Hemisphere. The United States believes that nations should control their own destinies and that the nations of Latin America should be closely allied with the United States—whether they are willing or not. Furthermore, the United States has repeatedly demonstrated its willingness to use force to achieve its goals in the hemisphere.

In 1994 President Clinton enforced the long-standing practice of U.S. intervention in the region by sending U.S. forces to Haiti, a country they had gone to many times before. Haiti had been ruled by the Duvalier family dictatorship for decades during the Cold War, and so long as the dictators remained loyal to the United States, U.S. leaders did little to undermine this dictatorship. With the end of the Cold War, however, the dictatorial regime in Haiti was pushed out and a new, democratically elected regime was established under President Jean Bertrand Aristide, a former Catholic priest. However, this elected government was driven from power in a military coup in 1991. Subsequently, Clinton ordered U.S. forces to occupy Haiti, remove the military government, and reestablish civilian rule. He argued that this action was necessary to promote democracy both in Haiti and throughout the region. He also said it was a required act in order to protect the human rights of Haitian citizens. Only then, he claimed, could Haiti's extensive political and economic problems be solved.

Opponents of Clinton's policy, including Congressman William Clinger (R-PA), argued that there were no serious U.S. interests at stake in Haiti. Thus, there was no reason to send U.S. forces there. In addition, they complained that Clinton had used U.S. forces without getting congressional support; consequently, the legitimacy of this action might be undermined. Finally, many critics noted that the United States had supported Haitian military dictators for decades. They therefore doubted that the United States was suddenly interested in the human rights of ordinary Haitians. Instead, they claimed that Clinton undertook this action to protect U.S. economic interests in the area.

Militarily, the occupation of Haiti was quite easy. The Haitian military melted away. However, in the transition to civilian rule, mobs of former soldiers looted, committed murder, and otherwise terrorized civilians. Since there were not enough troops on the island to police every intersection, much violence ensued. In time, Aristide was returned to power, and elections for a successor government have been held and enforced. Most U.S. forces were withdrawn from Haiti by 1996, although some remain on the island. Haiti remains the poorest country in the Western Hemisphere.

More broadly, the United States maintains its prerogative to intervene in Central and South American nations at will. U.S. forces conduct military operations against suspected drug targets throughout Colombia, for example, and openly support some candidates in local elections while opposing others. This policy is largely supported by the American people.

CLINTON'S REMARKS IN A TELEVISION ADDRESS TO THE NATION

September 15, 1994

[J]ust four years ago, the Haitian people held the first free and fair elections since their independence. They elected a parliament and a new president, Father Jean Bertrand Aristide, a Catholic priest who received almost 70 percent of the vote. But eight months later, Haitian dreams of democracy became a nightmare of bloodshed.

General Raoul Cedras led a military coup that overthrew President Aristide, the man who had appointed Cedras to lead the army. Resistors were beaten and murdered. The dictators launched a horrible intimidation campaign of rape, torture and mutilation. People starved; children died; thousands of Haitians fled their country, heading to the United States across dangerous seas. At that time, President Bush declared the situation posed, and I quote, "an unusual and extraordinary threat to the national security, foreign policy and economy of the United States."

. . .

I know that the United States cannot—indeed, we should not—be the world's policemen. And I know that this is a time with the Cold War over that so many Americans are reluctant to commit military resources and our personnel beyond our borders. But when brutality occurs close to our shore, it affects our national interests. And we have a responsibility to act.

Thousands of Haitians have already fled toward the United States, risking their lives to escape the reign of terror. As long as Cedras rules, Haitians will continue to seek sanctuary in our nation. This year, in less than two months, more than 21,000 Haitians were rescued at sea by our Coast Guard and Navy. Today, more than 14,000 refugees are living at our naval base in Guantanamo. The American people have already expended almost $200 million to support them, to maintain the economic embargo, and the prospect of millions and millions more being spent every month for an indefinite period of time looms ahead unless we act.

. . .

Our mission in Haiti, as it was in Panama and Grenada, will be limited and specific. Our plan to remove the dictators will follow two phases. First, it will remove dictators from power and restore Haiti's legitimate, democratically-elected government. We will train a civilian-controlled Haitian security force that will protect the people rather than repress them. During this period, police monitors from all around the world will work with the authorities to maximize basic security and civil order and minimize retribution.

. . .

I know many people believe that we shouldn't help the Haitian people recover their democracy and find their hard-won freedoms, that the Haitians should accept the violence and repression as their fate. But remember: the same was said of a people who, more than 200 years ago, took up arms against a tyrant whose forces occupied their land. But they were a stubborn bunch, a people who fought for their freedoms and appealed to all those who believed in democracy to help their cause. And their cries were answered, and a new nation was born—a nation that, ever since, has believed that the rights of life, liberty and the pursuit of happiness should be denied to none.

October 25, 1994. http://www.pub.whitehouse.gov/uri-res/12R?urn:pid//oma.
eop.gov.us/1994/9/15/6/.text.

OPPOSITION TO U.S. POLICY TOWARD HAITI

October 8, 1994

Mr. William Clinger (R-PA). Mr. Chairman, I rise to express my views on the current U.S. military occupation of Haiti.

My position on U.S. policy toward Haiti is clear and simple. I neither supported President Clinton's initial deployment of U.S. troops to Haiti nor do I support the current U.S. military occupation of the troubled nation. No compelling U.S. interests were at stake in Haiti. No American lives were at risk, and the United States had no vital strategic or economic concerns there. While the United States should always be committed to democracy and support democratically elected leaders, I question whether placing U.S. service men and women in Haiti to restore President Aristide is an appropriate use of our military forces.

Furthermore, it is my belief that, as commander-in-chief, President Clinton had an obligation to build public support for his policy before placing one American service member in harm's way. He should have clearly articulated our national interests and security objectives in Haiti, and allowed Congress to fully and publicly debate and vote on the merits of his policy. President Clinton's decision not to seek public or congressional support prior to the invasion and occupation of Haiti was a serious failure on his part, because if he had, the United States might not be in the troublesome position we are in today.

Although I feel U.S. military intervention in Haiti is a mistake, and U.S. troops should be withdrawn as soon as possible, I strongly oppose any congressional action to set a deadline for withdrawal or any attempt to cut off funds for military operations in Haiti.

Under the two previous administrations, I consistently joined my Republican colleagues in fending off Democratic attempts to tie the hands of the President in executing U.S. foreign policy. I argued that Congress must give the President latitude to properly carry out his responsibilities as our commander-in-chief, especially when U.S. troops are in a hostile environment. It would be contrary to my beliefs and hypocritical for me now to support any resolution that severely restricts the President's authority over foreign policy and military affairs by mandating the withdrawal of U.S. troops.

The Congressional Record. October 6, 1994: E 2278.

PEACEKEEPING IN RWANDA (MARCH 1998)

The wholesale genocide that took place in Rwanda in 1994 presented the first, but sadly not the last, challenge for U.S. policy makers in the post–Cold War era. After a series of atrocities in which members of one ethnic group attacked members of the other, full-scale civil war broke out. Between 500,000 and 1,000,000 Tutsi tribespeople were killed by Hutu tribal members in less than three months. During the Cold War, the United States had regularly ignored slaughters like those that occurred in Rwanda: questions of peoples' human rights were suppressed in favor of not starting a U.S.–Soviet conflict. After the end of the Cold War in 1991, however, this fear evaporated: there was no Soviet Union. Yet there are limits to U.S. capacity; America has neither the troops nor the money to police the entire world. Although the United States has intervened in the countries that used to make up Yugoslavia, in the heart of Europe, what to do in areas not so directly important to the United States remained a question.

At the time of the Rwanda genocide, the United States did little but sit on the sidelines and say "stop." After being criticized for this decision, President Clinton reversed policies in 1998 and stated that the United States had a moral obligation to help people anywhere in the world whose rights were being violated. He called for war criminals to be prosecuted, an international response force to be developed to intervene whenever violence breaks out, and for potential conflicts to be anticipated to prevent violence before it breaks out. Only then, Clinton argued, would the peoples of the world have a chance to live decent lives.

Journalist Michael Kelly and other critics of Clinton's policies argued that Clinton's pledge was not credible. The United States had many opportunities to enforce Clinton's ideas: the world was filled with violence and suffering. In all cases except those in Europe, however, the United States had failed to intervene to prevent bloodshed. Other critics argued that the United States had neither the resources nor the right to solve all moral and political crises on earth. Both types of critics agreed that the United States should not claim the moral high ground in international affairs since it was not consistent in supporting human rights.

Lacking resources, political support, and any idea of how it could help end the ethnic slaughter there, the United States never intervened in Rwanda. This decision was relatively popular with most Americans for at least two reasons: first, Americans tend to oppose military interventions in those areas in which the nation lacks vital interests, and second, Americans have not intervened in areas where the population being threatened is largely black, particularly in sub-Saharan Africa, since a 1965 intervention in Liberia. Accordingly, while human rights leaders criticized Clinton for his Rwanda decisions, very few ordinary Americans or other political leaders did.

The general pattern of U.S. intervention in Europe and nonintervention in the rest of the world has continued in the aftermath of Clinton's pronouncement. In 1999 genocidal slaughter occurred in Sierra Leone without U.S. intervention. Even Liberia, a country in which the United States has intervened in the past, and with which it has a unique relationship (it was settled by freed U.S. slaves in the 1850s), experienced a brutal civil war in 1998–1999 with no U.S. involvement. In addition, Russia has invaded and suppressed a rebellion in a former territory, Chechnya, and the United States could do little. Americans say that they care about human rights, but either from a lack of capacity, resources, or concern about areas outside Europe, the U.S. does not send its forces to areas beyond Europe or Latin and South America.

CLINTON'S REMARKS TO GENOCIDE SURVIVORS, ASSISTANCE WORKERS, AND U.S. AND RWANDA GOVERNMENT OFFICIALS

March 25, 1998

I have come today to pay the respects of my nation to all who suffered and all who perished in the Rwandan genocide. It is my hope that through this trip, in every corner of the world today and tomorrow, their story will be told; that four years ago in this beautiful, green, lovely land, a clear and conscious decision was made by those then in power that the peoples of this country would not live side by side in peace.

During the 90 days that began on April 6 in 1994, Rwanda experienced the most intensive slaughter in this blood-filled century we are about to leave. Families murdered in their home, people hunted down as they fled by soldiers and militia, through farmland and woods as if they were animals.

From Kibuye in the west to Kibungo in the east, people gathered seeking refuge in churches by the thousands, in hospitals, in schools. And when they were found, the old and the sick, women and children alike, they were killed—killed because their identity card said they were Tutsi or because they had a Tutsi parent, or because someone thought they looked like a Tutsi, or slain like thousands of Hutus because they protected Tutsis or would not countenance a policy that sought to wipe out people who just the day before, and for years before, had been their friends and neighbors.

The government-led effort to exterminate Rwanda's Tutsi and moderate Hutus, as you know better than me, took at least a million lives. Scholars of these sorts of events say that the killers, armed mostly with machetes and clubs, nonetheless did their work five times as fast as the mechanized gas chambers used by the Nazis.

It is important that the world know that these killings were not spontaneous or accidental. It is important that the world hear what your President just said—they were most certainly not the result of ancient tribal struggles. Indeed, these people had lived together for centuries before the events the President described began to unfold.

These events grew from a policy aimed at the systematic destruction of a people. The ground for violence was carefully prepared, the airwaves poisoned with hate, casting the Tutsis as scapegoats for the problems of Rwanda, denying their humanity. All of this was done, clearly, to make it easy for otherwise reluctant people to participate in wholesale slaughter.

Lists of victims, name by name, were actually drawn up in advance. Today the images of all that haunt us all: the dead choking the Kigara River, floating to Lake Victoria. In their fate we are reminded of the capacity in people everywhere—not just in Rwanda, and certainly not just in Africa—but the capacity for people everywhere to slip into pure evil. We cannot abolish that capacity, but we must never accept it. And we know it can be overcome.

The international community, together with nations in Africa, must bear its share of responsibility for this tragedy, as well. We did not act quickly enough after the killing began. We should not have allowed the refugee camps to become safe haven for the killers. We did not immediately call these crimes by their rightful name: genocide. We cannot change the past. But we can and must do everything in our power to help you build a future without fear, and full of hope.

We owe to those who died and to those who survived who loved them, our every effort to increase our vigilance and strengthen our stand against those who would commit such atrocities in the future—here or elsewhere. Indeed, we owe to all the peoples of the world who are at risk—because each bloodletting hastens the next as the value of human life is degraded and violence becomes tolerated, the unimaginable becomes more conceivable—we owe to all the people in the world our best efforts to organize ourselves so that we can maximize the chances of preventing these events. And where they cannot be prevented, we can move more quickly to minimize the horror.

So let us challenge ourselves to build a world in which no branch of humanity, because of national, racial, ethnic or religious origin, is again threatened with destruction because of those characteristics, of which people should rightly be proud. Let us work together as a community of civilized nations to strengthen our ability to prevent and, if necessary, to stop genocide.

. . .

We applaud the efforts of the Rwandan government to strengthen civilian and military justice systems. I am pleased that our Great Lakes Justice Initiative will invest $30 million to help create throughout the region judicial systems that are impartial, credible, and effective. In Rwanda these funds will help to support courts, prosecutors, and police, military justice and cooperation at the local level.

We will also continue to pursue justice through our strong backing for the International Criminal Tribunal for Rwanda. The United States is the largest contributor to this tribunal. We are frustrated, as you are, by the delays in the tribunal's work. As we know, we must do better. Now that administrative improvements have begun, however, the tribunal should expedite cases through group trials, and fulfill its historic mission.

We are prepared to help, among other things, with witness relocation, so that those who still fear can speak the truth in safety. And we will support the War Crimes Tribunal for as long as it is needed to do its work, until the truth is clear and justice is rendered.

. . . We must make it clear to all those who would commit such acts in the future that they too must answer for their acts, and they will. In Rwanda, we must hold accountable all those who may abuse human rights, whether insurgents or soldiers. Internationally, as we meet here, talks are underway at the United Nations to establish a permanent international criminal court. Rwanda and the difficulties we have had with this special tribunal underscores the need for such a court. And the United States will work to see that it is created.

http://www.pub.whitehouse.gov/uri- . . . /oma.eop.gov.us/1998/3/26/3.text.2

"NEVER AGAIN? OH, NEVER MIND"

The Washington Post, January 12, 2000

Mr. Michael Kelly. Bill Clinton arrived in Rwanda in March 1998 carrying heavy baggage. Four years earlier, Hutu tribal militias in Rwanda had slaughtered at least a half-million and perhaps more than a million members of the Tutsi tribe. The slaughter was no overnight event. Armed for the most part with only clubs and machetes, the militias spent 90 days butchering their way through the country.

Despite abundant news coverage of the genocide and repeated entreaties for help, the United States took no effective steps to stop the killing. In his speech in Kigali, Clinton offered an explanation for this: ignorance. He told the survivors that, although "it may seem strange . . . all over the world there were people like me sitting in their offices, day after day, who did not fully appreciate the depth and the speed with which you were being engulfed by this unimaginable terror."

This statement was not remotely true. As has been documented by objective observers, the U.S. government followed the progress of the genocide in Rwanda closely. Clinton himself was fully apprised; the president knew what was going on as first hundreds, then thousands, then hundreds of thousands were murdered. And neither is it true that Clinton was guilty of mere inaction in the face of genocide, that he only "did not act quickly enough [to stop the killing] after the killing began," as he put it. In fact, he acted promptly, and repeatedly, to personally deny urgent requests from the United Nations to send even a very small force of non-American troops into Rwanda. On May 24, with the Red Cross estimating the number of murdered in Rwanda at 400,000 and climbing, Clinton—still blocking the deployment of U.N. troops—said: "We cannot solve every such outburst of civil strife or militant nationalism simply by sending in our forces."

So, in Kigali, facing the survivors of a massacre he had refused to intervene against, it is understandable that the president felt the need to promise better in the future. He said the leaders of the world must "organize ourselves so that we can maximize the chances of preventing these events, and where they cannot be prevented, we can move more quickly to minimize the horror." "And," he said, "we must make it clear to all those who would commit such acts in the future that they too must answer for their acts, and they will."

At the time the president spoke, the West African nation of Sierra Leone was in danger of being overrun by the so-called troops of the so-called Armed Forces Revolutionary Council, a junta dedicated to overthrowing the government of Ahmad Tejan Kabbah, elected in 1996. By late 1998, the situation was grave; Nigerian troops imported into Sierra Leone with the support of an alliance of African governments were losing ground to the rebel army, 10,000 frequently drugged amateurs commanded by Sam "General Mosquito" Bockarie, a former hairdresser.

In January 1999, nine months after Clinton spoke, General Mosquito's troops took Sierra Leone's capital of Freetown, and the United States closed its embassy. In the aftermath of victory, the rebels waged a campaign of terror against the innocent civilian population of Sierra Leone, murdering and raping indiscriminately and, in a particularly cruel practice, cutting off the hands of men and boys. All told, the rebels have murdered, maimed or raped an estimated 10,000 people in Sierra Leone, with many children among their victims.

As *The Washington Post*'s managing editor, Steve Coll, argued in a detailed and convincing article this week, the United States could have averted this slaughter by providing weapons and other support to the Nigerian troops in Sierra Leone. "No such scenario was ever seriously entertained," writes Coll. "State Department officials say it was hardly even discussed at the White House." Nor did the United States intervene with force to stop the slaughter. Never again must we be shy in the face of the evidence? Never mind.

The second promise of Kigali, that of accountability, went swiftly by the boards, too. What did the United States do to punish General Mosquito and his killers? It lent its strong support to a peace agreement, signed in Lome, the capital of Togo, on July 7; the agreement provides blanket amnesty for the hairdresser-general and his band of merry handchoppers.

The president is partially right. It is easy to say, Never again. But in this case, at least, it wouldn't have been really so hard to make it so.

The Washington Post, January 12, 2000, A 19.

AIR STRIKES ON SUDAN AND AFGHANISTAN (AUGUST 1998)

In August 1998, U.S. embassies in Kenya and Tanzania were destroyed by car bombs. In each case, a few American and many local citizens were killed. After a long investigation, U.S. intelligence sources identified the bombers as being associated with a former U.S. ally, Osama bin Laden. bin Laden, a Saudi Arabian billionaire, had helped the United States funnel aid to several groups of anti-Soviet fighters that formed to oppose the Soviet invasion of Afghanistan in 1979. However, when the Soviet Union pulled its forces out of Afghanistan, the United States cut off the aid it was giving to groups like that led by bin Laden. Osama bin Laden then turned against the United States and began attacking American targets across the world.

In response, President Clinton ordered U.S. aircraft to bomb a pharmaceutical factory in Sudan. Clinton argued that it was really making chemical weapons that bin Laden's group might use in a terrorist attack. In addition, U.S. missiles struck several bases inside Afghanistan that were described as terrorist training camps. bin Laden was expected to be at one of these camps; however, he had left shortly before the strike hit. Clinton argued that terrorist attacks had to be met with violent responses: if terrorists felt they could attack U.S. targets with impunity, all Americans would be at risk.

Opponents of the strike, including Congressman Ed Whitfield (R-KY), pointed out that there was little evidence, if any, that the Sudan factory was either producing chemical weapons or was associated with bin Laden's group. As a consequence, they feared that the United States had destroyed Sudan's only plant for producing helpful drugs on a rumor, and thereby had increased the Sudanese people's suffering. Other critics commented that the people who feel the negative effects of a U.S. strike become angry at the United States. Such people then volunteer to join anti-U.S. groups and commit violence. Thus U.S. violence stimulates violence against the United States.

The U.S. air strikes were moderately effective. Many trainees at the Afghani camp were killed, but bin Laden remains alive. The Sudanese plant was never proved to have made chemical weapons, and many people in Sudan remain angry toward the United States. In addition, while the American people supported this raid, the fact that it came just as Special Prosecutor Kenneth Starr was releasing the results of his investigation into the Monica Lewinsky affair led many people in the United States and in the rest of the world to refer to these strikes as "Monica's War"— an attempt by the president to direct attention away from his domestic troubles. If this was Clinton's strategy, it did not work: he was subsequently impeached and tried for his actions in the Lewinsky affair.

After the raid, incidences of major bombings against U.S. targets overseas declined for a period, largely as a result of increased security. Attacks like those bin Laden's group committed have led to a redesign of new U.S. government facilities: in the future, U.S. buildings will be kept well back from main roads and will have only a limited amount of glass, which tends to cause the most damage when a car bomb explodes. In October 2000, a U.S. Navy vessel, the USS *Cole*, was attacked by a boat filled with explosives while it was refueling in the harbor of Aden, Yemen. Seventeen sailors were killed, and many more were wounded, possibly by people allied with Osama bin Laden. This may signal a rise in terrorist attacks against U.S. targets worldwide.

CLINTON'S ADDRESS TO THE NATION

August 20, 1998

Today I ordered our Armed Forces to strike at terrorist-related facilities in Afghanistan and Sudan because of the imminent threat they presented to our national security.

I want to speak with you about the objective of this action and why it was necessary. Our target was terror. Our mission was clear—to strike at the network of radical groups affiliated with and funded by Osama bin Laden, perhaps the preeminent organizer and financier of international terrorism in the world today.

The groups associated with him come from diverse places, but share a hatred for democracy, a fanatical glorification of violence, and a horrible distortion of their religion to justify the murder of innocents. They have made the United States their adversary precisely because of what we stand for and what we stand against.

A few months ago, and again this week, bin Laden publicly vowed to wage a terrorist war against America, saying—and I quote—"We do not differentiate between those dressed in military uniforms and civilians. They're all targets. Their mission is murder and their history is bloody."

In recent years, they killed American, Belgian and Pakistani peacekeepers in Somalia. They plotted to assassinate the President of Egypt and the Pope. They planned to bomb six United States 747s over the Pacific. They bombed the Egyptian embassy in Pakistan. They gunned down German tourists in Egypt.

The most recent terrorist events are fresh in our memory. Two weeks ago, 12 Americans and nearly 300 Kenyans and Tanzanians lost their lives, and another 5,000 were wounded when our embassies in Nairobi and Dar es Salaam were bombed. There is convincing information from our intelligence community that the bin Laden terrorist network was responsible for these bombings. Based on this information, we have high confidence that these bombings were planned, financed, and carried out by the organization bin Laden leads.

America has battled terrorism for many years. Where possible, we've used law enforcement and diplomatic tools to wage the fight. The long arm of American law has reached out around the world and brought to trial those guilty of attacks in New York and Virginia and in the Pacific. We have quietly disrupted terrorist groups and foiled their plots. We have isolated countries that practice terrorism. We've worked to build an international coalition against terror.

But there have been, and will be, times when law enforcement and diplomatic tools are simply not enough, when our very national security is challenged, and when we must take extraordinary steps to protect the safety of our citizens. With compelling evidence that the bin Laden network of terrorist groups was planning to mount further attacks against Americans and other freedom-loving people, I decided America must act.

And so, this morning, based on the unanimous recommendation of my national security team, I ordered our Armed Forces to take action to counter an immediate threat from the bin Laden network. Earlier today, the United States carried out simultaneous strikes against terrorist facilities and infrastructure in Afghanistan. Our forces targeted one of the most active terrorist bases in the world. It contained key elements of the bin Laden network's infrastructure and has served as a training camp for literally thousands of terrorists from around the globe. We have reason to believe that a gathering of key terrorist leaders was to take place there today, thus underscoring the urgency of our actions.

Our forces also attacked a factory in Sudan associated with the bin Laden network. The factory was involved in the production of materials for chemical weapons.

. . .

I want you to understand, I want the world to understand, that our actions today were not aimed against Islam, the faith of hundreds of millions of good, peace-loving people all around the world, including the United States. No religion condones the murder of innocent men, women and children. But our actions were aimed at fanatics and killers who wrap murder in the cloak of righteousness; and in so doing, profane the great religion in whose name they claim to act.

My fellow Americans, our battle against terrorism did not begin with the bombing of our embassies in Africa; nor will it end with today's strike. It will require strength, courage and endurance. We will not yield to this threat. We will meet it, no matter how long it may take. This will be a long, ongoing struggle between freedom and fanaticism; between the rule of law and terrorism. We must be prepared to do all that we can for as long as we must.

America is and will remain a target of terrorists precisely because we are leaders; because we act to advance peace, democracy and basic human values; because we're the most open society on Earth; and because, as we have shown yet again, we take an uncompromising stand against terrorism.

But of this I am also sure. The risks from inaction to America and the world would be far greater than action, for that would embolden our enemies, leaving their ability and their willingness to strike us intact. In this case, we knew before our attack that these groups already had planned further actions against us and others.

http://www.pub.whitehouse.gov/uri-res/I2R?urn:pdi//oma.eop.gov.us/1998/4/21/4.text.1

DISTURBING NEW DETAILS IN AFTERMATH OF U.S.
EMBASSY BOMBINGS

September 23, 1998

Mr. Ed Whitfield (R-KY). Mr. Speaker, I rise today to bring to the attention of the Congress and the American people disturbing new details of national policy decisions made in the aftermath of the bombing of the U.S. embassies in East Africa last month. This emerging information focuses on the Clinton administration's decision to retaliate against terrorists it suspected of carrying out the embassy attacks and in particular the decision to attack a pharmaceutical factory in the Sudan suspected of producing chemical weapons for the use of the terrorists led by Mr. bin Laden.

This new insight is contained in an article in the September 21, 1998 issue of the *New York Times* by reporters Tim Weiner and James Risen. It raises serious questions regarding the accuracy of intelligence information on which the decision was made and the credibility of statements made by senior officials in the Clinton administration as they sought to justify their decisions after the bombing in which it is estimated 20 to 50 people were killed.

The article reconstructs how a group of 6 senior administration officials and the President picked the bombing targets. It is based on interviews with participants and others at high levels of the national security apparatus and recounts how an act of war was approved on the basis of fragmented and disputed intelligence.

I quote from the article: Within days of the attack, some of the administration's explanations for destroying the factory in the Sudan proved inaccurate. Many people inside and outside the American government began to ask whether the questionable intelligence had prompted the United States to blow up this factory under false information.

I note that today former President Jimmy Carter asked for a congressional investigation about this matter.

Quoting further, Senior officials now say their case for attacking the factory relied on inference, as well as evidence that it produced chemical weapons for Mr. bin Laden's use. However, in analyzing more closely the efforts of those officials to justify their actions, it should be noted that since United States spies were withdrawn from the Sudan more than 2 years ago reliable information about the plant was scarce. In fact, in January 1996, weeks after American diplomats and spies were pulled out of the Sudan, the CIA withdrew as fabrications over 100 reports furnished to it by an outside source regarding terrorist threats against U.S. personnel in the Sudan.

A month after the attack, the same senior national security advisors, who had described the pharmaceutical plant as a secret chemical weapons factory, financed by bin Laden, are now conceding that they had no evidence to substantiate that claim or the President's decision to order the strike. It is now clear that the decision to bomb the factory was made amidst a three-year history of confusion in the intelligence community and conflicting foreign policy views within the administration regarding the Sudan.

The Congressional Record. September 23, 1998: H 8508.

PEACEKEEPING THROUGH BOMBING IN KOSOVO (MARCH 1999)

Several years after the crisis in Bosnia, Kosovo, another region of the former Yugoslavia, exploded in ethnic violence when Serb forces worked to drive the historically Muslim Kosovars from the region. This time, in contrast with the Bosnian case, the United States responded with military force. At first, it engaged in a months-long bombing campaign against Serb targets in Kosovo and in Serbia itself. After a peace agreement was reached, it, along with several other nations, sent troops in to serve as peacekeepers among the warring groups.

President Clinton advanced this policy for several reasons. He feared that a war in central Europe might spill over Kosovo's borders and affect many other countries, including several U.S. allies. He also pointed to the "ethnic cleansing" process by which Serb forces were clearing Muslim Kosovars out of their homes in an effort to "purify" Kosovo in violation of international law and human rights. Taken together, he felt that these reasons justified a substantial U.S. commitment to peace in Kosovo.

Like others who opposed Clinton's policy, Senator Kay Bailey Hutchison (R-TX) feared that U.S. involvement in the region would cause more problems than it would solve. What if, for example, Serbs attacked Americans? Would the United States go to full-scale war? In addition, they complained that the president had undertaken this action in violation of the War Powers Act, a 1973 law that requires presidents to get approval from Congress if U.S. forces would be in danger for more than sixty days. Finally, critics noted that both sides in Kosovo had committed atrocities; in choosing sides, the United States was inevitably allying itself with people who might have committed immoral acts.

The bombing campaign against Serb forces was the first time in international history when a set of nations attacked another for its violations of international human rights law. It was ultimately successful: Serbia agreed to pull its forces out of Kosovo in 1999. This, too, was a first: never before had airpower alone served to deter an aggressor from operating in a hostile country. (Unfortunately, a U.S. bomb hit and destroyed the Chinese embassy in Serbia, killing several Chinese citizens and causing a major controversy between the United States and China.)

U.S. and other forces are serving today as peacekeepers in Kosovo. Sadly, as of 2000, Kosovar forces are engaged in a campaign of reverse ethnic cleansing and are attempting to drive Serbs from Kosovar territory. The peacekeeping forces are stuck between the proverbial rock and a hard place, with enemies on both sides. No major war broke out in Europe, and the leader of Serbian forces, Slobodan Milosevic, was forced from office after he lost a rigged election and faced a popular uprising. Additionally, no clear policy has emerged about when U.S. forces ought to intervene and why. Peacekeeping remains one of the most highly contentious, highly intractable—and unsolvable—problems in contemporary U.S. military policy.

CLINTON'S REMARKS AT MEMORIAL DAY SERVICE

May 31, 1999

Today, there is a new challenge before us in Kosovo. It is a very small province in a small country, but it is a big test of what we believe in. Our commitment to leave to our children a world where people are not uprooted and ravaged and slaughtered en masse because of their race, their ethnicity or their religion; our fundamental interest in building a lasting peace in an undivided and free Europe, a place which saw two world wars when that dream failed in the 20th century; and our interest in preserving our alliance for freedom and peace with our 18 NATO allies.

All of us have seen the hundreds of thousands of innocent men and women and children driven from their homes, the thousands singled out for death along the way. We have heard their stories of rape and oppression, of robbery and looting and brutality. And we saw it all before, just a few years ago, in Bosnia. For four long years, until NATO acted, combining with the resistance of Bosnians and Croations, to bring the Dayton peace agreement and to turn the tide of ethnic cleansing there.

How did this all happen? Well, 10 years ago the Berlin Wall fell, ending communism's cruel and arbitrary division of Europe, unleashing the energies of freedom-loving people there, after two world wars and the Cold War, to be united in peace and freedom and prosperity. But that same year in Serbia, Slobodan Milosevic became the last hold-out against a Europe free, united and at peace, when he stripped away the rights of the Kosovars to govern themselves. He then went to war against the Croations and the Bosnians. And in the wake of that, after four years, a quarter of a million people were dead, 2.5 million people were refugees—many of them still have not gone home. There was a stunning record of destruction, told not only in lives, but in religious, cultural, historical and personal buildings and records destroyed in an attempt to erase the existence of a people on their land.

In Kosovo we see some parallels to World War II, for the government of Serbia, like that of Nazi Germany, rose to power in part by getting people to look down on people of a given race and ethnicity, and to believe they had no place in their country, and even no right to live. But even more troubling, we see some parallels to the rumblings all around the world where people continue to fall out with one another and think they simply cannot share common ground and a common future with people who worship God in a different way or have a slightly different heritage.

. . .

Just look around here today at the kinds of people who are wearing the evidence of their service to our country. We are a stronger country because we respect our differences and we are united by our common humanity. Now, we cannot expect everybody to follow our lead—and we haven't gotten it entirely right, now. We don't expect everybody to get along all the time. But we can say "no" to ethnic cleansing. We can say "no" to mass slaughter of people because of the way they worship God and because of who their parents were. We can say "no" to that, and we should.

It is important that you know that in Kosovo the world has said "no." It's not just the United States, or even just our 18 NATO allies with us. People on every continent—Arabs and Israelis are sending assistance, Protestants and Catholics from Northern Ireland; Greece and Turks; Africans, Asians, Latin Americans. Even those whose own lives have been battered by hurricanes and other natural disasters and who have hardly anything to give are sending help, because their hearts have been broken and their consciences moved by the appalling abuses they have seen.

Our objectives in Kosovo are clear and consistent with both the moral imperative of reversing ethnic cleansing and killing, and our overwhelming national interest in a peaceful, undivided Europe which will ensure we will not have to send large numbers of young Americans to die there in the next century in a war. The objectives are that the Kosovars will go home; the Serb forces will withdraw; an international force, with NATO at its core, will deploy to protect all the people, including the Serb minority, in Kosovo. And, afterward, to avoid future Bosnias and future Kosovos, we will learn the lesson of the Marshall Plan and what we did for eastern Europe after the Berlin Wall fell, by working with our European allies to build democracy and prosperity and cooperation in southeastern Europe so that there will be stronger forces pulling people together than those that are driving them apart.

I know that many Americans believe that this is not our fight. But remember why many of the people are laying [sic] in these graves out here—because of what happened in Europe and because of what was allowed to go on too long before people intervened. What we are doing today will save lives, including American lives, in the future. And it will give our children a better, safer world to live in.

In this military campaign the United States has borne a large share of the burden, as we must, because we have a greater capacity to bear that burden. But all Americans should know that we have been strongly supported by our European allies; that when the peacekeeping force goes in there, the overwhelming majority of people will be European; and that when the reconstruction begins, the overwhelming amount of investment will be European. This is something we have done together.

http://www.pub.whitehouse.gov/uri-res/I2R?urn:pdi://oma.eop.gov.us/1999/6/2/7.text.1

OPPOSITION TO CLINTON'S POSITION ON KOSOVO

March 22, 1999

Mrs. Kay Bailey Hutchison (R-TX). Mr. President, I rise today to talk about the situation in Kosovo. We have been watching this situation unfold for days, actually months—actually, you could say thousands of years. But it is coming to a head in the very near future, perhaps in hours. As I speak today, Richard Holbrooke is talking to Slobodan Milosevic and trying to encourage him to come to the peace table. I hope he is successful, and I know every American hopes that he is successful. But what I think we must talk about today is what happens if he is not.

What happens if Mr. Milosevic says, "No, I am not going to allow foreign troops in my country," and if he says he is going to move forward with whatever he intends to do in the governance of that country? I think we have to step back and look at the situation and the dilemma which we face, because there is no question, this is not an easy decision. What comes next?

Basically, the President has committed the United States to a policy in NATO to which he really does not have the authority to commit. The consequences are that we have to make a decision that would appear to walk away from the commitment he made without coming to Congress, and that is not a good situation. I do not like having to make such a choice, because I want our word to be good. When the United States speaks, I want our word to be good. Whether it is to our ally or to our enemy, they need to know what we say we will do.

But the problem here is, the President has gone out with a commitment before he talked to Congress about it, and now we have really changed the whole nature of NATO without congressional approval. We are saying that we are going to bomb a sovereign country because of their mistreatment of people within their country, the province of Kosovo, and we are going to take this action, basically declaring war on a country that should not be an enemy of the United States and in fact was a partner at the peace table in the Dayton accords on Bosnia.

So now we are taking sides. We are turning NATO, which was a defense alliance—is a defense alliance—into an aggressive, perhaps, declarer-of-war on a country that is not in NATO. Mr. President, I just do not think we can take a step like that without the Congress and the American people understanding what we are doing and, furthermore, approving of it.

There is no question that Mr. Milosevic is not our kind of person. We have seen atrocities that he has committed in Kosovo. But, in fact, there have been other atrocities committed by the parties with whom we are purporting to be taking sides. The Albanians have committed atrocities as well, the Kosovar Albanians. So we are now picking sides in a civil war where I think the U.S. security interest is not clear.

I think it is incumbent on the President to come to Congress, before he takes any military action in Kosovo, to lay out the case and to get congressional approval. What would he tell Congress? First of all, before we put one American in harm's way, I want to know: What is the intention here? What is the commitment? What happens in the eventuality that Mr. Milosevic does not respond to bombing, that he declares he is going to go forward without responding to an intervention in his country? What do we do then? Do we send ground troops in to force him to come to the peace table? And if we did, could we consider that is really a peace? What if NATO decides to strike and an American plane is shot down? What if there is an American POW? What then? What is our commitment then?

. . .

That is why so many of us in Congress are concerned and why we realize the dilemma. We understand that this is not an easy black and white decision. We are talking about a commitment that the President has made. I do not like stepping in and saying that we shouldn't keep a commitment the President has made. Overriding that great concern is the consequence of not requiring the President to have a plan and a policy that will set a precedent for the future. I think we could explain it by sitting down with our European allies and saying, first of all, if we are going to change the mission of NATO, this must be fully debated and fully accepted by every member of NATO within their own constitutional framework. If we are going to turn NATO from a defense alliance into an affirmative war-making machine, I think we need to talk about it.

. . .

There was a way to go into Bosnia, but Kosovo is very different. Kosovo is a civil war in a sovereign nation. There are atrocities. There have been atrocities on both sides. We are picking one side, and we are doing it without a vote of Congress. I do not think we can do it. I do not think the President has the right to declare war, and under the Constitution, he certainly does not. And under the War Powers Act, it takes an emergency. This is not an emergency. We are not being attacked. United States troops are not in harm's way at this point.

The Congressional Record. March 22, 1999: S 3039–3041.

NUCLEAR TEST BAN TREATY (OCTOBER 1999)

In the aftermath of the Cold War, and as the total numbers of nuclear weapons held by the United States and Russia began to be reduced substantially, interest in a nuclear test ban treaty was rekindled. Historically, nations with nuclear weapons had tested them to first prove that they could create a working nuclear device, and then to assess whether the weapons were safe over time—could they still explode years after they were built, were they leaking too much radiation, and so on. By the 1990s, however, increasingly sophisticated computers could account for these problems without actually testing a nuclear device. Additionally, by the 1990s, the United States and Russia were worried less about an attack from each other and more about nuclear proliferation—an increase in the number of nations capable of producing and using nuclear weapons. Thus they negotiated a nuclear test ban treaty in an attempt to slow down proliferation and to reduce the chances that a test explosion might be interpreted as an attack by an enemy power.

President Clinton supported the internationally sponsored test ban treaty both as a tool to control proliferation and as a cost-saving measure. He argued that if nations could not test, they could not prove they could create nuclear weapons. Opponents would not feel the need to develop their own weapons forces, and proliferation would be slow. In addition, he pointed out that weapons testing is extremely expensive and dangerous: special bunkers have to be built to contain the explosions, and radiation might leak out. Computers could be used for the same purpose. Finally, he insisted that the United States must ratify a treaty that was popular worldwide if it did not want to become isolated internationally.

Opponents of the test ban treaty, including Senator Jesse Helms (R-NC), argued that it was unreasonable to trust other nations to comply with the ban. They could develop more powerful weapons and thereby threaten the United States. Other critics also pointed out that the occasional nuclear explosion would serve as a reminder to potential enemies that should they attack the United States, it had the capacity to annihilate them. Testing, then, was as much a political as a scientific necessity.

The U.S. Senate rejected the test ban treaty 51 to 48 in 1999. (The Constitution requires that treaties be passed by a two-thirds vote of the Senate, or 67 of 100.) Technically, then, the United States does not have to comply with the treaty's requirements. However, by using his power as commander in chief, President Clinton has maintained his policy of banning nuclear tests, a policy that has been in place during his term of office. Interestingly, this issue was not a major issue in the 2000 presidential campaign. Ultimately, that fact may serve as a sign of how far the nation has come in the twenty years covered in this volume: when Ronald Reagan became president, the nation was close to nuclear war with the Soviet Union; when Clinton left office, there was no Soviet Union and nuclear weapons barely registered as issues of concern in contemporary politics.

CLINTON'S RADIO ADDRESS TO THE NATION

October 9, 1999

On Tuesday, the Senate plans to vote on whether to ratify the nuclear test ban treaty. Today, I want to emphasize why this agreement is critical to the security and future of all Americans.

Just imagine a world in which more and more countries obtained nuclear weapons and more and more destructive varieties. That may be the single, greatest threat to our children's future. And the single, best way to reduce it is to stop other countries from testing nuclear explosives in the first place. That's exactly what the test ban treaty will do.

The treaty is even more essential today than it was when President Eisenhower proposed it more than 40 years ago, or when President Kennedy pursued it. It's more essential, even, than when we signed it three years ago. Because, every year, the threat grows that nuclear weapons will spread—in the Middle East, the Persian Gulf and Asia, to areas where American troops are deployed, to regions with intense rivalries, to rogue leaders and perhaps even to terrorists.

The test ban treaty gives us our best chance to control this threat. A hundred and fifty-four countries have already signed it, including Russia, China, Japan, Israel, Iran and all our European allies. Many nations have already ratified it, including 11 of our NATO allies, including nuclear powers France and Britain. But for two years after I submitted the treaty to the Senate for ratification, there had been absolutely no action.

. . .

The stakes are high. If our Senate rejected this treaty outright, it would be the first time the Senate has rejected a treaty since the Treaty of Versailles, which established the League of Nations after World War I. We all know what America's walking away from the world after World War I brought us—in the Depression and the Second World War. If our Senate rejected this treaty, it would be a dangerous u-turn away from our role as the world's leader against the spread of nuclear weapons. It would say to every country in the world, well, the United States isn't going to test, but we're giving all of you a green light to test, develop and deploy nuclear weapons.

Last year rival nuclear explosions by India and Pakistan shook the world. Now both countries have indicated their willingness to sign the test ban treaty. But if our Senate defeats it, can we convince India and Pakistan to forego more tests? America has been the world's leader against the proliferation of nuclear weapons for more than four decades. If our Senate defeats it, we won't be anymore. If our Senate defeats it, what will prevent China, Russia or others from testing and deploying new and ever more destructive weapons?

Some oppose the treaty because they say we still need to test nuclear weapons ourselves to make sure they're reliable. But this week, 32 American Nobel Prize winning physicists, and other leading scientists told the Senate that America doesn't need to test more nuclear weapons to keep a safe and reliable nuclear force. After all, we stopped testing back in 1992. And now we're spending about $4.5 billion a year on proven program, using our advanced technology to maintain a superior nuclear force without testing. Since we don't need nuclear tests to protect our security, this treaty does not require us to do anything we haven't already done.

It's about preventing other countries from nuclear testing; about constraining nuclear weapons development around the world, at a time when we have an overwhelming advantage.

. . .

Some also say these treaties are too risky because some people might cheat on them. But with no treaty, other countries can test without cheating and without limit. The treaty will strengthen our ability to determine whether other countries are engaged in suspicious activity, with on-site inspections and a global network of over 300 censors, including 33 in Russia, 11 in China, 17 in the Middle East. We could catch cheaters and mobilize the world against them. None of that will happen if we don't ratify the treaty.

. . .

So I say to the senators who haven't endorsed it, heed the best national security advice of our military leaders. Hear our allies who are looking to us to lead. Listen to the scientists; listen to the American people who have long supported the treaty. And since you're not prepared for whatever reason to seize the priceless chance to fulfill the dream of Presidents Eisenhower and Kennedy for a safer world, delay the vote on the treaty, debate it thoroughly, and work with us on a bipartisan basis to address legitimate concerns. And then you'll be able to vote yes for our country, and our children's future.

http://www.pub.whitehouse.gov/uri-res/I2R?urn:pdi://oma.eop.gov.us.1999/10/12/2.text.1

OPPOSITION TO THE COMPREHENSIVE TEST BAN TREATY

October 12, 1999

Mr. Jesse Helms (R-NC). I feel obliged to observe that the United States has already flirted with an end to nuclear testing—from 1958 to 1961. It bears remembering that the nuclear moratorium ultimately was judged to constitute an unacceptable risk to the nation's security, and was terminated after just three years. On the day that President Kennedy ended the ban—March 2, 1962—he addressed the American people and said:

We know enough about broken negotiations, secret preparations, and the advantages gained from a long test series never to offer again an uninspected moratorium. Some urge us to try it again, keeping our preparations to test in a constant state of readiness. But in actual practice, particularly in a society of free choice, we cannot keep top flight scientists concentrating on the preparation of an experiment which may or may not take place on an uncertain date in the future. Nor can large technical laboratories be kept fully alert on a standby basis waiting for some other nation to break an agreement. This is not merely difficult or inconvenient—we have explored this alternative thoroughly and found it impossible of execution.

This statement is very interesting. It makes clear that the fundamental problems posed by a test ban remain unchanged over the past 27 years. The United States certainly faces a Russian Federation that is engaging in "secret preparations" and likely is engaging in clandestine nuclear tests relating to the development of brand-new, low-yield nuclear weapons. The United States, on the other hand, cannot engage in such nuclear modernization while adhering to the CTBT [Comprehensive Test Ban Treaty].

Likewise, the Senate is faced with the same verification problem that it encountered in 1962. As both of President Clinton's former intelligence chiefs have warned, low-yield testing is undetectable by seismic sensors. Nor does the United States have any reasonable chance of mobilizing the ludicrously high number of votes needed under the treaty to conduct an on-site inspection. In other words, the treaty is unverifiable and there is no chance that cheaters will ever be caught.

This is not my opinion. This is a reality, given that 30 of 51 countries on the treaty's governing board must approve any on-site inspection. Even the President's own senior arms controller—John Holum—complained in 1996 that "treaty does not contain . . . our position that on-site inspections should proceed automatically unless two-thirds of the Executive Council vote 'no.'" Instead of an automatic green light for inspections, the U.S. got exactly the opposite of what it requested.

But most importantly, in 1962 President Kennedy correctly noted that the inability to test has a pernicious and corrosive effect—not just upon the weapons themselves (which cannot be fully remanufactured under such circumstances)—but upon the nation's nuclear infrastructure. Our confidence in the nuclear stockpile is eroding even as we speak. Again, this is not my opinion. It is a fact which has been made over and over again by the nation's senior weapons experts.

. . .

So as I listen to these claims that the United States is "out of the testing business," I make two basic observations. First, we are only out of the testing business because President Clinton has taken us out. There is no legal barrier today to conducting stockpile experiments. The reason is purely political. Indeed, the White House is using circular logic. The United States is not testing because the White House supports the test ban treaty; but the White House is claiming that because we are not testing, we should support the treaty.

Second, I remind all that the United States thought it was out of the testing business in 1958, only to discover how badly we had miscalculated. President Kennedy not only ended the 3-year moratorium, but embarked upon the most aggressive test series in the history of the weapons program. If Senators use history as their guide, they will realize that the CTBT is a serious threat to the national security of the United States.

The Congressional Record. October 12, 1999: S 12402–12404.

RECOMMENDED READINGS

Balman Jr., Sid. "Clinton Torn Over What to Do in Somalia." *United Press International* [Washington News, BC cycle], October 4, 1993.

Becker, Elizabeth. "Clinton Says Aid Proposal Is Urgent for Colombia Drug Effort." *New York Times,* January 12, 2000, A4N, A4L.

Bennett, William J. *The Death of Outrage.* New York: Simon and Schuster, 1998.

Bethell, Tom. "Liberals Go to War (Decision to Bomb Yugoslavia)." *American Spectator* 32, no. 7 (1999): 18.

Bombardieri, Marcella. "Wagging Dog? Fine, Some Say (US Strikes Back/Reaction and Fallout/the Local Response)." *Boston Globe,* August 22, 1998, A8.

Broder, John M. "Israel and Syria Agree to Begin Intensive Peace Talks in January." *New York Times,* December 17, 1999, A1N, A1L.

Brooks, Alexander D. "Megan's Law: Constitutionality and Policy." *Criminal Justice Ethics* 15 (1996): 56–66.

Campbell, Colin, and Bert A. Rockman, eds. *The Clinton Legacy.* New York: Chatham House, 2000.

Cannon, Carl M. "From Bosnia to Kosovo." *National Journal* 33, no. 14 (1999): 13.

———. "Judging Clinton." *National Journal* 32, no. 1 (2000): 14.

Cerniello, Craig. "Senate Rejects Comprehensive Test Ban Treaty; Clinton Vows to Continue Moratorium." *Arms Control Today* 29, no. 6 (1999): 26.

"Clinton Goes on Trial; Senate Urged to Excise 'Cancer in Body Politic.' " *Record* [Bergen County, N.J.], January 15, 1999, A1.

Clymer, Adam. "Senate Panel Kills Financing for National Service Program." *New York Times* [late edition], September 12, 1995, A18.

Crossette, Barbara. "Rwanda Genocide Seen as Worsened by U.N. Inaction; Panel Cites U.S. Lapses; 800,000 Died in 1994, Experts Report, as Western Powers Played Down Problem." *New York Times,* December 17, 1999, A1.

Currie, Elliott. "What's Wrong with the Crime Bill?" *Nation* 258, no. 4 (1994): 114.

Deibel, Terry L. *Clinton and Congress: The Politics of Foreign Policy.* New York: Foreign Policy Association, 2000.

Drew, Elizabeth. *Showdown: The Struggle between the Gingrich Congress and the Clinton White House.* New York: Simon and Schuster, 1996.

"The Economy: Do Presidents Matter?" *Investor's Business Daily,* August 7, 1998, A4.

Fyodorov, Vasily. "Clinton's 'Chinese Factor.' " *Moscow News* 24, June 11, 1993, 4.

Garay, Ronald. "Televising Presidential Impeachment: The US Congress Sets the Stage." *Historical Journal of Film, Radio and Television* 19, no. 1 (1999): 57.

Gellman, Barton. "Clinton Sets 2-Phase Plan to Allow Gays in Military; Ban to End While Formal Order Is Delayed." *Washington Post,* January 22, 1993, A1.

Gillespie, Nick. "Presidential Drift: Clinton's Haiti Policy Has No Anchor." *Reason* 26, no. 3 (1994): 6.

Gingrich, Newt. *To Renew America.* New York: HarperCollins, 1995.

Healey, Jon, and Thomas H. Moore. "Clinton Forms New Coalition to Win NAFTA's Approval." *Congressional Quarterly Weekly Report* 51, no. 46 (1993): 3181.

Hedges, Stephen J., Peter Cary, Bruce B. Auster, and Tim Zimmermann. "The Road to Ruin: Washington's Bosnia Policy and the Many Causes of Failure." *U.S. News & World Report,* December 12, 1994, 59.

Ingwerson, Marshall. "Iraq Strike May Address Key Concern on Clinton." *Christian Science Monitor,* 1 June 29, 1993, 1, F4.

"Issues: How Clinton's Values Translate into Policies." *USA Today,* August 7, 1996. http://www.usatoday.com/elect/es/es369.htm.

Jaschik, Scott. "Clinton's National-Service Plan Disappoints Students and Colleges; They Say Program Will Benefit Few People and Divert Money from Key Aid Programs." *Chronicle of Higher Education* 39, no. 36 (1993): A27.

Jones, Charles O. *Clinton and Congress, 1993–1996: Risk, Restoration, and Reelection.* Norman: University of Oklahoma Press, 1999.

Kahn, Joseph. "White House Steps Up Efforts for China Trade Deal; an Issue with a Knack for Making Strange Bedfellows." *New York Times,* January 11, 2000, C4.

Kirkpatrick, Jeane J. "The Clinton Tirade: An Internationalist Responds." *National Review* 51, no. 22 (1999): 17.

Kirschten, Dick. "McClinton v. McGingrich." *National Journal* 26, no. 45 (1994): 2592.

Klaidman, Daniel. "A Reluctant Campaigner: How a Workaholic General Is Fighting the Drug War on His Terms, not Clinton's." *Newsweek,* October 21, 1996, 36.

Krauss, Clifford. "GOP Struggles to Unify Attack on Clinton Plan." *New York Times,* March 2, 1993, A19.

Kudlow, Lawrence A. "Clinton Eyes Surplus to Reinvent Great Society." *Insight on the News* 15, August 2, 1999, 28.

Kurtz, Howard. *Spin Cycle.* New York: Simon and Schuster, 1998.

Maggs, John. "China Trade Deal: No Fortune Inside." *National Journal* 31, no. 37 (1999): 2569.

Mallaby, Sebastian. "The Bullied Pulpit: A Weak Chief Executive Makes Worse Foreign Policy." *Foreign Affairs* 79 (2000): 2.

Marcus, Ruth, and Daniel Williams. "Show of Strength Offers Benefits for Clinton; Response to Iraq Seen Bolstering Administration Diplomacy and at Home." *Washington Post*, June 28, 1993, A1.

Page, Susan, and Beth Belton. "Clinton Takes Credit for a Robust Economy." *USA Today*, October 15, 1996. http://www.usatoday.com/elect/ep/epd/epdc082.htm.

Pear, Robert. "Clinton to Seek $110 Billion for Uninsured; Favoring the Incremental Plan of His Vice President." *New York Times*, January 20, 2000, A14.

"The President's Policy on Gays in the Military: A Mixed Reaction from Gay/Lesbian, Political, Military and Religious Leaders." *Boston Globe*, July 20, 1993, 12.

Robinson, Linda, and Bruce B. Auster. "After Talking Tough, Getting Tough?" *U.S. News & World Report* May 9, 1994, 48.

Rosenburg, Eric. "Reagan's 'Star Wars' Vision Finds Life under Clinton." *National Journal* 31, no. 20 (1999): 26.

Rozell, Mark, and Clyde Wilcox, eds. *The Clinton Scandal and the Future of American Government*. Washington, D.C.: Georgetown University Press, 2000.

Sanger, David E. "Clinton Sends Envoys to Try to Close a Deal on Opening Chinese Markets to the U.S." *New York Times*, November 9, 1999, A12.

Schmitt, Eric. "Senate Kills Test Ban Treaty in Crushing Loss for Clinton, Evokes Versailles Pact Defeat; Vote Is 51 to 48; Last-ditch Proposal to Put Off Action Fails along Party Lines." *New York Times*, October 14, 1999, A1(N), A1(L).

Shapiro, Joseph P. "Can Washington Cure Sick Nursing Homes?" *U.S. News & World Report*, August 3, 1998, 25.

"The Showdown (NAFTA)." *Economist*, special edition, November 13, 1993, 23.

Shull, Richard K. "Parental Vigilance Still Beats Any Law." *Indianapolis News*, May 21, 1996, A5.

Skocpol, Theda. *Boomerang: Clinton's Health Security Effort and the Turn against Government in U.S. Politics*. New York: Norton, 1996.

Smith, Eric L. "Will You Be Better Off in Four More Years?" *Black Enterprise*, January 1997, 54.

Smith, Tony. "In Defense of Intervention." *Foreign Affairs* 76, no. 6 (1994): 34.

Starr, Paul. "The Clinton Presidency, Take Three." *American Prospect*, January/February 1997, i. 30. http://www.prospect.org/archives/30/fs30star.html.

Stevenson, Richard W. "Clinton Wants $2 Billion Expansion in Tax Credit for Working Poor." *New York Times*, January 12, 2000, A17.

"Under the Gun." *New Yorker*, March 22, 1993, 4.

Weatherford, M. Stephen, and Lorraine M. McDonnell. "Clinton and the Economy: The Paradox of Policy Success and Political Mishap." *Political Science Quarterly* 111, no. 3 (1996): 403–436. http://64.33.36.250/index.php3.

Woodward, Bob. *The Agenda: Inside the Clinton White House*. New York: Simon and Schuster, 1994.

Zook, Jim. "President's National-Service Legislation Survives Republican Attacks in Congress." *Chronicle of Higher Education* 39, no. 47 (1993): A22.

BIBLIOGRAPHY

Ackerman, Frank. *Reaganomics: Rhetoric vs. Reality*. Boston: South End Press, 1982.

Allen, Charles F., and Jonathan Portis. *The Comeback Kid: The Life and Career of Bill Clinton*. New York: Birch, 1992.

Anderson, Martin. *The Ten Causes of the Reagan Boom, 1982–1997*. Stanford, Calif.: Hoover Institution on War, Revolution and Peace, Stanford University, 1997.

Baker, Peter. *The Breach: Inside the Impeachment and Trial of William Jefferson Clinton*. New York: Scribner, 2000.

Bennett, William J. *The Death of Outrage: Bill Clinton and the Assault on American Ideals*. New York: Free Press, 1998.

Budget, U.S. http://w3.access.gpo.gov/usbudget

Burns, James MacGregor. *Dead Center: Clinton-Gore Leadership and the Perils of Moderation*. New York: Scribner, 1999.

Busby, Robert. *Reagan and the Iran-Contra Affair: The Politics of Presidential Recovery*. New York: St. Martin's Press, 1999.

Campbell, Colin, and Bert A. Rockman, eds. *The Clinton Legacy*. New York: Chatham House, 2000.

Cannon, Lou. *President Reagan: The Role of a Lifetime*. New York: Simon and Schuster, 1991.

Coulter, Ann. *High Crimes and Misdemeanors: The Case Against Bill Clinton*. Washington, D.C.: Regnery, 1998.

Cronin, Thomas, and Michael Genovese. *The Paradoxes of the American Presidency*. New York: Oxford University Press, 2001.

Dallek, Matthew. *The Right Moment: Ronald Reagan's First Victory and the Decisive Turning Point in American Politics*. New York: Free Press, 2000.

Dallek, Robert. *Ronald Reagan: The Politics of Symbolism*. Cambridge, Mass.: Harvard University Press, 1984.

Daynes, Byron, and Glen Sussman. *The American Presidency and the Social Agenda.* Upper Saddle River, N.J.: Prentice Hall, 2001.

Drew, Elizabeth. *On the Edge: The Clinton Presidency.* New York: Simon and Schuster, 1994.

Edwards III, George C., John H. Kessel, and Bert Rockman, eds. *Researching the Presidency.* Pittsburgh: University of Pittsburgh Press, 1993.

FirstGov, the portal to all U.S. government websites. http://www.firstgov.gov.

Fischer, Beth A. *The Reagan Reversal: Foreign Policy and the End of the Cold War.* Columbia: University of Missouri Press, 1997.

FitzGerald, Frances. *Way Out There in the Blue: Reagan, Star Wars, and the End of the Cold War.* New York: Simon and Schuster, 2000.

Frendreis, John, and Raymond Tatalovich. *The Modern Presidency and Economic Policy.* Itasca, Ill.: F.E. Peacock, 1994.

Genovese, Michael. *The Power of the American Presidency, 1789–2000.* New York: Oxford University Press, 2001.

Greene, John Robert. *The Presidency of George Bush.* Lawrence: University Press of Kansas, 2000.

Hagstrom, Jerry. *Beyond Reagan: The New Landscape of American Politics.* New York: Penguin Books, 1989.

Hill, Dilys M., and Phil Williams. *The Bush Presidency: Triumphs and Adversities.* New York: St. Martin's Press, 1994.

Hyland, William. *Clinton's World: Remaking American Foreign Policy.* Westport, Conn.: Praeger, 1999.

Karaagac, John. *Between Promise and Policy: Ronald Reagan and Conservative Reformism.* Lanham, Md.: Lexington Books, 2000.

Lagon, Mark P. *The Reagan Doctrine: Sources of American Conduct in the Cold War's Last Chapter.* Westport, Conn.: Praeger, 1994.

Laham, Nicholas. *The Reagan Presidency and the Politics of Race: In Pursuit of Colorblind Justice and Limited Government.* Westport, Conn.: Praeger, 1998.

———. *Ronald Reagan and the Politics of Immigration Reform.* Westport, Conn.: Praeger, 2000.

Light, Paul. *The President's Agenda.* Baltimore: Johns Hopkins University Press, 1982.

Lowi, Theodore J. *Democrats Return to Power: Politics and Policy in the Clinton Era.* New York: Norton, 1994.

Rozell, Mark J. *The Press and the Bush Presidency.* New York: Praeger, 1996.

Schier, Steven E. *The Postmodern Presidency: Bill Clinton's Legacy in U.S. Politics.* Pittsburgh: University of Pittsburgh Press, 2000.

Schmertz, Eric J. *President Reagan and the World.* Westport, Conn.: Greenwood Press, 1997.

Scott, James. *Deciding to Intervene: The Reagan Doctrine and American Foreign Policy.* Durham, N.C.: Duke University Press, 1996.

Scott, James, ed. *After the End: Making U.S. Foreign Policy in the Post–Cold War World.* Durham, N.C.: Duke University Press, 1998.

Skowronek, Stephen. *The Politics Presidents Make.* Cambridge, Mass.: Belknap, 1993.

Sloan, John W. *The Reagan Effect: Economics and Presidential Leadership.* Lawrence: University Press of Kansas, 1999.

Smith, Hedrick. *The Power Game: How Washington Works*. New York: Ballantine Books, 1988.

Stockman, David. *The Triumph of Politics: The Inside Story of the Reagan Revolution*. New York: Avon, 1986.

Warshaw, Shirley. *The Domestic Presidency: Policymaking in the White House*. Boston: Allyn and Bacon, 1997.

White, John Kenneth. *The New Politics of Old Values*. Lanham, Md.: University Press of America, 1998.

Wills, Garry. *Reagan's America*. New York: Penguin Books, 2000.

Woodward, Bob. *The Agenda: Inside the Clinton White House*. New York: Simon and Schuster, 1994.

———. *The Choice: How Clinton Won*. New York: Simon and Schuster, 1994.

INDEX

Abraham, Katherine, 151
Abshini, David, 100
Afghanistan air strikes, 263–68
Aging population, 9–10
Air traffic controllers strike, 24–28
Air travel, taxes on, 161
Alaska, USS, 71
Americans with Disabilities Act of 1990 (ADA), 116, 127–31
America's Watch, 103
Americorps, 193–97
Anti-Ballistic Missile (ABM) Treaty, 84–86, 106–7
Aristide, Jean Bertrand, 255–56
Arms control: under Bush, 171–75; under Kennedy, 69; under Reagan, 68–72, 84–85, 103–8; Soviet violations of, 107
Arms Control and Disarmament Agency (ACDA), 107
Arms sales, to Iran, 98–99
Armstrong, William, 63
Aschauer, David, 122

Baker, James, 168
Balanced budget amendment, 40–45, 152–56
Ball, George, 78

Barca, Peter, 157, 159–61
Beirut, Lebanon peacekeeping mission, 72–79, 98
Bennett, Charles, 176, 179–82
Bentsen, Lloyd, 220
Berlin Wall, fall of, 114
Bickel, Alexander, 61
bin Laden, Osama, 263–68
Bishop, Maurice, 80–81
Blecker, Robert, 122–23
Block, Fred, 121–22
Bockarie, Sam "General Mosquito," 262–63
Boland amendment, 102
Bonker, Don, 34, 38–40
Bork, Robert, 55–62, 145–46
Bosnia peacekeeping mission, 249–54
Brady, James, 222–24
Brady, Sarah, 223–24
Brady Bill, 189, 222–26
Brown, Harold, 86
Brown, Walter L., 180
Budget, balancing the: Bush, 152–56; Reagan, 40–45
Budget deficits: under Bush, 154; under Clinton, 208–9; effects on presidents, 18, 41; under Reagan, 16, 20, 41–43

Budget surpluses, under Clinton, 191, 209, 240–44
Bunning, Jim, 240, 242–44
Burton, Dan, 127, 129–31
Bush, George H. W.: Americans with Disabilities Act, 116, 127–31; balanced budget amendment, 152–56; budget deficits, 4, 116; drug control, 123–27; economic plan, 118–23; economic support for former Soviet Union, 175–82; education reform, 135–41; Family and Medical Leave Act, 131–35; on Haiti, 256; invasion of Panama, 115, 162–66; on the Middle East, 76; nomination of Clarence Thomas, 141–47; North American Free Trade Agreement, 157–61; Persian Gulf War, 115–16; Somalia involvement, 246, 248; Strategic Arms Reduction Treaty, 171–75; Tiananmen Square protests, 115; timeline, xix–xx; on voodoo economics, 23, 118; welfare reform, 147–52
Bush, George W., 213, 235

Campaign contributions, 45, 190
Capital gains taxes, 119, 123, 243
Carter, Jimmy, 97, 267
Cedras, Raoul, 256
Chechnya, 259
Cheney, Dick, 204
China. See People's Republic of China
Christopher, Warren, 248
Chun Ziming, 201
Church, F. Forrester, 92, 95–98
Civil rights: Bork nomination, 60–61; disabled Americans, 116, 127–29; sex-related crimes and, 231; sexual preference, 203, 205. See also Racial discrimination
Clean Air Act, 116
Clean Water Act, 116
Clinger, William, 255, 257–58
Clinton, Hillary, 212
Clinton, William (Bill): Family and Medical Leave Act, 132; first election of, 114; gun control, 189, 222–

26; Haiti intervention, 254–58; health care reform, 212–17; homosexuals in the military, 188–89, 202–8; investigation and impeachment, 234–40; Kosovo bombing, 268–73; Megan's Law, 230–34; NAFTA, 157, 217–22; National Service, 193–97; nuclear test ban treaty, 273–78; Republican victory in Congress, 190; Rwanda peacekeeping mission, 189, 258–63; Somalia peacekeeping mission, 189, 245–49; Sudan and Afghanistan air strikes, 263–68; tax cuts and budget surplus, 240–44; timeline, xxi–xxiii; trade with China, 191, 197–202; welfare reform, 51, 148; Yugoslavia and Bosnia peacekeeping, 189, 249–54
Clinton-Gephardt bill, 215–17. See also Health care
Coalitions of voters, 10
Cold War, 5–6, 114
Cole, USS, 264
Coleman, Ronald D., 222, 224–26
Coll, Steve, 263
Collins, Cardiss, 99, 102–3
Constitutional amendments, 40–45, 152–56
Contra funding, 102–3
Cox, Christopher, 212, 215–17
Crime control: gun control, 223, 225; nomination of Robert Bork, 58; sex-related crimes, 230–34; war on drugs, 123–27, 226
Cultural homogenization, 7–8
Currency stabilization fund, 178–79

D'Amato, Alfonse, 226, 229–30
Danforth, John, 143
Dasbach, Steve, 232–34
Day of Reckoning (Friedman), 121
Death taxes, 21–22, 243
Defense spending: under Bush, 120; under Clinton, 208; in the former Soviet Union, 181–82; under Reagan, 16, 42–43, 84–88
Demographics of U.S., 8–10
Détente, 5

Disabled Americans, 116, 127–31
Diversity of population, 8–10
Divided government, 3–4
Drug control: under Bush, 123–27, 163; under Clinton, 226–30
Dukakis, Michael, 113

Economic plans: under Bush, 118–23; under Clinton, 208–12; under Reagan, 20–24
Education reform: under Bush, 135–41; under Clinton, 197, 210, 242
Edwards, Harry, 147
Endara, Guillermo, 164
Energy taxes, 209
Enterprise zones, 28–33, 63
Environmental Protection Agency (EPA), 116
Estate taxes, 21–22, 243
Exceptionalism, 12
Export-Import Bank, 178

Family and Medical Leave Act of 1990, 131–35
Family-oriented policies: child care, 120; Family and Medical Leave Act of 1990, 131–35; tax cuts as, 20, 33–34, 36–37; welfare reform and, 51
Federal employees' right to strike, 24, 26
Fleming, Lauren, 211
Ford, Kenneth, 93
Foreman, Fred, 58
Foster, Vince, 234
Franks, Gary, 193, 195–97
FREEDOM Support Act of 1992, 176–79
Free trade. See Trade agreements
Friedman, Benjamin, 121–23

Gays and lesbians in the military, 188–89, 202–8
Gemayel, Amine, 75
Gephardt, Richard, 20, 23
Geren, Pete, 250, 252–54
Gilman, Benjamin, 245, 248–49
Ginsburg, Douglas, 56
Glasnost, 105

Globalization, 7–8
Gonzalez, Charles, 72, 77–79
Gorbachev, Mikhail, 173–75
Gore, Al, 190, 213, 236
Gorton, Slade, 208, 210–12
Governments: purpose of, 11–12; role of leaders, 13–14; unique characteristics of U.S., 12
Gramm-Rudman bill, 40–41, 42
Grechko, Marshal, 86
Greenspan, Alan, 244
Grenada, invasion of, 77, 79–83
Gun control, 189, 222–26

Habib, Phil, 75
Haiti intervention, 254–58
Hart, Gary, 41, 43–45, 79, 82–83
Head Start, 140
Health care, 188–89, 196, 212–17
Helms, Jesse, 171, 274, 276–78
Higgenbotham, A. Leon, 147
High Intensity Drug Trafficking Program, 228
Hill, Anita, 142
History, choice of issues in, 1–2
Hittle, Brig. Gen. James D., 179–81
Holbrooke, Richard, 271
Holum, John, 277
Holzer, Harry, 151
Homemakers, tax code and, 36
Homosexuals in the military, 188–89, 202–8
Hoover, Herbert, 180–81
Hostages, in Lebanon, 98–101
Housing and community development, 62–67
Human rights struggles: Americans with Disabilities Act, 128; apartheid in South Africa, 88–92; contras' use of land mines, 103; Kosovo, 268–73; range of opinions on, 6; Rwanda intervention and, 258–59; in the Soviet Union, 106; trade with China, 197–98, 201–2
Humberger, Edward, 32
Hunter, Duncan, 203, 206–8
Hussein, Saddam, 100, 167–68
Hutchison, Kay Bailey, 268, 271–73

Immigration reform, 45–50
Impeachment calls: for Clinton, 191, 234–40; for Reagan, 99
India, nuclear tests in, 275
Inner cities, improvement of, 28–29, 31–33, 63
Intermediate-range nuclear forces treaty, 17, 103–8
International Monetary Fund (IMF), 178
Iran-contra scandal, 73, 98–103
Iraq, policy towards: under Bush, 115–16, 166–68; under Clinton, 190
Ireland, peace efforts in, 189–90
Israel, importance to United States, 75–76

Jefferson, Thomas, 154
Jones, Paula, 235

Kabbah, Ahmad Tejan, 262
Kaiser, Robert, 87–88
Kamenev, Leo, 181
Kanka, Megan, 233
Kelly, Michael, 258, 261–63
Kemp, Jack, 151
Kennan, George, 180–81
Kennedy, Anthony, 56
Kennedy, John F., 69, 276–78
Kennedy, Ted: on Bork nomination, 56, 59–62; on education reform, 136, 139–41; on invasion of Panama, 162, 165–66
Kenya embassy bombing, 263, 265, 267
Kosovo bombing, 268–73
Kurtz, Howard, 221
Kuttner, Robert, 118, 121–23
Kuwait, invasion by Iraq, 115–16, 166–68

Laffer Curve, 15–16
Latino population of U.S., 46, 48–49
Leaders, role of, 13–14
Leahy, Patrick, 68, 70–72
Leamond, Goat, 119
Lebanon peacekeeping mission, 72–79, 98

Lesbians in the military, 188–89, 202–8
Levin, Sander, 218, 220–22
Lewinsky, Monica, 191, 235–37, 264
Liberia, 259
Libertarian Party, Megan's Law opposition by, 232–34
Libya, bombing of, 92–98
Litvanov, Maxim, 180
Losing Ground (Murray), 52

Marine barracks attack (Lebanon), 72–79
Marriage penalty, 21
Marshall, Thurgood, 141
Martinez, Matthew, 46, 48–50
Mazzoli, Romano, 152, 155–56
McFarlane, Bud, 75
McMickle, Marvin, 141, 145–47
Medicare Part C, 217
Medicare reform, 240–41
Megan's Law, 230–34
Merit Schools program, 137–38
Methodology of book, 10–14
Middle East policy: under Clinton, 189–90; under Reagan, 72–79
Milosevic, Slobodan, 250, 269–72
MIRVs, 68
Mobile Enforcement Teams program (MET), 228
Model Cities Program of the 1960s, 30
Monroe Doctrine, 254
Moyers, Bill, 52
Munnell, Alicia, 122–23
Murray, Charles, 52
MX Peacekeeper missile, 68–72

National Security Council (NSC), 101–2
National Service Trust Act of 1993, 193–97
New American Schools program, 137
New world order, 166–67
Nicaraguan contras, 98–103
Nitze, Paul, 86
Nixon, Richard M., 234
Noriega, General Manuel, 115, 162–64
North American Free Trade Agree-

ment (NAFTA): under Bush, 157–61; under Clinton, 157, 217–22

North Atlantic Treaty Organization (NATO), 176, 251–52, 270–73

Nuclear arms: in China, 199; intermediate-range nuclear forces treaty, 103–8; in Iraq, 168; negotiated reductions in, 17–18, 68–72; START, 171–75; test ban treaty, 273–78

On Borrowed Time (Peterson), 121

Operation Bootstrap, 32

Operation Desert Storm. *See* Persian Gulf War

Organization of American States (OAS), 158, 162, 166

Pakistan, nuclear tests in, 275

Panama, invasion of, 115, 162–66

PATCO strike, 24–28

Peace Corps, 196

Peacekeeping missions: Bosnia, 249–54; Kosovo, 268–73; Lebanon, 72–79, 98; Rwanda, 189, 258–63; Sierra Leone, 189, 259, 262–63; Somalia, 189, 245–49; Yugoslavia, 189, 249–54

Pease, Donald, 118, 121

Pell, Claiborne, 92, 95

Pell Grants, 140–41

People's Republic of China: bombing of embassy by U.S., 269; most-favored-nation status, 191, 197–202; prohibition of forced labor exports, 202; Tiananmen Square protests, 115, 199, 201

Perot, Ross, 157

Pershing II missiles, 104

Persian Gulf War, 4–5, 115–16, 166–71

Peterson, Peter G., 121, 123

Political action committees (PACs), 45

Presidency, U.S.: budget deficits and surpluses, 4–5; changing demographics, 8–10; end of the Cold War, 5–6; era of divided government, 3–4; globalization, 7–8; importance of context, 2–3; linkage of politics and personality, 2

Presidential libraries, 13

Pressler, Larry, 106–8

Privacy rights, 56

Pro-family policies. *See* Family-oriented policies

Professional Air Traffic Controllers Organization (PATCO), 24–28

Proxmire, William, 84, 87–88

Proxy wars, 5

Puerto Rico, Operation Bootstrap in, 32

Qadhafi, Mu'ammar, 93–95, 98

Racial discrimination: in housing, 64; Robert Bork on, 60–61; South Africa sanctions, 88–92. *See also* Civil rights

Rangel, Charles, 166, 169–71

Reagan, Ronald: air traffic controllers strike, 24–28; arms control and the MX missile, 68–72; balancing the budget, 40–45; Bork nomination, 55–62; budget deficits, 4, 18; change in Soviet policy, 5–6; enterprise zones, 28–33, 63; first economic plan, 20–24; Grenada invasion, 77, 79–83; housing and community development, 62–67; immigration reform, 45–50; intermediate-range nuclear forces treaty, 103–8; Iran-contra scandal, 98–103; Lebanon peacekeeping mission, 72–79, 98; legacy of conservative ideology, 18–19, 190; Libya bombing, 92–98; South African sanctions, 88–92; Strategic Defense Initiative, 84–88; support of repressive authoritarian governments, 18–19; tax reform act, 33–40; timeline, xvii–xix; welfare reform, 50–55

Reagan Doctrine, 17, 79, 98

Reighley, Jerry, 130

Reno, Janet, 190

Rhetoric, importance of, 14

Richardson, Bill, 124, 126–27

Riemer, David, 148, 150–52

Risen, James, 267

Roukema, Margaret, 53–55, 131, 133–35

Russia, economic aid to, 175–82

Rwanda peacekeeping mission, 189, 258–63

SALT I Treaty, 85

SALT II Treaty, 68, 70–72

Saudi Arabia, Persian Gulf War and, 166–67

Savings rate, 121–23

School vouchers, 136

Scowcroft, Brent, 115

Sex-related crimes, 230–34

Sexual affairs of Clinton, 191–92, 234–35

Sexual harassment, 142, 189–90, 234–35

Sexual orientation, 188–89, 202–8

Sierra Leone peacekeeping mission, 189, 259, 262–63

Simon, Paul, 148, 150–52

Simpson-Rodino bill, 48–49. See also Immigration reform

Social Security, budget surpluses and, 240–41

Somalia intervention, 189, 245–49

Souter, David, 143–44

South Africa, economic sanctions on, 88–92

Soviet Union: assistance towards former countries of, 114, 175–82; change towards, under Reagan, 5–6, 17; policy of containment towards, 5; Reagan Doctrine, 6, 17; SALT II Treaty, 68, 70–72

Special prosecutors, 190–91, 234

Speeches by Bush: Americans with Disabilities Act, 128–29; balanced budget amendment, 153–54; drug control, 124–26; economic aid to the former Soviet Union, 176–79; economic plan, 119–21; education reform, 137–39; Family and Medical Leave Act of 1990, 132–33; invasion of Panama, 163–64; nomination of Clarence Thomas, 142–44; North American Free Trade Agreement,

158–59; Persian Gulf War, 167–69; START talks, 172–73; welfare reform, 149–50

Speeches by Clinton: drug control, 227–28; economic growth plan, 209–10; gun control, 223–24; Haiti intervention, 255–57; health care reform, 213–15; homosexuals in the military, 204–6; impeachment trial, 236–38; Kosovo bombing, 269–71; Megan's Law, 231–32; NAFTA, 218–20; National Service, 194–95; nuclear test ban treaty, 274–76; Rwandan intervention, 259–61; Somalia involvement, 246–48; Sudan and Afghanistan air strikes, 264–66; tax cuts and budget surpluses, 241–42; trade with China, 198–200; Yugoslavia and Bosnia peacekeeping, 250–52

Speeches by Reagan: air traffic controllers strike, 25–26; arms control and reduction, 69–70; Bork nomination, 57–58; budget deficit, 41–43; enterprise zones, 29–31; federal tax reduction legislation, 21–23; Grenada invasion, 80–82; housing and community development, 63–65; immigration reform, 47; intermediate-range nuclear forces treaty, 105–6; Iran-contra controversy, 100–102; Lebanon peacekeeping mission, 73–76; Libyan bombing, 93–95; South Africa sanctions, 90–91; Strategic Defense Initiative, 85–86; tax reform, 35–38; welfare reform, 51–53

SS-20 missile, 108

Starr, Kenneth, 190–91, 234, 264

Star Wars (SDI), 84–88, 107

Statue of Liberty inscription, 50

Stokes, Louis, 141, 145

Strategic Arms Reduction Treaty (START), 17, 107, 171–75

Strategic Defense Initiative (SDI), 84–88, 107

Student loans, 210

Sudan air strikes, 263–68

Sullivan rules, 89, 91

Sumner, William, 24, 27
Sun, Lena, 201
Supply-side economics model, 15–16, 118
Support for East European Democracy (SEED) Act of 1989, 177
Supreme Court nominations: Bork, Robert, 55–62; Thomas, Clarence, 116, 141–47
Syria, 75

Talent, James, 235, 238–40
Tanzania embassy bombing, 263, 265, 267
Tax code revision: Clinton, 209–11; progressivity concept, 34, 38; Reagan, 17, 21–24, 30, 33–40; significance of, 20
Tax cuts: under Bush, 118–19, 123; capital gains, 119, 123, 243; under Clinton, 240–44; under Reagan, 15–16, 20–24, 33–34
Tax incentives, in enterprise zones, 28–33, 63
Tax increases: Bush, 116, 118–20; Clinton, 188–89, 208–11, 216; Reagan, 21
Teacher certification, 138
Thomas, Clarence, 116, 141–47
Tiananmen Square protests, 115, 199, 201
Tibet, Chinese abuses against, 199
Timelines: Bush, xix–xx; Clinton, xxi–xxiii; Reagan, xvii–xix
Tower Special Review Board, 100–101
Trade agreements: China, 197–202; NAFTA, 157–61, 217–22; Peru, 227
Tribe, Laurence, 45
Trickle-down economics, 15–16, 20, 118
Trident submarines, 68–69, 71

Unemployment, welfare reform and, 150–52
United States, unique characteristics of, 12

Vento, Bruce, 24, 26–28
Volunteering, pay for, 196
Voodoo economics, 23
Vouchers, for housing, 63–64

Wang Juntao, 201
War on drugs. See Drug control
War Powers Act: Bosnia bombing, 268; Grenada invasion, 79–80, 82–83; Kosovo intervention, 273; Lebanon peacekeeping, 73, 77–79; Persian Gulf War, 167, 170–71; Somalia peacekeeping, 245, 248–49
Wealth, distribution of: data on, 122–23; in globalization, 7; in tax cut proposals, 23
Weinberger, Caspar, 253
Weiner, Tim, 267
Weiss, Ted, 20, 23–24, 28–29, 31–33
Welfare reform: under Bush, 147–52; under Clinton, 51, 148; under Reagan, 28–29, 50–55
Whitewater investigation, 189–90, 234
Whitfield, Ed, 264, 267–68
Wolf, Frank, 198, 200–202
Wolpe, Howard, 89, 91–92
World Bank, 178
World Trade Organization (WTO), 198
Wu, Harry, 202

Yavlinsky, Grigory, 180
Yeltsin, Boris, 174
Yugoslavia, 189, 249–54, 268–73

Zero option, 105

About the Authors

LANE CROTHERS is Associate Professor of Political Science at Illinois State University. He specializes in political culture, political leadership, and the presidency. He has published works on leadership in police and social work agencies, rhetoric and presidential policy-making, and political culture.

NANCY S. LIND is Associate Professor of Political Science at Illinois State University. Her specializations include the bureaucracy, including interactions of the presidents with administrative agencies, public administration, and public policy. Her publications have focused on issues of violence, the role of the NCAA in setting administrative standards for colleges and universities, and economic development.